P9-DCC-590

MARRIAGE WITHOUT CHILDREN

MARRIAGE WITHOUT CHILDREN

Diana Burgwyn

HARPER COLOPHON BOOKS
Harper & Row, Publishers
New York, Cambridge, Philadelphia, San Francisco
London, Mexico City, São Paulo, Sydney

Lines on pages 158–159 are from "Waiting" by Jane Cooper, copyright © 1973, 1974, by Jane
Cooper, which originally appeared in *American Poetry Review.* Reprinted with permission of
Macmillan Publishing Co., Inc.

A hardcover edition of this book is published by Harper & Row, Publishers, Inc.

MARRIAGE WITHOUT CHILDREN. Copyright © 1981 by Diana Burgwyn. All rights reserved.
Printed in the United States of America. No part of this book may be used or reproduced in any
manner whatsoever without written permission except in the case of brief quotations embodied
in critical articles and reviews. For information address Harper & Row, Publishers, Inc., 10 East
53rd Street, New York, N.Y. 10022. Published simultaneously in Canada by Fitzhenry &
Whiteside Limited, Toronto.

First HARPER COLOPHON edition published 1982.

ISBN: 0-06-090940-4   (previously ISBN: 0-06-014882-9)

82 83 84 85 10 9 8 7 6 5 4 3 2 1

For my mother,
Rae Stambul,
with love and gratitude

Contents

Acknowledgments

The heart of this study lies in the roughly one hundred interviews with people who shared with me the stories of their voluntarily and involuntarily childless lives. I would like to thank them not only for providing the basic material of this book but for enriching my life through their candor, warmth, and generosity. They extended courtesies far beyond those expected of interviewee to interviewer, driving me miles to my next taping, preparing elegant brunches, housing me overnight, sending me relevant clippings in the mail. I hope I have returned their trust by capturing their essence faithfully in the pages which follow.

Several professionals in the fields under study—psychologists, psychiatrists, sociologists, educators, demographers, social workers, executives of various organizations—gave to me of their time and wisdom; each is mentioned by name in the course of the book.

One group which opened wide its doors to me, providing staff assistance, library facilities, and an introduction to its full membership, was the National Alliance for Optional Parenthood in Washington, D.C.; in particular, I wish to acknowledge Gail McKirdy, former acting director. Equally helpful was Barbara Eck Menning, founder and executive director of Resolve, a nationwide organization which deals with matters of infertility. The staff of the Free Library of Philadelphia provided courteous and continual research assistance.

As for that circle of friends and relatives who nurtured me through this project and believed fully in it before a page was written, there is no adequate way for me to thank them and no appropriate way to list them here. Suffice it to say that they know who they are and are aware of my gratitude. One among them, Judith Kaufman, read the entire manuscript and offered sound and astute criticism.

Introduction

Childlessness has been studied and talked about with enormous interest in recent years. No longer is it automatically considered a deprivation, although for those who want children and are unable to have them it *is* a deprivation—usually a major one. But, for most people, parenthood or nonparenthood has become a matter of personal choice. And, despite some lingering prejudice toward those who choose the latter route, they are acknowledged on the whole to have made a normal, rational decision. Once referred to as the "invisible minority," the voluntarily childless are now far from reticent. Indeed, the subject of whether or not to have children has become a staple of cocktail parties and scientific seminars alike.

In the wake of this new interest, decision-making books, clinics, and workshops, which attempt to help couples decide whether they truly want children and would be good parents, have sprung up around the country. Much attention also has been focused upon childless career women who, toward the end of their childbearing years, confront with urgency the issue of motherhood. In a sense these preoccupations have taken the place of the subject that for years filled medical and popular journals: the plight of the infertile woman (rarely were infertile men featured), whose life consisted of weary treks from one doctor to another, one painful test after another, in the quest for parenthood.

What is often ignored even today is the fact that there is a life *after* the childbearing years for both the voluntarily and involuntarily childless. What happens then? What is the childless (or childfree, as some of the more zealous nonparents call it) existence like in the years, the decades that follow?

This book began as an after-the-fact exploration of my own childlessness, which had been voluntary. My husband and I were absorbed in our separate careers and in helping each other's career, had limited funds, and felt a certain unfamiliarity with and disinclination toward child care. We were in our early thirties when we married, so there were not many years left for a change of heart. In keeping with the tenor of the times—the early 1970s, when voluntary childlessness was less a topic for intensive scrutiny—we talked only infrequently about children, finding it easier to push off the ultimate decision.

Not until the age of thirty-eight, when I suddenly was faced with the need of a hysterectomy, did I begin to think more deeply about childlessness, what it meant then and what it might mean for the rest of my life. For, though I was childless by choice, the fact that I was now physiologically unable to bear children was quite a different matter.

It was at that stage of my life that this book began to take form through the questions I asked myself: What are the middle years like without children? Does career become less meaningful as time goes on? Is the childless couple more or less intimate than the parent couple? Are pets really child substitutes? Why do some sterile people choose not to adopt? How different are the feelings of voluntarily and involuntarily childless couples in later years? Is old age lonelier without children? And, most important: how can a couple maximize their childless state, whether it is by choice or imposed?

In 1979, by which time I was actively researching the subject of childlessness, I was separated from my husband, an event which had relevance to the planned book and which brought difficult new questions: Are childless people in a better or worse position emotionally than parents in the event of a separation or divorce? Do many among them feel that having had a child might have saved the marriage? Do widowed people react similarly to divorced people as regards their childlessness?

Determining answers to these and many other questions became the purpose of this book.

A major consideration was how to approach the subject and what boundaries to draw. I felt that a composite technique would be most effective: utilizing scientific data from authorities in the field (obtained through both personal meetings and use of published materials), along with pertinent historical and literary references, and, finally, a large number of tape-recorded interviews with childless people throughout the nation.

For the latter I traveled to New England, the Middle Atlantic States, the South, Midwest, Northwest, and California. Most of the interviews were done in urban areas because that is where the majority of people without children live. Correspondence and phone conversations increased the geographic spread somewhat.

Those interviewed were friends of mine, friends of friends, referrals by professionals, and members of organizations with which I had made contact, such as Resolve and the National Alliance for Optional Parenthood. Frequently, people I interviewed led me to others.

Though this study can be characterized as random rather than controlled, I tried to achieve a variety in religious, ethnic, and social background; in profession; in life style. Most of those interviewed were well educated, and none could be considered poor by government standards. I did not talk with anyone younger than the middle twenties, when marriages seemed established and continued nonparenthood a strong possibility. My oldest interviewee had just celebrated her ninetieth birthday.

When both partners in a marriage were willing to be interviewed, I saw them either together or separately, as they wished. At times I talked only with husband or wife. In cases of divorce I spoke to only one of the former partners, not attempting to contact the estranged spouse.

Second and third marriages are included when both partners have remained childless. Occasionally I interviewed couples of whom one partner had a child from a previous marriage, but only when such children were grown and living elsewhere. A number of childless widows and widowers were among my subjects.

Beyond the scope of this book, because their life situations were different enough to make comparisons invalid, were childless couples living together unmarried, couples whose children had died, and never-married single people without children.

My interviews were not heavily structured or based on a rigid questionnaire, for what I sought was individual life stories from which I hoped certain trends and patterns would emerge.

The roughly one hundred people with whom I spoke were, almost without exception, eager to talk and share ideas. Their stories constituted dramas rich in experience and emotion.

Some couples voluntarily childless had been accused of being selfish and abnormal; one woman told me her mother had compared her to "a pig wallowing in the mire." A law student was offered a very hefty sum by his father-in-law as bribery for reproduction. Others had loving parents who said: "Look, times are tough today; I wouldn't want children myself if I were you."

I met couples in conflict because one wanted and the other did not want children. I talked with perfectly nice people who admitted the inadmissible: they don't like children. I saw those who had had miscarriages and sterilizations and false pregnancies; there was even one "perfect abortion."

Among the involuntarily childless were couples who had tried for years to have a child but could not and, for a variety of reasons, did not adopt. Of these, some had achieved lives of mature fulfillment; others were unable to shed a pervasive sadness. Some had learned to cope with pain through humor. "Well," said one man, "if we get too curious about what our child would have looked like we'll go down to the police station and have a composite drawing made up!"

I met men and women for whom human offspring were unnecessary and undesired because their work constituted their children. I met old people who had generations of children not their own running playfully through their lives. I talked with several confused couples in their twenties and thirties who have so many options open to them that they don't know which to choose.

Some people admitted that our interview had raised new issues and prompted surprising responses. "Why you never told me that!" said one astonished wife to her husband after hearing his analysis of her voluntary childlessness. And a middle-aged composer, musing over what he had said earlier, commented more to himself than to me: "Interesting that I would have preferred a little girl to a little boy . . ."

Among the interviewees were many who allowed me to use their real names. Others, wishing to remain anonymous, asked that I conceal their identities through fictitious names and, at times, changes in professions and cities as well. The former will be identifiable to the reader because they are referred to initially by both given name and surname (e.g., "Henry Jones" or "Linda Brown"); in the latter cases I use only a fictitious given name (e.g., "Jane" or "Bill"). When disguising geographic location and profession, I have attempted to make appropriate substitutions.

There are a few stumbling blocks in a study such as this. One is that childless people can only imagine what their existence would have been like as parents. They cannot speak with firsthand experience. But, because the subject of this book is childlessness, I made no serious effort to counter or verify expectations of parenthood with the realities as expressed by mothers and fathers.

The fact that people do not fall into easy categories also presents a problem to the writer. Even the nomenclatures "voluntarily childless" and "involuntarily childless" are too facile. They do not take into account the many shadings of feeling and turns of fate that cause people to become nonparents. (To cite just one example, what category is valid for the woman who has two abortions prior to being married, then tries unsuccessfully to conceive?) Though I do use standard terminology for the sake of organization, I have tried in presenting individual life stories to give emphasis to the complex issues that lie behind nonparenthood.

Studies of this kind suffer from a mathematical skewness in that it is much more difficult to find voluntarily childless people in mid- and late life than it is to find those of similar sentiments in their twenties and thirties. Infertility is a different matter; there are many individuals at every stage of adult life who have experienced this unfortunate condition.

Readers should bear in mind that the life of childless couples today—be the childlessness by choice or imposed—is far different than it was ten, twenty, or forty years ago, especially for women. Hence, although comments made by older people may have as much emotional relevance now as they ever did, they should be considered in light of changing times.

I was, during the writing of this book, bothered by the transitory, elusive nature of what I had sought to make permanent. I made imaginary phone calls to one individual and another to ask whether they were still childless, married, sterilized, of the same sentiments. I questioned myself as well. What would *I* have said into that microphone two years ago had I been interviewed by someone else? Surely not the same story as today.

But we can only deal with what we know and are at a given moment. Tomorrow we will change. In precisely this potential lies a major excitement of life.

"Why do you want to talk to me?" asked the oldest person among my interviewees, a charming and alert widow of ninety. "Everybody's different," she said. "We are all different."

What, Mollie was asking, could she possibly say that would be applicable to someone else: a thirty-five-year-old career woman who is attempting to decide whether or not to have children, a young man faced with infertility, or a childless divorcée lonely in mid-life?

But, although we *are* all different, we are also alike. Other people, in revealing themselves to us, can produce chords of responsiveness, waves of empathy, shocks of recognition. It is my hope that readers of this book, be they parents or nonparents, will find themselves mirrored in the various lives described and that this, in turn, will lead to new and helpful insights.

Many people asked me as I neared completion of the book what conclusions I had reached. They were hoping, as I had hoped, for definitive, eternal, unambiguous truths about nonparenthood. But such is not possible. Childlessness is a complex and fluid state. It has its own richnesses and poverties and is viewed differently by the childless as their life circumstances evolve. If parenthood is understood to be productive of many differing and even contradictory emotions within the same individual, why should not childlessness be the same?

This is not to say that I have no findings at all. At least I have found clues, directions. I trust that they are implicit within the text, but perhaps they deserve emphasis here.

The most obvious is that the choice of parenthood or nonparenthood is one of the most important decisions of a lifetime. It should be made with that full recognition and with as honest an evaluation as possible of one's deepest needs, goals, abilities, and limitations.

Perhaps it is a truism, but for me it was a valuable one, that childlessness need not be considered a definitive state, even after the childbearing years are past. Many people do not have their own offspring but fill their working and personal lives with others' children. Some remarry and develop a close relationship with the new mate's children. I interviewed one woman in her sixties, the widow of a famous writer, who had recently adopted a baby girl. "The oldest single grandmother in America," she laughingly calls herself.

The word "adaptability" comes to mind as I write of this woman. We humans are, I think, more adaptable than we sometimes give ourselves credit for. Denied children because they are infertile, some people develop such a fulfilling life that they decide childlessness was possibly the best course after

all. Bored in mid-life, many voluntarily childless couples decide to take advantage of their freedom by assuming new and
challenging careers.

Several professionals with whom I spoke told me they feel
that the majority of people can adjust quite well to life either
as a parent or nonparent. "Not being a parent doesn't mean
that you wouldn't have made a good one," said one psychiatrist, "but that there are other priorities in a hierarchy of
interests." Commented another: "Most people can make a
satisfying life with or without children so long as certain vital
human needs are met: the need to control one's life in certain
ways, the need for nurture, intimacy—someone to care for
and be taken care of by physically and emotionally."

Perhaps the most significant conclusion for me was that
whether or not one is a parent is in the end less crucial than
what one does with the given situation. People without children, whether the reason for the childlessness was dedication
to career, bad timing, the desire to limit responsibilities, or
blocked fallopian tubes, can, as the interviews in this book
illustrate, lead wonderfully constructive lives—lives that, even
if they do not involve children directly, vitally affect future
generations of children.

D.S.B.

Philadelphia,
May 3, 1981

MARRIAGE WITHOUT CHILDREN

1

Marriage Without Children: Then, Now, and Tomorrow

Childlessness was not considered a fit subject for conversation until quite recently, and when people did talk about it they were usually sympathizing with the plight of the infertile woman. That men could have a similar problem was unthinkable. And that some people didn't *want* to have children was the most inadmissible possibility of all.

It is not surprising that the revolution in ideas regarding parenthood and nonparenthood which has occurred over the last two decades was so long in coming. To begin with, there used to be far less choice in the matter. Infertile people tended to suffer in silence—a response due both to embarrassment and to the fact that the science of diagnosing and treating such a condition had not progressed to nearly the state it has reached today. For those who preferred to limit their families or not have children at all, methods of birth control were few and dissemination of information about them scanty. Besides, motherhood defined a woman's very role in life, while fatherhood added greatly to a man's stature in both home and community. To question this was to defy nature itself.

The roots of society's push toward parenthood lie deep in history. During the centuries, the millenniums, of agrarian society, when lives were short, infant mortality high, and physical labor arduous, the continuation of the species was a matter of grave concern. Children were needed—as many as could be begotten. In response to this need, different societies developed their own methods for encouraging and even demand-

ing large-scale procreation. As far back as twentieth-century-
B.C. Babylon, according to author Elizabeth M. Whelan, the
Code of Hammurabi attempted to increase the number of
births by outright legislation, while in ancient Rome, somewhere between 18 B.C. and A.D. 9, Caesar Augustus decreed
that mothers had the right to wear distinctive clothing and
ornaments. The situation hadn't changed much by the seventeenth century: Spanish men who married early and had large
families benefited from tax advantages, and Frenchmen of the
nobility who had ten or more children—legitimate ones, that
is—received annual pensions.[1]

Religion played a large part in convincing people of their
duty to "be fruitful and multiply" (the words of God first cited
in Genesis). Roman Catholicism, with its view that the sole
purpose of sexual intercourse is procreation, is among the
most doctrinaire of faiths. The Judaic dictum, as stated in the
Talmud, is no less clear: "He who has no children is as if he
were dead." A strict interpretation of both Catholic and Jewish law would, in fact, require annulment or divorce in cases
of intentional childlessness.

The Protestant faiths (with the exception of the fundamen-
talist sects) are more moderate in their views, despite the
chilling comment by sixteenth-century theologian Martin Lu-
ther: "If a woman grows weary and at last dies from childbirth,
it matters not. . . . She is there to do it."[2] Mormons, who are
neither Catholic nor Protestant, are among the most frankly
child-oriented religions; the birth rate in Utah, where most of
them are concentrated, is twice the national average.[3]

Complementing the influence of most religions has been the
philosophic view that parenthood is the only normal outcome
of adulthood: the ultimate affirmation of life itself. Here, traditional psychoanalysis, which took form at the end of the last
century under Sigmund Freud, has been one of the strongest
voices. Freud saw motherhood as being essential to the
healthy feminine psyche and went so far as to claim that the
drive toward pregnancy was, in fact, a desire to incorporate
and retain the penis. (This well-known theory of "penis envy"
is still the subject of much argument and, not surprisingly, has

been joined by theories of "womb envy.") Other psychoanalysts added fuel to Freud's fire. Among these were Helene Deutsch, author of the two-volume work *The Psychology of Women*, published in 1944, 1945. Deutsch described women as being basically passive and masochistic and claimed that pregnancy fulfills the deepest and most powerful female need; those without that need, according to Deutsch, have a "masculinity complex."[4]

Among the most famous modern proponents of the birth-for-all psychoanalytic school is Erik Erikson, whose idea is that there are eight stages in the normal progression through human life; failure to reproduce foils stage seven, which he calls "generativity": establishing and guiding the next generation. Erikson has made concessions about people who, because of special creative gifts, devote their lives to self-development instead of having children, but his implication is clear that this route is but second best.

It is no wonder, given such influences, that until recently our country—along with most of the world—was strongly pronatalist. Pronatalism: a new word in our vocabulary and one not fully accepted even today. (You will not find it, for instance, in the 1979 Second College Edition of *Webster's New World Dictionary of the American Language.*) But word and concept do exist. Pronatalism is generally defined as any attitude or policy that exalts motherhood and encourages parenthood for all.

During the last half century our country has witnessed a dramatically changing picture in birth statistics as well as in the development of a peculiarly American brand of pronatalism.

Looking back to the Depression decade of the 1930s, we find that spinsterhood and delayed marriage were common, with lifetime childlessness edging up toward 20 percent.[5] It is felt by present-day demographers that economic deprivation and pessimism about the future of the country contributed to the low birth rates of the period. That people knew anything at all about the prevention of pregnancy through such means as condoms and diaphragms was due largely to Margaret Sanger, who opened the first birth-control clinic in the U.S. in 1916 and went to jail nine times for her efforts (birth-control information was categorized as "obscene materials").

A number of scientists back in the Depression years assumed that children were simply being postponed until times improved. In fact, many of the expected children never did appear. Paul C. Glick, senior demographer in the Population Division of the U.S. Bureau of the Census, has speculated that "many of the women who delayed having those other children reached the point where they liked it better without them than they had thought they would."[6] If so, this is an attitude strikingly in keeping with today's.

Birth levels remained low in the United States during World War II, which saw men off to do battle and women taking their place in the factories. But after the war, in an atmosphere of economic confidence, patriotism, idealism, and traditionalism, America went into full pronatalist swing. Interestingly, as Glick reminds us, it was precisely that group of women born during the Depression who, having reached their childbearing years in the 1950s, created the "baby boom." It was they who set an all-time national record for early marriages, high birth rates, and one of the lowest figures ever for lifetime chiildlessness (6 percent of those who married).[7] The peak year for births was 1957, although fertility (which in this usage refers to the projected average number of children born per woman during a lifetime) did not diminish significantly until after 1960.

As noteworthy as the number of births was the propaganda that accompanied it, causing America to equate parenthood with bliss. This was a "togetherness" time, when any family problem was resolved within the half-hour television limits of *Leave It to Beaver, Father Knows Best,* or *I Love Lucy.* The real-life birth of Lucille Ball's baby Desi Arnaz, Jr., was tailored to TV so effectively that it constituted one of the all-time highs in audience ratings. By contrast, childless women in daytime soap operas were usually unhappy and frigid. Any TV (or real-life) characters who were resistant to parenthood were branded as immoral, abnormal, immature, selfish, irresponsible, neurotic, rejecting, unstable, divorce-prone, and a host of similarly unsavory qualities.

Women's magazines sang the same tune. *Redbook, McCall's, Good Housekeeping, Ladies' Home Journal, Family Circle,* and others beatified mother and child with unmistakable religious (Madonna and Child) parallels. Articles propounded having new babies as the way to save faltering marriages, and authors recounted with undisguised admiration the sagas of infertile women who had undergone years of medical and psychic agony in order to reproduce. Mother's and Father's Day, storks and trousseaus, bridal dresses and honeymoons—these were the stuff of American dreams.

As for advertisers, there was no way to escape their blandishments, whether it was floor wax, spaghetti, or life insurance they were selling. The message was: Buy this product or service to make your big, happy family even happier. And it met a receptive, if captive, audience among the same stay-at-home mothers who had been denied responsible jobs because employers assumed they would be useless once they reproduced (indeed, they *would* be, given such conditions as short, if any, maternity leave and only token help from their mates with child care). Their only hope was that they would be rewarded for all their years of maternal effort by having their children make suitable marriages and produce offspring, thereby elevating them to grandmotherhood. As for the fathers, they were busy getting ahead. This meant, especially if they worked for big companies, that they had to maintain the proper executive image: photograph of wife and children on desk, youth-oriented activities like Little League and Girl Scouts, a spacious suburban home with two cars and resident pets. Such constituted stability, dependability, character.

Income taxes, military benefits, health and life insurance plans—all these and more were weighted in favor of parents, giving concrete governmental and industrial support to the notion that parenthood stood for the decent life.

The result of this many-faceted pronatalism was to convince people that life without children was meaningless. A survey carried out in Detroit in 1960 by Robert Blood and Donald

Wolfe showed that marriages that were childless by choice were practically nonexistent; wanting one child was almost as rare as wanting none; and childless wives, except for the newly married, expressed frustration over their fate.[8]

And then something happened to change it all. Or, rather, several things.

The feminist or women's movement has played a major role in the transformation of America. There are various misconceptions concerning this very large and complex phenomenon, one of which is that it is against having children. This is not the case, though obviously in a many-stranded and diverse population such as this one there are differences of opinion on parenthood as on many other subjects. But basically the philosophy is one of choice: that couples be encouraged to choose whether or not they want children, based on individual needs and life styles. Feminists believe that women, if they decide positively, should be given all possible support and assistance by their mates and society to make parenthood a facet but not the mission of life. Conversely, if they decide negatively, they should be given every opportunity to explore alternative means of fulfillment.

Long before the feminist movement flowered in its contemporary form, there were women of foresight who espoused precisely this view. Among them was Charlotte Gilman Perkins, who, in her book *Women and Economics* (1898), urged women to work outside the home in order to gain economic independence; she called for the establishment of "cooperative apartments" in which a professional staff would be hired for housework and child care.[9] Then, in 1916, a clinical psychologist, Leta Hollingworth, who was married and childless, wrote a brilliant essay criticizing the society that values women only according to their maternal role.[10] In 1930 a voice was raised in London, that of Jean Ayling, who wrote a book called *The Retreat from Parenthood* in which she spoke of the adverse effects of full-time motherhood and the need for other satisfactions.[11] By the 1920s and 1930s the situation had improved somewhat, with more women going to college and professional schools and into careers that hitherto had been denied them.

It was after World War II and the often reluctant return of women from the factories into the home that their gains were eroded and their position as strictly wives and mothers reaffirmed. The need was great at that time for a strong spokeswoman. One appeared in the person of Simone de Beauvoir, French writer and longtime companion of philosopher Jean-Paul Sartre. In *The Second Sex,* published in English translation in 1953, de Beauvoir debunked the "maternal instinct" and decried the end of a woman's growth at around age twenty when, as wife and mother, "she stands with her life virtually finished," her talents unrealized and stifled.[12]

De Beauvoir's powerful message did not catch on immediately, for women, still under the influence of Freudian psychology and the post–World War II ambience, were playing their motherhood role to the hilt. But then, in 1963, Betty Friedan burst upon the scene with her book *The Feminine Mystique,*[13] which convinced women of the severe societal limitations under which they had been living. The rest is history. Banding together in such groups as the National Organization for Women (NOW), which was founded by Friedan in 1966, they began to seek the equality they had been denied in all walks of life. Well represented by many other writers of note, such as Germaine Greer and Kate Millett, who vigorously attacked the patriarchal system and its gods—Freud included—women sought new roads to fulfillment. Some, like Friedan, were mothers and happy with that choice, if not with the societal restrictions that motherhood placed upon them. Others did not wish the parental role at all.

The rise of the voluntarily childless wife ran parallel to the feminist movement as a whole. Several of these women were connected with the communications media and had much influence. Gael Greene was among the early ones; in 1963, writing in the *Saturday Evening Post,* she championed married life without children as being "wondrously satisfying."[14] Her tale must have been too much to bear, because three thousand letters came in—most of them angry. A few other nonmothers came forth in similar fashion, but none with the verve of NBC correspondent Betty Rollin, who wrote a provocative and feisty piece in *Look* seven years later. "Motherhood cleaned up sex!" chortled Rollin. As for religion: "If God were to speak to us in a voice we could hear, even He would probably say, 'Be fruitful. Don't multiply.' "[15]

Several others took up the cudgels in book form. Some works were not directly connected with childlessness but gave implicit encouragement to it. Among the first (1962) was *Sex and the Single Girl* by *Cosmopolitan* editor Helen Gurley Brown, who was herself married and voluntarily childless.[16] In the book she held out to women the pleasures of the swinging single life, exciting career, and late marriage—a female answer to the hedonist philosophy of *Playboy,* then almost ten years into its bunnyhood. More explicitly, a couple, Anna and Arnold Silverman, wrote *The Case Against Having Children* in 1971.[17] But it was young, glamorous Ellen Peck, a onetime schoolteacher and counselor, who became the biggest spokeswoman for the childfree life style. In her book *The Baby Trap,* published the same year, Peck extolled the joys of married life without children and damned parenthood with such statements as: "The men who don't have children talk about their wives. The men who have kids ask me out."[18] Though marred by a superficial champagne-breakfasts-and-Riviera-vacations image of the childless life, which in its way is as prejudiced as the women's magazines were back in the 1950s, *Baby Trap* was sorely needed. Peck admits to having written it for its shock value, and shock people it did. (She later edited a more judicious text on the subject with Judith Senderowitz, called *Pronatalism: The Myth of Mom and Apple Pie.*)[19]

It was time now for mothers to do some thinking, too. If parenthood was not all it had been proclaimed to be, maybe they had made a mistake. Maybe it was the women without children who were to be envied. Shirley Radl took this dragon by its thorny tail in her book *Mother's Day Is Over* (1973), revealing herself as a woman who loved her children but found motherhood to be agonizingly difficult and her own success at it questionable ("if being a mother means liking the job, I am a failure at it").[20] The book was written with sensitivity and freed many other women to admit that life with toddlers and teenagers was not quite so perfect as they had been led to expect.

In the 1970s, the so-called "maternal instinct," which had been a foundation stone of psychoanalytic theory, came in for a lot of jabbing—from men as well as women. "Women don't need to be mothers any more than they need spaghetti!" proclaimed Richard Rabkin, New York psychiatrist.[21] "Motherhood . . . a biological destiny? Forget biology!" opined sociologist Jessie Bernard.[22] And psychologist Nathaniel Branden claimed he had a number of women patients who had worked very hard to convince themselves they had a maternal instinct, in order to prove that they were "truly feminine"; three or four children later, he reported, they found the whole idea absurd.[23]

Suddenly it seemed that parents, rather than nonparents, were on the defensive. Many polls and questionnaires were developed around the theme of parental (dis)satisfaction. The one that distressed Americans most was a survey by syndicated columnist Ann Landers, who in 1975 asked her readers: "If you had it to do over again, would you have had children?" Some 70 percent of the 10,000 respondents said "No."[24] Landers, surprised herself at the results, admitted that characteristically she heard more from those with negative, rather than positive, feelings. Still, 70 percent was a rather large figure. The complaints of the disillusioned parents were many: children strapped them financially, interfered with their life style, were impossible to raise (especially in the teen years with drugs, pregnancies, crimes, and suicides common), and ignored them in old age. But behind most of the given reasons was a common thread: having been fed a gilded picture of parenthood in the post–World War II years, people were not prepared for the hard realities. It was to this disillusionment that they were reacting, as much as to the children themselves.

In any case, one learns not to take surveys like Landers's too seriously because there is usually something to refute them. *Better Homes and Gardens* did its own survey in 1978, and 91 percent of the parents who responded said they *would* do it again.[25]

That voluntary childlessness made the inroads it did in the late 1960s and '70s would not have been possible without the influence of other vital factors. Finances were among these: the dollar was not buying so much anymore and people were becoming frightened by the burgeoning costs of raising just one child from the cradle through college. With ever greater numbers of women in the work force out of choice as well as necessity, the job of mother seemed to many an onerous added responsibility. Ideas and ideals about the American family were giving way to new realities: the highest divorce statistics in our history, later marriages, postponed first children, more singles, freer sex both in and out of marriage (with recreation rather than procreation as the goal), more dependable birth control—especially the pill and sterilization. Of major import was the 1973 landmark decision by the Supreme Court legalizing abortion. Its implications were broad: that women could now make decisions about their own bodies and their long-term futures, that it was up to them to decide whether ending life after conception but before birth was or was not moral. In 1973 alone, 744,000 legal abortions were performed; in 1975 the annual figure jumped to over a million.

Another influence was at work, too: the belated realization that America cannot continue to multiply in population if we expect to have any control over the quality of life. So deeply had the pronatalist philosophy penetrated our existence along with a "pioneer view" of endless land and resources that we simply couldn't believe we were growing beyond capacity. But when the recognition finally came it did something important: lent social legitimacy to the childless married life.

It was thanks to the environmental movement, spearheaded by such individuals as biologist Paul Ehrlich, that overpopulation became a national concern. Ehrlich's book *The Population Bomb,* published in 1968,[26] was dramatic and alarming in its projections and spawned several organizations devoted to cutting down on the birth rate. Of these, Zero Population Growth (ZPG) is an important one. ZPG's goal is to stabilize the American population so that birth plus immigration will equal death plus emigration. In the 1960s ZPG became associated quite effectively with the slogan "Stop at Two"—children, that is.

I talked with Wendy Univer, who was head of the Philadelphia office of ZPG. "The fertility in our country is now averaging less than two children per woman—1.8, to be exact," she told me. "But the U.S. is continuing to grow by well over two million people every year because all those women born during the baby boom are of childbearing age.

"With only 5 percent of the world's population, we Americans use up over 30 percent of the energy produced in the world. Our population is projected to reach 260 million by the year 2000. What that could mean in terms of water and air pollution; unemployment; food, hospital and housing shortages, and urban crisis, is staggering."

ZPG is currently spending much effort to promote one-child and childfree families. The organization also continues to fight the argument that, in having smaller families, the educated upper classes will be overrun by the poor lower classes. In fact, studies like one by James A. Sweet at the University of Wisconsin have shown that, while there was a continuous decline in U.S. fertility on all levels of society after the baby boom, this has been most pronounced among depressed-income minority groups which previously had the highest fertility rates.[27]

Other researchers have attempted to evaluate the relationship between environmental factors and the decision to remain childless. One study, in 1971, by Susan O. Gustavus and James R. Henley, Jr., focused on childless couples of whom one or the other had been sterilized. The most common reason the subjects gave for their sterilization was "population concerns."[28] However, findings such as these are considered suspect by many researchers simply because the decision to have or not have children is so overwhelmingly personal. To say you are doing something for the good of humanity sounds much better than to admit that you just don't want children—especially when the method chosen to prevent birth is sterilization, which is subject to much criticism for its permanency. Canadian sociologist Jean E. Veevers, who is one of the world's leading authorities on voluntary childlessness, labels population concerns as an "ex-post facto justification" for non-parenthood.[29]

Veevers and other researchers have made another interesting statement: that most of the women in their studies said they did not become aware of the women's movement until after they had made the decision to eschew parenthood.[30] Feminism—like population concerns—thus provided ideological support of their choice, rather than impetus toward it.

In 1972 a nonprofit organization was founded whose specific purpose was to make the childfree life style a socially accepted and realistic option. Founded among others by Ellen Peck of *Baby Trap* and Shirley Radl *(Mother's Day Is Over),* the group was originally known as the National Organization for Non-Parents (NON); in 1978 the name was changed to the more conciliatory National Alliance for Optional Parenthood (NAOP). Among well-known personalities active in NAOP have been TV host Hugh Downs, theater critic John Simon, actress Shirley MacLaine, environmentalist Paul Ehrlich, and clinical psychologist Lee Salk.

I talked with Carole Baker, who for many years was executive director of NAOP. "Our initial purpose," Baker told me, "was to act as a support system to those who were thinking of not having children or who had already made that decision. We wanted to let these people know that they are not alone, not isolated deviants in our society or any more selfish than parents—because we are *all* selfish. NAOP also acts as an element of cultural change so that in the long run there won't be a need for an organization like ours."

The group's members around the country have been analyzed as being 64 percent women and 36 percent men, largely under thirty-five years of age, married, white, urban, politically liberal, not committed to a formal religion, and with an education and income level higher than the U.S. population as a whole.[31] The organization is not trying to limit its membership in such a fashion; rather, those attracted to NAOP and the childfree life it espouses tend to fit this profile. Very important to NAOP is its 19 percent parent contingent. Baker, herself the mother of two, says: "After all, parents know better than anyone else what parenting is all about, and we can present a realistic picture of it."

She continues: "I want my children to grow up in a context where being without children is just as acceptable as parenthood and where people do not expect to become parents unless they intend to offer the commitment that every child has a right to expect."

NAOP's biggest hit has been a brochure called "Am I Parent Material?" (1977), which challenges many of the standard reasons for childbearing and has given rise to workshops and study groups around the country. Among the brochure's stated wrong reasons for parenthood are because everybody's doing it, to give your own parents grandchildren, to have somebody to possess, so as not to be lonely in old age, to carry on the family name, to save the marriage, to prove you are a man or woman. Critics of this and similar lists say, not without some legitimacy, that they are rigid and pass moral judgment on a decision that cannot be totally explicable or even rational, while neglecting the *right* reasons for parenthood.

Baker is of the opinion that much more thought generally goes into the decision to remain childfree than the decision to have a child. "But that's beginning to change. And I would rather see someone regret being without children than regret being a parent. There are going to be lots of things in life that we miss out on; we can't do everything. We have to make choices. Choices involve tradeoffs.

"At NAOP we also want to get over the message to infertile people that not being able to have children, even though one wants them, is not the end of the world." NAOP has a good working relationship with the group called Resolve, composed of infertile women and men. I met one couple who belonged to both organizations, feeling that each membership needed an exposure to and compassion toward the other.

NAOP earned itself something of a reputation for disliking children, especially in the early years when, as NON and under Peck's leadership, it was more militant in its stance. Staff members at the Washington, D.C., headquarters told me they still meet people who, on hearing their affiliation, make such comments as: "Are you the people who give children away? That's awful!"

People who actively dislike children—they are called *misopedists*—are, in fact, pretty rare, W. C. Fields notwithstanding. (Fields, a crotchety, hard-drinking comic, achieved enduring notoriety by his statements denigrating everything from Philadelphia to children; among the latter was "Anybody who hates children and dogs can't be all bad.")[32] Admittedly, there have been exceptions throughout history of societies in which children were neither wanted nor loved. Anthropologist Margaret Mead uncovered one startling example of misopedists in New Guinea: the Mundugumors, a cannibalistic tribe in which the women detest childbearing and the men hate their wives for being pregnant.[33]

There is a tendency to focus accusations of parental neglect and indifference on the underdeveloped nations or on the lower classes of the developed world. But this is not verified by historical fact. Parisian scholar Elisabeth Badinter wrote a book published in 1980 called *Love Plus: The History of Maternal Love,* in which she described urban upper-class French mothers in the eighteenth century as shipping their infants off to wet nurses for four or five years.[34] Evidently they preferred opening salons to nursing babies, which, they complained, deformed their breasts and made the nipples flaccid. (The great statesman Talleyrand met such a fate; he was born, baptized, and shipped away all on the same day, returning to his mother at age four, lame from an accident.) In the early days of our own country children were harshly treated (the New England Puritans, for instance, considered children to be sinful creatures whose spirit had to be broken). As for our own time, child abuse by parents is hardly restricted to the underprivileged.

NAOP, except for the fringes of its membership—some of whom have left the organization since the name change and the decreasing influence of Ellen Peck—is neither against birth nor against children. It is simply opposed to the idea that everybody must have children. Unfortunately, in its attempts to gain publicity, NAOP has initiated certain activities that have confused people as to its sentiments. One was the decision to begin an annual Non-Parent's Day (August 1), first celebrated in 1974 at Central Park in New York City and featuring three women in white who danced a nonfertility rite.[35] *New York Times* humorist Russell Baker promptly wrote a column which envisaged mothers sending their childless daughters bouquets with cards reading: "Thanks to my daughter on Unmother's Day for not having any more children like her."[36]

Actually, some very solid citizens were involved in this event, including distinguished authors Alvin Toffler, Isaac Asimov, and Cleveland Amory, who called for the end of society's glorification of childbearing. At the ceremony and at succeeding ones, a nonfather and nonmother of the year were named. Among NAOP's more publicized nonparents was philanthropist and political activist Stewart R. Mott. Mott for years was an outspoken bachelor and ardent nonparent with a strong interest in NAOP, ZPG, and similar organizations. Then suddenly he got married. Mott informed me when I questioned him by phone that he remained supportive of NAOP and its goals but that his own "lukewarm attitude" toward children had been modified by his new wife's desire to have them, and she had won out. "We will be checking the temperature charts before long," he told me. However, true to ZPG, the Motts would "stop at two."

Now that it has made some real progress in dealing with pronatalist pressure as a whole, NAOP is putting its energies into other areas, such as attempts to cut down on the huge number of teen pregnancies and to make people aware of the magnitude of child abuse. Also high on its agenda is encouraging employers to provide concrete advantages to the childfree. Among the latter is a "creative" leave of absence, paralleling the maternity leave, which would enable employees to spend time away from the office in study or temporary assignment to other organizations. The Population Institute in Washington, D.C., already has such a program. NAOP also has lobbied successfully to have sterilization and even abortion benefits included in group insurance plans. A subject on which the organization has not yet taken a firm stand is all-adult housing, sensitive because of its discriminatory implications.

The National Alliance for Optional Parenthood has professional affiliations around the country with a network of psychiatrists, psychologists, and sociologists who maintain that being childfree enhances marriage. Conversely, their studies show that the first year after a baby's birth (especially that of the first child) often represents a crisis period in the marriage. Among such authorities is Angus Campbell, director of the Institute for Social Research at the University of Michigan, who found that young married couples without children expressed the greatest contentment with their lives, followed by two groups: older couples without children and older couples whose children are grown.[37]

As is common with studies of this kind, there are professionals on the other side of the fence who maintain that the birth of a child affects the marriage only slightly and temporarily in a negative sense, or even that it enhances the husband-wife relationship. Besides, they claim, whatever strains are endured are generally felt by parents to be worthwhile. Anthony Pietropinto and Jacqueline Simenauer, who did a massive survey of 3,900 married men and women across the nation, concluded in their book published in 1979 that "far more parents regard their children as having brought them closer together than as exerting a disruptive force in the marriage."[38]

However people assess their own childlessness or parenthood, there is a distinct attitudinal change regarding parenthood in general. A study by the Roper Organization, whose results were released in mid-1980, was informative on that subject: "Among the more significant findings is the overwhelming consensus that motherhood is no longer synonymous with marriage. While a majority of American women (94%) favor marriage, 82% do not feel that children are an essential ingredient for a happy marriage."[39]

Out of the quibbling has come at least one recognition: marriage without children is not destined to be unhappy and unfulfilled any more than marriage with children is assured of being an unqualified success. That is a big step forward.

The climate as we enter the 1980s seems on the whole more tempered, more measured, if not without certain contradictory signals. The vociferous parents have had their day—or, rather, their decades—on the podium, and the staunch nonparents have experienced their shorter time in the sun. We are at a stage where children are neither revered nor reviled and where parenthood and nonparenthood are seen in shades of gray instead of black and white. In substantial numbers, those of childbearing age are joining discussion groups which help them come to an understanding of their own deepest needs and motivations in this, one of life's most important decisions.

More and more one hears people admit to honest ambivalence regarding parenthood, not only before the decision is made, but after. Betty Rollin, among the most vigorous defenders of the childfree life, recently expressed to a reporter from *Time* magazine the feeling that in not having had children she has "missed something."[40] Conversely, parents show much curiosity—and even envy—about the childless life; no longer does it strike them as so abnormal. Yet, as NAOP's Carole Baker said: "Choices must be made in a society as complex as ours. And choice means sacrifice—you can't have it all."

Of much significance is the new openness by psychiatrists to voluntary childlessness as a viable and preferable life style for some people; no longer is it automatically labeled deviant and abnormal. As for the long-argued "maternal instinct," though there is still no real consensus as to whether it is physiological or psychological in origin, instinctual or rooted in learned behavior, most social scientists agree that in some women, in some form, it does exist. Still, as John Leo wrote in a *Time* article, it "almost certainly can be overridden by cultural influences."[41]

An intriguing shift in the feminist movement is also perceptible. In its current stage of development, the movement is looking at families as a whole—in particular, at the husbands who, back in the 1970s (which were dubbed the "Me Decade" by writer Tom Wolfe), got left behind. Fatherhood used to be a pretty clear-cut job for a man. As master of the household, with full responsibility for it economically, he was rarely required to take on other duties, such as housecleaning, babysitting, cooking. But, with wives' entry into the working world, men are learning to assume some of these responsibilities. This means the decision of whether or not to have children is more and more a joint one. Men have to consider such questions as: Will home duties jeopardize career development and force them to take a less-responsible, less-interesting position? Would more emphasis on family and less on the job be rewarding? Or would the switch in roles simply be asking too much? As one still childless man said to writer Nadine Brozan: "I'm willing to accept my share, but not more than my share. I don't want to be the mother."[42]

Statistics on parenthood and on plans for future parenthood traditionally have focused almost entirely on women. But with the loosening of strict maternal and paternal roles, we can expect to see the feelings of men expressed more openly and given far more attention. Even the subject of a paternal instinct is being studied by such scientists as Una Stannard, who sees men as having a drive toward fatherhood that is, in fact, more "maternal" than that of the mother herself.[43]

In keeping with this spirit of tolerance and objectivity, some once heavily pronatalist American institutions are viewing matters quite differently. I spoke with Carrie Gabriel, Mrs. America for 1979, which was revealing of this. Thirty-two years of age and voluntarily childless, Gabriel is a financial planner for Remington-Rand Corporation in Princeton, New Jersey. She told me that while not so many years ago the focus in the contest was mainly on "cooking and starching shirts," today the criteria are far different. Certainly there were mothers among the contestants, but, she said, "at least 30 percent who took part when I did in the thirty-to-forty age range were childless."

To be sure, there are still glaring instances of pronatalism, such as this statement which I quote from the book *Mother-In-Law* by Ann Serb, published in 1978: "Although it's very hard for any mother to believe, there are some people who do not want children for a variety of reasons. If selfishness is one of them—as the mother-in-law might strongly suspect—she'd better be grateful that no grandchildren will suffer from being raised by people who view them only as an inconvenience. It's the only comfort she's going to get. And that doesn't make her existence without grandchildren much easier to bear."[44]

Contrarily, there is the occasional misopedist with equally biased views. There was, for instance, an angry contribution to the Op-Ed page of the *New York Times* in 1980, sent in anonymously by a Manhattan attorney, age forty-four. It constituted an announcement to his wife, who wanted a child, that he did not: "My wife is urging, insisting, in fact, that we bring in an absolute stranger to live with us. . . . I'm not having any of it. No child. But there'll probably be a divorce."[45] One can only wonder if the wife learned about her upcoming single status through the *Times*.

Among the most tenacious pronatalist holdouts are the religions. Catholicism continues to adhere strongly to its pro-birth tenets, a stance that causes some to leave the faith; however, individual priests often quietly give support to those who opt for childlessness. Sometimes, caught between personal wishes and faith, people make odd but understandable choices. Psychiatrist Helen Edey wrote in an article: "Some Catholic couples I have talked to prefer voluntary sterilization to contraception because they have sinned once rather than having to confess repeated transgressions."[46]

Organized Judaism has become increasingly adamant on the subject of children. In June 1977 even the Reform Movement, which is the most liberal segment, took a clear stance urging Jewish couples to have at least two or three children. This is related to the thorny question of "Jewish survival" (particularly as a result of the atrocities of World War II) as well as to the fact that, in absolute numbers, Jews are decreasing—partly through intermarriage.[47] Once again, however, we find individual rabbis and theologians who support voluntary childlessness and give help to those who wish to retain both their faith and their freedom of personal choice.

Some people carry the matter of childlessness and religion a step further: into active lobbying. One of these is Elaine Burhop of Seattle, a voluntarily childless wife and member of the United Methodist Church. "I've taken it upon myself," she told me, "to initiate changes in the rules that are in the book of discipline of the United Methodist Handbook. So far we have been successful in having a state petition passed. If it is accepted nationally, this will mean that our church supports childless couples as having made a respectable and responsible decision."

Pronatalism among blacks is an extremely sensitive issue today. With the struggle for achievement having been so great, those who have climbed the slippery ladder of success are naturally desirous of passing on a better life to the next generation. Still, this puts great pressure on those who, for whatever reasons, prefer to remain childless.

I talked with Barbara Daniel Cox, executive director of the Women's Resource Network located in Philadelphia. She is a woman deeply concerned with the matter of voluntary childlessness for blacks. "I would say there certainly is peer pressure in the direction of parenthood," she told me. "Family is a very important value to most black people, and I think we buy into the traditional concept that woman is here to procreate. I know some childless women in mid-life, which is where I am, who are struggling with the issue: Can I, should I? will I? must I? And they are not very comfortable with who they are because other people might feel that if they don't reproduce they're not fulfilling their responsibility. I think a lot of traditionalism came out with the black power movement, and blacks became more focused upon their roots and keeping family life together."

According to Cox, black women are forming their own groups to discuss the parenthood question because those established by whites often prove unsuitable for their needs. She also feels that "black women want to hook up with black men emotionally more than white women do with white men. The quest for equality is at a different point for us."

A forty-year-old black woman who holds an executive position in an oil company and is married and voluntarily childless expressed similar sentiments to me. The black woman of achievement, she says, is under pressure to reproduce; often she does so whether or not she wants to. But then she finds herself in an intolerable position of having to raise the children alone while her husband struggles for career enhancement: "The black male is under such tension today just to survive, just to make it, to accomplish something in life, that it requires all of his energies. When you put him in a position where he has to take some of that energy and divert it to a family situation, it's as if there's nothing left. It can end up in hostility between partners and in forced responsibilities. 'I have enough in my job,' he says. 'Now I come home and you tell me I have another set of duties? No; I can't cope.'"

Studies in this area are few, but one in 1970 by Kiser and Frank revealed that black women over age twenty-five who had a college education or were married to professional men showed a lower fertility rate than white women in similar circumstances.[48]

As for the Latin community, it is particularly vulnerable to the pronatalist pressure of family, friends, and priests, according to Florida psychotherapist Dorita Marina. Latins, she says, are not organization joiners and resist various mental-health services which might influence them in the direction of nonparenthood. Even the most highly motivated, career-oriented Latin woman feels that if she gives up the role of mother there will be nothing left, according to Marina.[49]

Looking statistically at what has been happening in the United States on the birth scene, we find that the first half of the 1970s saw a continuation of the down swing that had

begun in the 1960s. The "birth dearth" or "baby bust," they
were calling it. In actual numbers, births reached a low point
in 1973 and then began to increase, especially after 1976.
(This increase is due, in part, to the fact that so many women
born during the "baby boom" have come into their childbearing years.) Fertility rates reached a historical low point in
1976, then began to fluctuate, with recent trends showing an
upward turn.

In May 1980 some rather dramatic figures were published
by the Bureau of the Census in a report entitled *Population
Characteristics: Population Profile of the United States: 1979:*
"Childlessness has risen sharply among women under thirty-
five," it claimed. "The proportion of childless increased from
24% in 1960 to 41% in 1979 for ever-married women twenty
to twenty-four years old, and from 13 to 26% for women
twenty-five to twenty-nine years old. Although it is not certain
at this point in time, it is likely that these large proportions of
young married women who are childless result from a decision
not merely to delay motherhood but to remain forever childless."[50]

That last prognostication may seem a very high one, but
several demographers would agree with it. Charles F. Westoff,
director of the Office of Population Research at Princeton
University and one of the most respected authorities in the
field, is among them.[51] Westoff believes that the factors which
led to the lowering of the birth rate in the 1960s and '70s are
irreversible and he suggests that if current rates persist, some
25 percent of women now of childbearing age will remain
permanently childless, setting an all-time U.S. record. Westoff
sees this trend as being characteristic of the developed world
as a whole. (The lowest birth rate of all is in West Germany,
where alarmists have predicted extinction by the year 2079.)
At the other extreme is China with 960 million inhabitants; so
serious is the overcrowding there that the government is offering such incentives as full wages at pension time to those who
remain childless.

There are a number of cogent reasons cited by scientists like
Westoff for continued, and growing, childlessness in the

United States. A basic one is the economy. Even with both partners working full time, double-digit inflation is making it very difficult for many young couples to raise even one child. Research by population economist Thomas J. Espenshade, author of a report published by the Population Reference Bureau in September 1980, concluded that, in terms of then-current prices, the average U.S. middle-income family was spending about $85,000 in direct, out-of-pocket expenses to see a child from birth through four years at a public university. To this one must add "opportunity costs," which reflect such factors as a reduction in the income of the mother and which, according to Espenshade, would add between $15,000 and $55,000, bringing the one-child total cost to a whopping $100,000–$140,000.[52]

The 64 million baby-boom children born between 1946 and 1961, who were raised in a period of unprecedented wealth and idealism, are now of childbearing age and coming up against these hard realities. Though some have achieved and even exceeded their career and financial expectations, others—especially the younger among them—have been forced to take on low-paying positions for which they are overeducated; some are not finding jobs at all. Because so many of them are flooding the market simultaneously, they also are competing with each other in such areas as housing. Here too they face disillusionment: soaring prices, high interest rates, and a shortage in homes.[53]

The baby-boom generation grew up with the expectation that their economic and social well-being would exceed that of their parents. Indeed, as futurist Alvin Toffler points out in his most recent book *The Third Wave,* surrogate fulfillment through one's children—the dream and likelihood that the next generation would do better than one's own—used to be a special gratification of parenthood. No more is this the case. Instead, young people are finding that their direction may well be down the ladder instead of up.[54] Struggling to maintain the life style to which they have become accustomed, many probably will defer having children, have just one child, or remain childless.

The growing importance to women of their careers, in connection not only with finances but with their personal development as well, will undoubtedly play its part in the decision of some couples to eschew parenthood. In the opinion of such population specialists as Westoff, only if the women's movement suffers a decided setback and/or financial conditions worsen to the point where a job crunch pushes younger and less-established women out of the executive and professional market will motherhood seem a preferable option to this group.

A good deal of media attention has been given in recent years to the phenomenon of late motherhood; this is a natural development given the contemporary woman's educational and career goals, her tendency to marry at a later age, and the development of highly sophisticated medical techniques which can detect fetal abnormalities common in the older mother-to-be. However, infertility does increase with age, even in men, though their reproductive ability drops off more slowly than women's. Hence, the desire for a pregnancy in the later years may not result in the reality of one. Another factor in the postponement of childbirth is referred to as "drift": the longer a couple waits, the more likely they are to become involved in other ego- and energy-involving activities and the less likely to give up a comfortable life style for the unknowns of parenthood.

Also relevant to future childlessness is the trend for couples to live together unmarried. This kind of arrangement has been around for centuries in quiet corners of society, but by 1979, according to a report by *Time* magazine, 1.1 million unmarried couples were cohabiting in the U.S.—double the number in 1970. Nathan Glazer, professor of education and social structure at Harvard, has written that he suspects such cohabitation is not replacing but "simply postponing marriage until such time as children are conceived."[56] Once again, however, postponement has a drift momentum of its own and can result in continued nonmarriage as well as permanent childlessness, especially as the law gives more and more weight to the economic rights of the cohabitants.

Also pointing in the direction of fewer children is the growing acceptance of homosexuality. Whereas in the past gay men and women characteristically married and had children to prove their "normalcy," now they feel much less pressure to do so. Martin Goldberg, M.D., director of marital therapy, training, and research at the Institute of Pennsylvania Hospital in Philadelphia, has an interesting theory which he expressed to me: "I think people's awareness of overpopulation is making homosexuality a lot more acceptable. We keep saying how much more liberal we are, but I'm convinced it's more that we are no longer threatened by the idea of people not reproducing themselves; instead, it's become desirable."

Yet another trend which has become quite common could have its own, if small, effect on parenthood. That is the growing numbers of older women, some of whom are past childbearing years, who become involved with and marry younger men.

Returning to infertility, the surprising truth is that, despite the incredible scientific progress made in this area, an estimated ten million people, or 15 percent of those of childbearing age, in the United States are now unable to reproduce, and only 40 percent of that number will eventually become natural (as versus adoptive) parents.

Because the Census Bureau does not distinguish between voluntary childlessness and childlessness due to infertility, an accurate statistical comparison is not possible. Compounding the difficulty is the fact that, at least until recent years, some couples who chose to be childless took refuge in claims that they were infertile, because voluntary childlessness was considered deviant and abnormal.[57]

Not everybody believes that birth rates will continue to plummet. One authority, at least, Richard A. Easterlin, professor of economics and a member of the population studies center at the University of Pennsylvania, foresees a virtual baby boom in the 1980s, along with an amelioration of many of the nation's social, political, and economic ills.[58] Easterlin is in the minority with this view. Veevers and Glick are two among many who agree with Westoff's opposite prognosis, if not necessarily with his high estimates of future childlessness.

Some, however, do point to certain changes in the national mood which could result in a leveling-off of childlessness. Sherry Barnes, former national director of population education for the Planned Parenthood Federation of America, told me she has sensed a swinging back to more conservative family trends in the last few years. Barnes sees delayed marriage, deferred first children, and fewer children per family as being more characteristic of the times than outright childlessness.

What are some of the conservative trends? Among the most significant is the concerted effort of the anti-abortion forces to overturn the 1973 Supreme Court decision legalizing abortion—an effort whose impetus was strengthened greatly with the election of Ronald Reagan and a like-minded Congress. Another sign is the subtly tightening restrictions on voluntary sterilization, which became a highly popular contraceptive method in the 1970s. Similarly, resistance to the Equal Rights Amendment represents a backlash to the feminist movement on the part of those women who are threatened by demands for the same career opportunities that men have and whose self-esteem is tied up with being mothers and housewives.

We live in a perplexing and contradictory age—a time which combines unorthodox living arrangements, unthinkable two decades ago, with stubborn traditionalism. Perhaps both extremes will prove to be unworkable. In any event, we Americans are confused: though skeptical of our old-time style of life and values, we are loath to give them up. A Gallup poll released in June 1980 revealed that almost half of all Americans believe that family life has deteriorated in the last fifteen years. Yet three women out of four view marriage with children as the "ideal" life, with one-third wanting to combine marriage, children, and a full-time job.[59]

The high rate of divorce and its effect on children has become a national obsession—so much so that scholars are trying to come up with new types of marriage to better protect children from the traumas of a broken home. This is not a new approach: decades ago, anthropologist Margaret Mead proposed a double system of marriage—the first a limited, early dissolvable form for those without children, and the second a long-term arrangement for parents.

Today, there are more complex ideas for a more complex society. *The New York Times* reported late in 1979 on the proposal of Judith Younger of Cornell Law School that there be three legally defined types of marriage which would center upon the matter of childbearing. "Dress rehearsal" marriage would be for the younger set (age sixteen minimum), "selfish marriage" for those twenty-two and up who want "personal fulfillment and mutual self-expression" but no children, and "marriage for children" for those who are willing to commit themselves to staying together until the children reach age eighteen.[60] Younger's concept may be reasonable, but the title "selfish marriage" surely is not. It represents a throwback to post–World War II pronatalism and the implication that, by definition, parents are unselfish. It also leads one to question how the infertile population would be categorized—perhaps as "involuntarily selfish marriage"?

It is not easy to decide whether or not to have or not have children, or how to live life after the decision is made. But those who are without offspring—whether by choice or not—have some clear advantages in the 1980s. The main one is that many other attractive options are available which hold promise for a rich and meaningful life. Another is that pronatalism, though not dead, is both laughable and passé.

The childless are finally in the mainstream of American life.

2

Childless by Choice: Making the Decision and Living With It

- "Our marriage is too good to tamper with."
- "Freedom, plain and simple."
- "I think I'd make a rotten parent."
- "Actually, I think I'd be a very good parent, but I don't want a twenty-year responsibility."
- "Money, money, money."
- "I've worked too long and hard in my career to give it up."
- "I guess I just didn't want to go against his [her] feelings, and he [she] was just dead set against kids."
- "The bottom line is: the disadvantages outweigh the advantages."

These are a handful among dozens of statements that people of varied ages made to me as their reasons for not having children. At first it seemed I might almost be able to chart them mathematically in order of frequency and importance. But the more I learned about the motivations, feelings, and relationships of voluntarily childless couples, the more complex and many-stranded appeared the reasons—positive and negative, overt and hidden—that lay behind this, one of the most important decisions of a lifetime.

The word I heard most often was "freedom." Whatever rationale is given for not having children, freedom is almost always among them—here spoken, there implicit: freedom to pursue career interests with commitment, to maintain a life style of spontaneity and mobility, to enjoy leisure time and to spend a lot of it in travel, to further one's education. "We've moved six times in our eleven years together," one voluntarily childless wife from Seattle said, "and never have we had to consider things like: should we find a house on a cul de sac, what's the school district like, and will we have enough money for shoes for the kids if my husband takes a lower-paying but more satisfying job.' Sometimes freedom means the opportunity to lead a contemplative, slow-paced life, indulging in hobbies from stargazing to pottery, and sometimes the opposite: a work-hard-play-hard existence. Freedom also can mean that one has the liberty to be away from the mate at times, either of necessity because of a work assignment or by choice like a summer vacation spent alone. (I met one woman in San Francisco who was going off by herself to house-sit for a week.)

Differently stated, the voluntarily childless desire freedom from the lifetime responsibility, the full-time occupation, that children entail. And that responsibility, many point out, is quite different in the 1980s than it used to be when life was simpler and children acted like children. "Today's twelve-year-old," a New England man said during our interview, "is yesteryear's twenty-one-year-old."

What is as important as the utilizing of one's freedom is the sense of it. Several researchers have noted that nonparents do not seem to be substantially freer in their life styles than parents but report they *feel* more free—and that perception is very important. As Jean Veevers, Canadian sociologist, writes in her recently published work *Childless by Choice:* "Options may not be exercised much but their existence is crucial."[1]

Closely allied with freedom for the voluntarily childless is the opportunity to "take risks"—another oft-repeated phrase. Granted, theirs is a selective kind of risk taking: perhaps moving to a foreign country or embarking on an unsure but exciting business venture. The risk they will *not* take is to bring into the world a human being whose life is subject to only transitory direction and control. A number of people who are highly successful professionally told me they don't like to be "out of control" of their lives and that this is a major factor in the decision to remain nonparents. In her popular novel

Fear of Flying, Erika Jong (who after the book's publication became a convert to late motherhood) says in the person of Isadora Wing: "I always wanted to be in control of my fate. Pregnancy seemed like a tremendous abdication of control. Something growing inside you which would eventually usurp your life."[2] Parenthood is, to be sure, a big gamble with uncertain odds, and the voluntarily childless aren't sure they want to try their luck, especially if life as a twosome is happy and fulfilling. "Why exchange a good thing, a known quantity, for a life we know nothing about?" they say.

Money. Where does that fit into the decision to be child-free? Certainly many people who intend to and do become parents put off having children because of insufficient funds. But with others postponing for monetary reasons often becomes permanent, at times because their income does remain limited but more characteristically because they have grown accustomed to various luxuries which would be jeopardized with parenthood.

Even in these difficult times, many couples without children continue to enjoy a high standard of living. One reason is that both are free—there it is again, that favorite word—to take on high-paying, responsible jobs. Another is that only a small part of the joint income is needed to buy services compensating for nonparticipation in housekeeping. The result is more spare cash for nonnecessities (entertainment, trips, advanced education, wardrobe) than working parents with heavy child-care expenses can afford.

Childlessness also means that the financial responsibility is less burdensome for each of the mates. By agreement, one might be the sole breadwinner for a time while the other devotes himself or herself to a personal goal, be that writing a novel or training for a new line of work. One couple interviewed by Kate Harper in her book *The Childfree Alternative* referred cheerfully to their life of "downward mobility,"[3] with both of them earning "less and less" but doing what makes them happiest. An engineer with whom I spoke in Chicago expressed a similar sentiment: "My father was a slave to the company he worked for. All for the sake of the kids. But

I won't have to do that. If I don't have $100,000 to retire on, we'll go up to Maine and open a little seashell shop or something."

How well even two-career childless couples will do financially in the future depends much on developments in the national economy. Some authorities are concerned that, if present trends continue, there will be few luxuries for any but the very rich and that many who want children simply will not be able to have them—i.e., children will themselves be a luxury.

Career, of course, does not just mean money. It can mean power, prestige, responsibility, excitement, growth, and a host of other tempting possibilities. Men are accustomed to being tantalized by the idea of a big career; some continue to revel in it, while others are getting tired of the rat race. For women, however, the opportunities are new—and heady.

Career goals are clearly a major reason for childlessness on the part of some women. Research by Beverly Toomey (Ohio State University) shows that many career-oriented women who eschew parenthood see themselves as being highly competent and independent and that most have had early and real career success to prove the validity of their self-assessment.[4] Some say they would like to have a family but do not believe that they can combine marriage, career, and motherhood effectively, especially since, whatever the good intentions of their husbands, women generally end up with primary responsibility for child rearing. A female graphics artist in North Carolina was alluding to this when she said to me: "I sometimes wonder, if I could have had the daddy role, might I have gone along with that? Like if I were a man and had married a woman who felt very strongly that she wanted children, I might have accepted being the secondary parent. But to be the primary one, I definitely wasn't interested."

Indeed, it takes a high energy and patience level to combine marriage, career, and parenthood, as well as an understanding and helpful mate and flexible working conditions. "The Superwoman image is beginning to irritate our readers," Kate Rand Lloyd, editor of *Working Woman,* told me. "In 1977 when I first came to the magazine, women were bedazzled by it, but after a couple of years they were saying, 'Come off it!' "

Realistic in their assessment of goals and limitations, many women recognize that if they were to shortchange a child in favor of career their guilt would be overwhelming. If, instead, they were to be the devoted mothers they would want to be, their professional life would suffer at least a temporary setback. Says Lloyd: "There is no question that women who take time off to have a baby trip on the career path. The woman who cannot stay late at the office is probably penalizing herself, especially in highly competitive fields such as law where sixty or seventy hours per work week is not uncommon. Clearly, women won't make it to that catbird seat unless they can work the same hours as a man."

Some career women who have a strong identification with the feminist movement cite related reasons for childlessness. An East Coast history professor, aged forty and divorced, has these sentiments:

"I've always had rather ambivalent feelings about having children. I think they probably come from accepting the viewpoint one finds in a patriarchy that motherhood is tantamount to inferiority. I didn't get this from my own mother. I must have absorbed it from the so-called culture. You grow up and you learn that girls can't do this and shouldn't do that and are not capable of the other. Consequently, you don't want to be associated with anything that girls do because you feel that will put you behind the eight-ball. You've also learned things about equality and independence, and you've taken your little social studies courses in elementary school and junior high school. So the last thing you want to do is to put yourself in a subordinate position. I think what women have unconsciously adopted is a patriarchal view that we are inferior and that what makes us inferior is what makes us women: childbirth and motherhood."

Obviously not all wives who choose to be childless consider career or the feminist movement as being integral to their decision. Some do not work at all and maintain a traditional marriage with the husband providing the entire income. Others look upon their employment as a job, not a career. They work for the money, for the structure and purpose this gives their day, for the pleasure of being with other people on a regular basis. A young woman from the South, sterilized, told me she fits into this category: "I enjoy working and I like having an interesting job, but I'm not one of those career-motivated people. I don't think I'd ever give up my fun time for a career."

Research on the relationship between childlessness and career on the part of men is more scanty. Generally, the literature shows that voluntarily childless women who are high achievers are married to men of similar ambition. However, Susan Bram claims in her doctoral dissertation (University of Michigan) that voluntarily childless men rate themselves as less dominant and less occupationally competitive than fathers and more supportive of the women's movement.[5] In the last few years there have been signs that men, increasingly disillusioned by career and desirous of a rich family life, are becoming frustrated and angry because the very women to whom they are attracted as potential mates are the ones who don't want children.[6]

Another major reason given for voluntary childlessness, especially by women, is the desire of the couple to maintain the special nature of their one-to-one relationship. They tend to see marriage without children as being happier than marriage with them (just as, conversely, most parents feel that childless marriages lack a basic purpose and hence are prone to unhappiness). Many scientific studies do support the view that children transform the nature of a marriage—and not always positively. The first child, in particular, demands a big adjustment, with the mates having less time and energy for each other and the husband often feeling displaced by the child. With growing children in the picture, the husband-and-wife relationship becomes less the focus as other groupings develop: each parent to the child or children, child to other child, and so on. On the other hand, when two adults make up the entire family, the opportunity for relating to each other is greatly facilitated.

What often develops among the childless is a marriage characterized by intimacy, dependency on, and even preoccupation with the other. Sometimes there is a gradual closing-out of the larger world. Veevers points out that focusing on the other adult to fulfill one's social and psychological needs can make one dangerously vulnerable to the continued existence and concern of that person. Also, in a troubled relationship such closeness can intensify the problem areas. However, in a good marriage this concentration of energies can, she says, maximize the relationship's strong points.[7] Many childless couples consider this intimacy to be worth the risks and claim it to be a major reason for their childless state. Others look upon it more as the result of having no children and are a bit wary, attempting to live instead with what Syrian poet Kahlil Gibran referred to as "spaces in your togetherness."[8] A young woman I spoke with from West Virginia is among them. "We're fairly close," she said, "but not one of those self-contained units."

Robert E. Gould, New York psychiatrist and professor at New York Medical College, told me he looks at the intimacy factor this way: "Many couples I've known who don't have children seem closer and more involved with their mates as friends. Of course, they are also more dependent on each other. They have more time to spend together—with less conflict."

The words "intimacy" and "nurture" are closely intertwined. But nurturing is usually associated with care for a younger, more dependent person—typically a child. When a couple decides not to have children, the need to nurture still exists and must somehow be satisfied. One way is to develop a closeness with other children, like those in one's family or circle of friends. Many do this. "Childless people make wonderful aunts and uncles," says Gould. A lot of energy can be invested, too, in friendships. Friends fulfill a deep emotional need and help make up a support system for the childless which, in older years, they may find particularly valuable. During the early years of a marriage, childless couples usually find it easier to make friends with their own kind; parents characteristically are too harried, financially pressed, and preoccupied with matters of childraising for the kind of socializing that the childless can enjoy.

Typical of childless marriages, and related to the quality of intimacy, is the tendency of the spouses to nurture each other. Often they act like children themselves—and they enjoy it. "At Christmas," said one wife, thirty-eight, "we shake our presents and sniff them and carry on like five-year-olds." This trait may become exaggerated when the partners are significantly different in age. Anita Landa, a developmental psychologist at Lesley College in Cambridge, Massachusetts, told me that she had seen several cases of voluntarily childless couples of widely disparate age in which the senior partner consistently served in a nurturing capacity to the junior one.

In his novel *Enemies, A Love Story,* Isaac Bashevis Singer, recipient of the Nobel Prize for literature, writes on a variation of that theme: the husband does not want a child, the wife does, and because she feels deprived she turns him into a child substitute. "He had frustrated her longing to bear children and so had taken the place of child for her," writes Singer. "She fondled him, played with him."[9]

It is difficult to draw the line on when childish behavior is merely fun and when it is an indication of an unwillingness or inability to be an adult—and hence an underlying reason for childlessness. "I don't know what I want to be when I grow up." I heard this many times, usually spoken in a jesting tone, during my interviews. What does it mean? Many things, perhaps: I don't want to be an adult; I don't *have* to be an adult if I am not a parent; I am not mature enough to be an adult and hence a parent.

Few human traits are more valuable than the sense of wonder, curiosity, and honesty of a child; good children's writers and artists, with or without children, possess these qualities in large measure. (Pamela Travers, who wrote *Mary Poppins,* J. M. Barrie, author of *Peter Pan,* and Dr. Seuss, who created such favorites as The Grinch and The Cat in the Hat, were all childless.) But childish behavior has its dangers, one being a difficulty in redefining the relationship with one's parents as adult to adult instead of adult to child. Voluntarily childless couples, then, may have to do consciously what comes to parents more naturally: grow up.

A stereotyped picture exists of the excessively emotional relationship between childless people and their pets. Jean Veevers claims this to be unsubstantiated among her interviewees, two-thirds of whom had pets (about the percentage of parents who do). Only in a minority of cases, she reports, were the animals child surrogates; in fact, many owners found pets to be unsatisfactory because they require the kind of care that children do.[10] Psychologist Landa, however, told me her clinical experience was rather different. "Many of my subjects felt that their relationship with pets was more intense than that of parents to their children. And they joked about it."

My interviews, admittedly random, leaned more in the direction of Landa's findings. "I just don't think babies are cute," said an elegant southern divorcée. "I mean I just have no desire to pick up somebody's little infant. I don't think they smell good. When they get to the stage where they are toilet-trained and I can talk to them, fine. But before that I would rather have a puppy. I think dogs are infinitely cuter."

Another childless couple had a beloved dog named "Son" who had his own room and a closetful of clothes; when Son reached thirteen, his "parents" told friends, they would be invited to a "Bark-Mitzvah." Yet another childless dog owner told me that when her marriage began to fall apart she and her husband considered getting a second dog. "Like having another baby to save the marriage," she said.

Those who have a strong attachment to their pets tend to express, in implicit contrast to children, the joys they bring ("They give you 100 percent love, without complaint") and the sadness ("They'll die before you, one after another; somehow that just doesn't seem right").

An advertisement from a Denver newspaper was sent to me by one of the people I interviewed. It left little doubt as to the sentiments of one woman, at least: "Dog sitter, toy poodle, needs loving day care while Mother works. 8–4:30. $10 a week."

One's own family background is integral to the decision about reproduction. Several studies indicate that there is a statistically large number of only children and eldest children among the voluntarily childless. The former, often unaccustomed to being around babies, tend to express trepidation in dealing with this unknown as well as an impatience with children. If they have led sheltered lives with parents who spoiled them precisely because they were the only ones, they may not be eager to give up that role or to make the kind of sacrifices their parents made for them. A dapper middle-aged college professor from San Francisco told me that, because his mother had married a man "who is not at all a loving type," she focused her affection on her only son. "She turned me into a Prince Charming. I was everything she wanted and that put tremendous pressure on me." As a result he became very self-centered. "I'm what matters," he said to me. "I feel if I am successful enough, I am image enough; I don't need kids."

The eldest child in a family, on the other hand, may have been saddled with a great deal of responsibility for younger siblings (sometimes a middle child in a large family falls into this same category). Though secure and competent in child care, he or she knows well the drudgery of it instead of the rosy picture that is our pronatalist heritage. Often these people are the ones who, even if they had what they describe as a happy family life and developed real love for the child or children they had to care for, don't want to go through it again with their own offspring. They also commonly feel that, as an aunt or uncle to their siblings' children, they have no need of their own. (Singer Dolly Parton, who was one of twelve, expressed precisely this sentiment to a reporter.)[11]

Millie and Grant are illustrative of similar views, though the precise circumstances are quite unusual. Millie, thirty-three, an art teacher, and Grant, thirty-four, an electronics engineer, live on what Grant calls "a very fertile street" in Manchester,

Vermont. It is the area where both were raised and where they met eighteen years ago. "Our getting together was kind of romantic," says Millie, an intense, petite brunette. "Basically," Grant corrects her, "she told me to drop dead!"

By the time she had graduated from high school Millie felt rather more kindly toward her handsome, dark pursuer, and they started dating. Though they considered marrying during college, they did not do so until graduation.

Millie's feelings about children while growing up were that "four was the magic number" (she was herself one of three). "But, as we got closer and closer to the wedding, I kept cutting down on the number until finally, when we were married, I thought, jeepers, it's okay to get pregnant now, only I don't *want* to."

It was hard to admit and analyze this change in her feelings, and Millie dealt with it by postponing . . . and postponing. Her reluctance was due in part to a growing fear—not based on any negative personal or family experience—of doctors, hospitals, and especially childbirth. There were also more positive reasons for not wanting children, the primary one being that she hesitated to introduce a new element into the marriage, which was characterized by fine communication, yet a lot of breathing space for both. The fact that Grant's work involved considerable financial risks was another consideration.

Millie and Grant did not arrive at nonparenthood easily. "There was nothing casual about this decision," she says, "and at times it still is very uncomfortable and unsettling for me." But that Grant had come to feel the same way independently was a big help. When the two read about the National Alliance for Optional Parenthood, they realized that a life without children wasn't so abnormal after all and might best suit their needs.

As they look back today at the reasons for what Grant calls "a 99.99999 percent surety that we'll remain childless," the two recognize something else of importance: the already-having-done-it factor. When both were in college and not yet married, Millie's sister-in-law suddenly died, leaving her firstborn, a son of six months. The shock to the family, a close-knit one, was great. Since Millie's brother was in no position to bring up a child alone, the baby remained with Millie and her parents, then in their fifties.

"So from age twenty to twenty-four," she recalls, "I had a child. We brought him up. And the funny thing is we were all nuts about him. He was a very, very easy child, very adjustable. My mother was first in charge and I was second. Basically, I was playing house in the most positive way, commuting to college every day, coming back at five, having dinner waiting for me on the table, with this little baby that couldn't wait to see me. Actually it's very much the position of a working father."

After the first few months of this new routine, Millie's parents, fatigued by the course of events and sudden change in life style, decided to take ten days away on vacation. Grant would be around to help during that time as he had been since the baby's arrival.

"This was the first time I had my nephew completely to myself," remembers Millie. "He was then about nine months old, which is an adorable stage. Bear in mind, I'd babysat and changed diapers and done everything that a mother would do by then.

"But when my parents took off on that Saturday morning and drove down the street and were no longer in sight, I took one look at the kid and realized I was in charge for ten days. I burst into tears and had a postpartum depression that lasted the entire time they were gone. I was a wreck. Oh, my God, all I can say is I was depressed. And I was bored. And I was scared. Here I was twenty years old . . . now there are *plenty* of mothers twenty years old. But I felt, I am alone and my mother isn't here to back me up! Those ten days, I'll never forget them."

Grant adds: "Hours of boredom and moments of sheer terror. You know, the kid's projectile vomiting, which was one of his tricks—like he's dying." Through it all, Grant did his best to help out. "I don't know how I could have coped if not for him," Millie says.

When her parents returned, life went back to normal. Millie

retained a close relationship with her nephew, delighting as he learned to walk and talk and teaching him to draw, while Grant introduced him to mechanical skills. Both felt the highs and lows of parenthood. "I know all those special feelings," says Millie.

Her brother remarried after a few years and took his son to live with him. The love between Millie, Grant, and nephew is still strong. But both partners say, "We've been parents." And they don't want to do it again.

Researchers have determined that childhood unhappiness is a potent factor in the decision to be a nonparent. This is not surprising; after all, if people do not remember their own youth positively and do not feel their parents enjoyed parenthood, why take the same route? Some, of course, try to repair the mistakes of the past by dealing more successfully with their own children. But others, especially those, according to psychologist Landa, who were victims of parental neglect and coldness in family relations, are likely candidates for voluntary nonparenthood.

Many women today perceive their mothers to have been martyrs in a male-dominated society, lacking in self-esteem, diminished by the role of housewife, and with no opportunity to develop their natural gifts in other directions. Daughters of such women are commonly among those who choose to follow the career path, relinquishing parenthood and fulfilling their mothers' unrealized dreams through their own achievements. They also typically say their mothers have admitted that, if times had been different, they too might have opted for childlessness.

The whole mother-daughter relationship has been studied with almost fanatical interest in our country in recent years. Largely responsible for setting this trend in motion was author Nancy Friday, whose book *My Mother/Myself* was published in 1977. Voluntarily childless and married to another author, William Manville, Friday focuses in the book on the lifelong struggle of the daughter to separate herself from the mother, a struggle that results from the daughter's growing realization of how much she is like the mother in both positive and negative qualities. The thought of having children, believes Friday, instills a great fear in some women of a too-close identification with their mothers; indeed, she contends, the actuality of motherhood reunites most women with their mothers, repressing the negative image they have tried to break away from.

Behind Friday's own rather typical reasons for childlessness —importance of career, not wanting to endanger her marital relationship—she admits there lurks such a fear: that she would become the "nervous, frightened mother" her own mother was to her. "Alone, I can control the helpless mother who lives inside me. A mother myself, I would become just like her."[12]

(Friday told me an amusing epilogue to her story: whereas in the past people warned her constantly of the miseries of nonparenthood, now that her writing has proven so successful they are quite silent on the matter.)

One's childhood experiences dictate to a large extent the world view one has an adult. A reason I heard on several occasions for not having children is what might be called the "state of the planet" or "why bring children into such a mess." Generally a secondary consideration which lends support to and justifies a decision made for other reasons, it is in that regard rather like overpopulation.

A Phoenix couple whom I interviewed were Jan, a psychotherapist of thirty-two, and Philip, a fine-arts professor five years older. Still unable to decide what their future will be as regards parenthood, they talked at some length about their differing world views. But not until the end of our meeting did a significant underlying reason for Philip's comments become clear.

Philip: "My major reservation, one which Jan does not share, is that I am not persuaded it's a great favor to bring a living being into existence at this moment in history. I think things are going to get worse. I'm not sure it's a favor to say to a child, 'Well, the air is running out, the nuclear holocaust is around the corner. Welcome aboard!' That may be rationalizing, masking other things. It doesn't absolutely make up my mind, but it does make me very frightened. Now I'm not talking about things like cancer. I'm talking about something more abstract. Something to do with hope and promise and a sense that you'd be working toward some vision, some goals. What I feel today is a contraction of possibilities."

Jan: "I grew up with a much different sense of certainty, a certainty given me by my parents that everything will be all right, can be worked out. I realize that perhaps that view belongs to childhood."

Philip: "It's very much a part of our general personality structures. I am emotionally conservative and cautious, and I can find the black lining in any cloud. Jan can find the silver lining in Hurricane Ethel!"

Jan: "Philip sees the world picture. I tend to think of things more narrowly. I spend my whole work time on individual growth and development. I see people who are doing really well come out of difficult backgrounds and people who aren't doing well come out of seemingly normal backgrounds."

And then this comment from Philip: "My parents were divorced when I was three. I'm sure a lot of my attitudes come from not having two parents. It's hard for me to imagine what I'd be like as a father because I never had a father I can remember. I'm sure that's the most powerful single element in my feelings."

Shortly after I spoke with Philip, I read a statement about the quality of life made by the famous historian Will Durant, who was both a father and grandfather and, judging by his memoir, a delighted one. Interviewed at the age of ninety-four, he commented wryly: "The world situation is all fouled up. It always has been. It always will be. I see no reason for change."[13]

Among the deepest and most repressed reasons for not wanting children are those dictated by fear. Author Nancy Friday revealed one of them in the mother-daughter relationship. Another is the fear of passing on a physical disease or weakness, real or imagined. Sometimes this subject is so sensitive that couples do not even seek out medical advice on the likelihood of transmitting such a defect to offspring. Emotional illness, still viewed with shame and secrecy, can be even more frightening. One man in his fifties whose family history contained several incidents of psychiatric disorder, and whose own life had been marked by severe bouts of depression, told me the major factor underlying his professed reasons for not wanting children (money, career, disinterest in fatherhood) was fear of passing on his own sickness and despair: "I wanted the agony to stop here."

One might expect that in our medically sophisticated era the dread of childbirth would be a thing of the past. Not so. Millie, who had a "postpartum depression" while in charge of her nephew, had such a fear. Other women told me that this was a potent factor in their decision. Sometimes it masked a deeper concern. "My mother always told me childbirth was so easy," said one. "Yet I am terrified of the pain. My two sisters have a congenital and debilitating hip ailment, and my mother suffered a special kind of pain in dealing with those two deformed children. I didn't want to go through that suffering, and so I think I translated that in my own mind into the fear of childbirth."

Some women—and men, too—see pregnancy as being unattractive and embarrassing and childbirth as ugly and disgusting. Their idea of a mother is someone who is sagging, old, and without sex appeal. One man admitted that the idea of impregnating his wife was "scary as hell."

Concern that one's marriage is in trouble is another reason for childlessness. Robert Chester of the University of Hull, England, first recognized, in 1974, that childlessness could be an index of unsatisfactory marital adjustment, rather than a causative factor in the breakdown of marriages,[14] the traditional view.

Sometimes the avoidance of parenthood enables couples to stay together in relative equanimity: cases, for instance, where one mate is so needy and demanding that he or she could not tolerate any nurturing of a child by the spouse. At other times the marriage ends anyway. I was told by one divorced woman that she had had an abortion while married, pretending to herself and the outside world that her husband was not yet sufficiently established careerwise to support a child; shortly afterward he left her. Much later, she finally admitted that it was her premonition of the separation that was the real reason behind the abortion. In any event, the decision to remain childless because of marital instability is a wise preventive move in every sense from the purely financial to the potential psychic damage to a child of divorce.

Sexual maladjustments can play a role in childlessness. The phenomenon of "virgin wives" is well known to psychiatrists: marriages which never have been consummated even though the partners may have been together for years. Often they cannot bear to admit this reason for the childlessness and pretend they are infertile, even to the extent of attempting adoption. Others seek professional help and may end up having children; still others remain "voluntarily" childless for life.

There are also marriages in which intercourse is unsatisfactory and infrequent, with the partners feeling a sense of diminished sexuality. This, in turn, affects negatively their perception of both self and mate as prospective parents. They may even fear they are incapable of impregnation, conception, or childbirth, so "Why bother?" Martin Sturman, Philadelphia endocrinologist, told me that in his practice infrequency of sexual intercourse has been a significant cause of childlessness. "It's not infertility," he says, "nor is it being childless by choice."

Childless couples who have a poor sexual relationship tend to be sensitive to the comments of others, even though these may be quite innocent. One forty-five-year-old woman told me every time people ask her if she has children she feels they are prying into her sex life and guessing at its inadequacy. Looking at parents, she can't help wondering how many of their children were planned and how many simply the product of more unrestrained lovemaking than her own.

Aside from problems like these, no real differences have been determined by researchers about the quality of marital sex between nonparents as compared with parents. It is not unusual, however, for nonparents to wonder if they could have had children had they wanted them. Several childless women who chose to have abortions admitted to me that, even though they do not regret the operation, they also do not regret the pregnancy: "It was nice to know that I had all the necessary equipment." Similarly, one woman after another revealed that she would love to experience pregnancy and childbirth—but not the job of parent that followed. As one thirty-eight-year-old wife said: "I feel the whole thing of carrying and delivering a baby is very womanly, very sexual. What can you do that is more womanly? Intercourse? Well, that's just animal instinct."

Prejudice against the childless sometimes is directed specifically, if covertly, to the area of sex. Ironically, the two most common attitudes are contradictory: one, that when people are childless by choice there is something the matter with their drive or performance and, two, that they indulge in too much sex and are "loose"—a holdover from the religious tenet that sex without at least the occasional goal of procreation is sinful.

"I think you have to feel very secure within yourself sexually not to have children," says Ruth, a Pasadena real-estate agent. "When a family lays guilt trips on you it usually relates to your masculinity or femininity. I overheard my husband's mother on a visit here. She was talking to the cleaning lady no less, and asking if she had children. Then she said, 'A family without children is barren.' What really infuriated me was that she was a guest in my home."

In response to such prejudice the voluntarily childless sometimes feed the second of those pronatalist criticisms, emphasizing all the time and energy they have for lovemaking, the ease and spontaneity of the act without children crawling around underfoot, and even the offbeat settings. (A study by W. M. James in 1974 did, in fact, support this contention. Couples without children have intercourse more frequently than couples with children, James concluded.)[15] Angered, parents fight back. What about "the rapture of stolen moments," wrote one mother in a letter to *Newsweek.*[16]

Not much research has been done on infidelity among the

voluntarily childless, but Veevers has broached the issue and feels there is no direct relationship, though many of her subjects alluded to extramarital affairs, from one-night stands to liaisons of several years. She concludes: "Since involvement in extramarital sex is known to be associated with low religiosity and other unconventional attitudes [attitudes common to the voluntarily childless], presumably the rates are somewhat higher among childless persons than among others."[17]

Choosing to be childless does not necessarily mean that one does not like children. Very often, in fact, nonparents enjoy young people enough to spend their working lives with them in schools, nurseries, churches, adoption agencies, hospitals, and summer camps. Why, then, don't they have their own? In many cases because the daytime responsibility—and the overtime—are enough. Says Nancy Craig of St. Louis, a teacher: "I get my parenting instincts taken care of at school. That's about all I can handle." A male college professor from San Francisco is more blunt: "I don't see how people who work with kids can have their own and survive. I'd come home and kill 'em."

Frank, a kindergarten teacher from Chicago, takes precisely the opposite view. He and his wife have postponed parenthood because of finances, but, at age thirty-one, he is chafing at the bit: "I know a lot of times when I'm working with kids I get frustrated," he says, "but the frustration comes from having them only a certain number of hours a day and not being able to accomplish a lot that I would like to do. With kids of my own I would have an entirely different role. I'd be seeing that other half I never see now."

A surprisingly large number of people claim that they enjoy children only at certain stages of development and forgo parenthood for that reason. They may like the teenager but not the toddler, the baby but not the college student. Others like young people of all ages but don't feel they or their mates would be good parents. Some cite lack of confidence and self-esteem, and feel the job of parenting is beyond their capability. One woman said to me about her husband: "He's a wonderful uncle—children love him—but as a disciplinarian he's a washout. He's the kind who winds them up and plays with them, then lays them back on their mothers."

Close contact without full-time responsibility is precisely what many childless people want when they seek out the offspring of relatives, friends, and neighbors, serving as babysitters, nonjudgmental confidants, companions at baseball games, and even godparents. And these friendships can work very well. An instructor in modern dance, whose husband directs high school plays, said this: "There are always kids around who are hungry for adults, other than their parents, to whom they can relate. Alan and I fulfill that role now. I think we always will." Another woman, a credit analyst from Louisville, Kentucky, feels this way: "I will be utterly frank about it. I don't want the day-to-day burden of children. I love what I skim off the top of other relationships with kids, like those in my family."

Not all childless adults go around being friends to children. Some are indifferent to children, feel uncomfortable around them, and say children make them nervous. A few even feel they are capable of child abuse. (Actress Katharine Hepburn, who is divorced and childless, once commented: "I'd have made a terrible parent. The first time my child didn't do what I wanted I'd kill him.")[18] A real feeling of antipathy toward children is more rare, but when it exists, it is the most potent reason of all for avoiding parenthood.

Ludmilla, forty-one, is a Russian émigré, childless, who left a prestigious publishing job in Moscow five years ago to come to the United States with her photographer husband Boris. They live now in a spacious loft apartment in Philadelphia, Boris's starkly poignant photographs of Soviet life filling the walls. Three lithe cats skittered across the wooden floor as Ludmilla and I talked over a table crowded with cheese, wine, bread, and, of course, vodka.

Ludmilla does not like children. One would never guess it because children like her and seek her out. Broad-faced, with large green eyes and severely cropped blond hair, she speaks in a rich and rolling voice. I noticed on first meeting her that she has a limp but forgot it quickly, so graceful is her manner.

"As a child I became a cripple," Ludmilla explained. "This happened when I was four years old. It was war, 1942. We used to live in a basement. It was such a terrible life, maybe six people in one room. Moscow was bombed and we had nothing to eat. I was very weak, fell down in the street and injured my knee. From that I developed tuberculosis. I spent six years in a sanatorium in bed. After I was out I was a cripple with crutches, and they tortured me. All the children, they tortured me. They took away everything I had—my books, my toys. I couldn't run, I couldn't do anything. They were so cruel all the time, I hated them. I couldn't fight back. I started at a very early age to dislike children.

"Even now, can you imagine, I am forty-one, and when I see children I go away from them. I feel they can say something to me. I better avoid it. I'm afraid of them.

"We have an expression in Russia: everybody is afraid to die alone, and nobody is afraid to die with children because children will always give you a glass of water. I see it a different way. Okay, I think, what if I have children and maybe they will *take away* the water?"

There is another kind of pain in Ludmilla's life. She has had several abortions, both during a first marriage that ended in divorce and in her present marriage to Boris. She had the abortions because she didn't want to have children, and now she fears children even more because in Russia all the abortions were done without anesthesia. "The first time you sleep with a man and you are pregnant. In Russia we did not have birth control, we had no anti-baby pills, we had nothing. All the time I make love I think of abortion. You can't imagine the pain. It was terrible, so terrible. . . .

"The first months after my divorce when I start dating Boris, I get pregnant again. Can you imagine? What to do? What to *do?* The same story again and again. Still no anesthesia, still the same pain. What remains? Nothing. And you still *hate children!*" Suddenly Ludmilla was struck by the humor behind the pain and she roared with laughter.

"All together I think I have eight abortions. Boris, for two years he says, 'Let's have this baby or that one.' I say, 'No way.' I don't want children. I don't like them. I can't stand them. I am afraid they will ask me why I am not like everybody else, that they will be cruel to other people who are cripples. I am afraid my child will be cruel to other children.

"Sometimes I think I am not normal because I could make children. My God, I could have eight children now. No, twice I have *twins!* Yes, the doctor told me. Oh my God, that is how many children?"

The most stress-filled time for decision making is usually when the wife reaches her thirties and begins to realize that her childbearing years will eventually come to an end. Some women begin to panic earlier, in the late twenties; others put off the issue by continually extending the cutoff date for consideration of pregnancy. Men generally have an easier time of it; even though they may be deeply committed to their marriages, they have the comforting underlying recognition that there is no absolute biological end to their own fertility.

There are some serious issues to consider regarding parenthood at this stage. If the couple have lived together without children for several years, they most likely have established an ingrained and enjoyable life style and are somewhat set in their ways. Often they are less than willing to take on the lower standard of living that would result from new expenses along with a possible reduction in or elimination of the wife's income. An older couple have to face the probability that they will have less energy, patience, and flexibility with youngsters. The prospect of being a graying, paunchy father and a menopausal career-woman mother at a sixth-grade school play is not likely to seem appealing. Worry over a difficult pregnancy and possible birth defects plagues many, even in an era of advanced medical techniques. Another concern is that one child might be all that a couple can handle; if so, that may be fine for some—the one-child family is no longer considered an aberration. Nonetheless, some professionals still consider it to be the most unwieldy family size—"a typical triangle in that one person usually feels left out," according to Martin Goldberg, Philadelphia psychiatrist.

Why, then, do people even consider having a child at this late stage? Why is it that, although the overall U.S. birth rate has not risen, the rate among women in their early thirties *has* grown? (*Newsweek* reported in March 1981 that the number of first births among women of that age, mostly among urban and professional women, has jumped by 37 percent in recent years.)[19] Sometimes the answer lies in career disillusionment. I talked with Philadelphia psychologist Margaret Baker, whose specialty is the two-career couple. "In your twenties and thirties you still have a great deal of idealism," says Baker. "You feel you can pretty much make your dreams come true. I don't think it's until the late thirties and even forties that you begin to realize there are going to be limitations. And, even if you have accomplished what you set out to do, the rewards might not meet your expectations."

As one's own parents grow older and die, mortality becomes a very real concern and the passing on of one's genetic heritage, one's knowledge, one's possessions, more meaningful. "I don't have a strong maternal instinct," says Ginny Hyde, a childless divorcée who is a ticket agent for a major airline, "but now that I'm thirty-four and my parents are in their seventies, all of a sudden I realize what they mean to me. It's like I want to give to somebody else the love they gave to me."

What is life about anyway, couples begin to ask at this stage. Oriana Fallaci, the Italian journalist, wrote in a compelling novel called *Letter to a Child Never Born:* "What good is it to fly like a seagull if you don't produce other seagulls who will produce others and still others who may fly?"[20]

The fact that their childbearing years are finite strikes many women with unanticipated force. "This is the first time in my life that I've had to confront the reality that there's a limit, a biological, physical limit," said a California psychologist, "and that the risks beyond it are great. And I don't like that."

Adds her husband, a newspaper writer: "If we were to wait and have a child later and there were some damage to the baby or to my wife, I don't know how we could ever work through the guilt."

Various names have been coined to describe women at the end of the childbearing years. Marilyn Fabe and Norma Wikler wrote a book about them with an apt title, *Up Against the Clock;* and Kate Harper, in her collection of interviews with childless people, referred to this stage by its German name, *Torschlusspanik* ("closing-time panic").[21] What can make the decision even harder is, paradoxically, all the information available about late motherhood. The literature is flooded with emotional arguments on both sides. On the one hand, there are idyllic reports by glamorous career women who had their first child late in life; on the other, there are warnings such as one by Johanna Garfield, whose glow has worn off. Writing in *McCall's,* this "'60s pioneer of late motherhood" reminds us: "The age forty (and by now possibly fifty) ear is simply not attuned to decibel counts once thought to be heard only by dogs, or to casual chitchat between five-year-olds about contraception, or to language . . . that makes Henry Miller sound like Mother Goose."[22]

Some deal with this perplexing time by falling into what has been described as "panic pregnancy" ("accidental pregnancy" is a variation on that theme) or the opposite "childlessness by default" or by "inertia." But when a decision is carefully and honestly made it usually is followed by a sense of relief; the *in*decision is what is exhausting. If the scales have tipped in favor of continued childlessness, the couple may continue as they are or take this opportunity to scrutinize their life together, discussing how it might be altered to assure continued growth and fulfillment in the years to come.

The above assumes that couples are in agreement over whether or not to have children. But what if they are not? Psychiatrist Robert Gould looks at the issue quite bluntly: "As I see it, if one of the two doesn't want a child, it's as if both of them don't want a child."

It is surprising how many couples give almost no time to determining before the marriage how the prospective mate really feels about offspring. Some among these are lucky: they have similar views and the subject never becomes a source of conflict. A happy, well-adjusted secretary of fifty-two whom I met in Atlantic City told me that she and her husband hardly ever discussed having children. "There was only one time I remember, down at our vacation cabin. It must have been six or seven years after we were married. I leaned out the back door—I was kind of teasing him—and I said, 'Hey, are you sure about children? Do you want them or not?' And he said quietly, 'Oh, well, Eve, I really don't think so because we've gone a long way now.' I suppose maybe I'd been around someone who'd asked me the question and it must have been strong on my mind at that point. I remember being totally satisfied and relieved with his answer."

Other couples, in discussing parenthood, find there are differences between them but ignore these, hoping they will go away. Sometimes they do—one partner comes around to the other's beliefs. And sometimes they don't, in which case the result can be divorce or, especially if the marriage has lasted for several years, an accommodation to the stronger partner. Among my interviews was one unusual case in which the wife, fifty-three, announced that she was voluntarily childless, and the husband, fifty-seven, went on to inform me that he was *in*voluntarily so. "I'm the unhappy one," he stated flatly. They explained that she, in deference to his wishes and to the baby-oriented philosophy of the time, had tried to become pregnant but did not—an outcome which was a relief to her but left him with an emptiness that still lingered.

Particularly painful are cases in which the mates are in agreement regarding children early in the marriage, only to learn later—perhaps years later—that one or the other has undergone a total change in attitude. If such differences persist, trouble may well lie ahead for the marriage, and if a pregnancy should occur, either accidentally or by design, the decision about whether to carry or abort the fetus can stir up deep anger and pain. "Some of the most severe and unhappy marital conflicts that I have dealt with have involved this very issue," says psychiatrist Goldberg.

I did not speak with any couples who expressed a decided and threatening difference of opinion regarding children.

However, I did interview one woman of twenty-nine, married for eight years and residing in Columbia, South Carolina, who was developing in the direction of wanting children, while her husband was clearly still not interested in the prospect. He was unavailable for an interview, so the comments which follow are the wife's alone.

Shy in manner, Gail, a physicist, spoke in a soft, sometimes barely audible voice, concealing her tenseness with a constant giggle. We sat on the floor amidst large Indian print pillows, among which she appeared especially petite and vulnerable, her long hair falling across her face.

"When we got married, we really didn't discuss having children. I don't think it's unusual for men who are in their early twenties to think that they will never want children, then as they get older and more mature to come to the decision that they *do* want them. I just assumed that someday he would come around to that and that I would be there at the same time."

But so far Bernie, her husband, has not made that transformation. "Maybe when he is out of graduate school and is working in the real world like I am, he may feel differently. Graduate school has a way of becoming a goal in itself."

Gail admits to some ambivalence on her own part and says that she is the kind "that could have swung either way." That she hasn't been "struck by lightning" with the desire for motherhood makes her feel she can also cope with nonmotherhood. But some of her comments seem to suggest otherwise.

"I think periodically of all that I would want to teach my child and how I would do things for my child. My husband feels differently. He says you have to create your own life and that you can't work through someone else. I remember once I said how great children would be and he came down strongly against it. I got real turned off by his attitude. But I'm not convinced I want children so much that I can let them create a major conflict between us.

"I'm very close to my family even though they're all thousands of miles away. That's one basic difference between Ber-

nie and me. His family has a different attitude—they're not
into grandchildren and cousins and so on. They are just people
who happen to be related.

"I have a hard time imagining what my life would be like
if I were fifty-five and without any children. I wonder about
the quality of a married life without children. If I were to force
the issue, I'm sure Bernie's reply would be negative. Of
course that's not the way I deal with situations. I think he has
to come to that on his own. I feel very married and very
committed to this relationship for my lifetime. I hope we can
make it last, but sometimes I wonder what the statistics say."

Decision making about parenthood is easy only for some.
Many find it difficult. I talked with Diane Elvenstar, Los Angeles clinical psychologist who holds a doctorate from the
University of California at Los Angeles and who is originator
and leader of one of the more imaginative decision-making
workshops in this area. Voluntarily childless and married to a
speech pathologist, Elvenstar told me that the purpose of her
sessions is "to resolve conflict, both internal and between
partners and to reduce the amount of stress involved in the
decision." With this goal she has formulated a lengthy and
intriguing set of written materials which concentrate on and
quantify in graph form the values, expectations, and feelings
of participants. She feels her biggest contribution has been "to
zero in on the emotional component."

Having worked with over two hundred couples thus far,
Elvenstar describes her workshop members as falling within
three categories: two-career couples with the wives in their
thirties, couples in conflict or with one expressing uncertainty,
and couples inclined in one direction but needing confirmation of that choice. Her sessions are characterized by a lot of
carefully structured play-acting at home, where both partners
pretend for three days that a pregnancy has been achieved and
for another three days that they are unable to have children.
How does each feel? Even such details as the wife not being
allowed to drink coffee during her pretend pregnancy are
strictly adhered to.

Elvenstar described a few of her couples to me. "One woman came to the workshop after the three days of 'pregnancy' and it turned out she'd done nothing but cry solid. She was miserable. Her face was a mess, totally red, and she had to stay home from work. It made her decide, of course, that she didn't want children.

"Another woman cried the whole time of the 'pregnancy' but for a different reason: she'd been on the pill for a long time and was afraid if she went off it she'd be infertile, and that scared her to death. She realized during our seminar how desperately she wanted a child and how she had been evading that. Her husband had been on the fence, but when he saw her going through all that turmoil, he decided he wanted a child because he loved her so much." Elvenstar also has her couples test their parent potential by borrowing a child during a full work week; she asks that they choose one of the age they most dread dealing with.

Though seminars such as this one can help clarify the issues and draw out important marital conflicts whose resolution is vital to the decision about children, some professionals are skeptical about various of the techniques used. Sociologist Veevers is among those who believe that borrowing someone else's child is not representative enough of a real parent-child relationship to be valid.[23] Elizabeth Whelan, a demographer and public health specialist who started her own decision-making group, is critical of attempts to quantify and rationalize emotions, claiming that in her own case she eventually took a "leap of faith"[24] in deciding to have a baby. Similarly, Bill Bernardy of St. Louis, who has been professionally involved with Planned Parenthood, listened to *his* inner voice which told him: "I don't feel that gut-level desire to have children."

The paths to voluntary childlessness have been studied most comprehensively by Jean Veevers. Though her research was carried out mostly in Toronto and London, similar findings have been reported by U.S. researchers. In my own interviews around the country I found a large number of people who had arrived at their childless state in precisely the ways she described.

The first group, which Veevers estimates to comprise one-third of the voluntarily childless, clearly and definitively make their choice before marriage and independent of the spouse-to-be.[25] In fact, most of them do so in early adolescence (researcher Sharon Houseknecht calls them "early articulators" because they not only feel but express clearly this preference). Some undergo a sterilization; others predicate the marriage on continued childlessness. Typically such individuals are women. Trudy Rosenthal, a teacher of nursing, now in her thirties and living in Virginia with her insurance agent husband, is one. "As odd as it may sound," she told me, "I've never envisaged myself wearing maternity clothes or pushing a baby carriage. By age sixteen I was wondering if I could successfully avoid what seemed the predetermined fate of motherhood."

It is considered more unusual for men to decide with surety at a young age never to become fathers. Most of the husbands who agree before a marriage to remain childless, claims Veevers, associate that with the decision to marry a particular woman, their own sentiments being neither strongly pro nor con.[26] I did, however, meet a few men whose commitment to nonparenthood had been clear from adolescence. The wife of one told me that early in their relationship she, expecting that they would be parents like everyone else they knew, began to effuse over "the beautiful children we would have." "*What children?*" he responded.

The majority (two-thirds) of the voluntarily childless reach this stage, according to Veevers, through a much more prolonged series of postponements. First they intend merely to delay having a family until a specific goal—career, financial, educational—is attained. Next they postpone more vaguely and for an indefinite period ("when we're feeling less pressed for time," for instance). The third stage is an open acknowledgment of the possibility of permanent childlessness, with a weighing of the pros and cons.[27] Frequently, this stage coincided in my interviews with the recognition that "Gee, we don't *have* to have kids!"—a recognition that may have been facilitated by exposure to other childless couples who served as role models. Receptive to the possibility of permanent non-parenthood, many start to look more critically at the lives of their parent friends and to recount such sagas as this one: "We were in the elevator and saw these two screaming kids hanging on to their mother. We looked at each other and said, 'Do we want that?' " Others talk about waiting for the "overwhelming urge" for parenthood to hit—but they suspect it may not. The last stage is an acceptance of permanent childlessness. Usually this is implied rather than explicit.[28]

Of the postponers, more than one-half of Veevers's subjects related their decision to the given marriage, indicating that with another mate they might well have felt differently. This, she feels, does not imply a lack in the relationship but openness to the potential of living differently. Another of her findings was that for one-half of the postponers the final decision against children was reached mutually, for one-fourth it was at the husband's initiative, and for one-fourth at the wife's.[29]

The seven-year marriage of attorney Stuart Kaufman, thirty-four, and Judith, an educational consultant of thirty-eight, is illustrative of two situations studied by Veevers: nonparenthood reached more at the wife's initiative and the realization that with different mates both might have elected to become parents.

Theirs is a stable relationship, with a lot of time spent in nurturing each other. Judy has a perceptive, quietly probing nature: she looks at life and people with compassion but without sentiment. Stuart is quick, witty, sophisticated in his tastes. The two live in a suburb of Philadelphia with a ladylike dog of Dutch descent and a mischievous cat named Arnold Katz, who, they claim, has been through ten of his nine lives. ("What? *Child* substitutes?" Stuart responds to my question in mock horror. "These precious fur angels? Say hello to the lady, children.")

Judy grew up having to do without many material possessions. She also had to take on considerable responsibility for her two sisters, which left her with a lot of confidence in her ability with children but few illusions about motherhood. Having achieved a good education, she was able to assume a responsible position entailing travel and to buy many things she had been deprived of before. Eventually it began to seem that children would be almost an intrusion. Yet Judy was and continues to be ambivalent about the subject. She thinks often of what she is missing: pregnancy, childbirth, the knowledge of what her child and Stuart's would be like.

Stuart says he never thought much about having a family and wouldn't have except in terms of his mate. "I can't remember once in my childhood or adolescence discussing the subject with anybody, which leads me to believe that I didn't have much interest in it then. But I always sensed from Day One that Judy was not going to have kids."

This remark, made while we were taping our interview, surprised Judy. "What? We never even discussed it before we were married!"

Stuart explains: "I don't think of you as the kind who would have a kid and then farm it out to a bunch of other people. You'd worry about it, you'd have to give up your career and take on a part-time job which would not be very interesting or challenging, driving yourself crazy, kid crazy; Arnold would probably be shredding you with his claws after a week of this. Really, it's not that I've been keeping these feelings a secret from you, but I never thought about it until just now."

Judy admits he is right. She *wouldn't* want to give up her hard-earned career accomplishments or the niceties of life. Staying at home doesn't appeal to her, nor does "farming out" a child—unless, that is, she was assured of full-time, high-quality care and regular housekeeping help. "If I'd married someone older, more established financially, then maybe I'd feel differently," she says.

Stuart continues: "By the same token, I think I would have been very willing to go ahead and have kids if you had really wanted them because that would go a long way to determining what my attitude would be toward the whole project." He does not feel deprived by the decision, just sometimes a bit nostalgic. "Maybe it's nice to have a kid at the dinner table? Somebody to talk to? to chuck under the chin? mop up after?"

Yet Stuart, too, is not without mixed feelings. He likes his business trips to Rio and realizes he could not take these so freely with a baby in the house. He sees the parenthood package as including an ever-present *au pair* girl—an amenity that is not possible in their present small home. Perhaps in five or six years his financial position will be such that he could have it all. Had he married someone four years younger than he is instead of four years older, they could have waited.

But Judy can't. The biological clock ticks on. So both continue as they are, doing interesting, valuable work and building a good life for themselves and the "fur angels."

"Someday," says Stuart cheerfully, "we will find ourselves old and childless, and we will never have decided to be that way."

Judy laughs. "That about sums it up."

Some couples who choose to be childless receive support and even encouragement from their intimates, including parents. One husband in his thirties told me: "A number of our friends' parents have said to them in one way or another, 'I love you very much, I'm glad you're here, but if I had it to do over again, I wouldn't have children.' " The reasons for such comments vary greatly: children have entailed too much work and money, caused marital discord, prevented them from fulfilling their own career dreams, and so on. Today's opportunity to choose freely between parenthood and nonparenthood, many parents feel, is a positive and long overdue development.

But many are not nearly so accepting. Indeed, reactions to voluntary childlessness can be highly critical and even hostile. The most common accusation nonparents face from family, friends, co-workers, and the media, according to a survey of the National Alliance for Optional Parenthood population by Barnett and MacDonald,[30] is that of selfishness. The childless react in different ways to this. Andy, a thirty-four-year-old government employee, says this: "I think the people who would call us selfish are, first of all, those who see having a child as a sacrifice because they're not very happy as parents themselves, so they want to know why we're not making the same damn sacrifice for the preservation of the species. I don't think those who are happy about having children would ever think to call anyone selfish for not having them. Would I call you selfish if you don't have a piano? It's up to you. I enjoy having a piano. I don't consider it a sacrifice to have the thing around here."

A second common criticism of the voluntarily childless is that they are inviting loneliness in old age. This is a difficult statement to counter since it is entirely possible that the childless *will* be lonely in old age. But there is no guarantee that parents will be able to avoid a similar isolation. Psychologist Nathaniel Branden made this comment in an interview with the director of the National Alliance for Optional Parenthood: "First they tell you you're selfish if you don't want to have children. Then . . . they start threatening you with how lonely you'll be in your old age if you don't have children to take care of you. . . . Not exactly an appeal to 'selfless' motives! The whole thing is such an absurd rationalization."[31]

There are a host of other pronatalist comments, ranging from the self-serving "Where have we failed you?" to "You're just the kind who *should* be having children." (Many voluntarily childless people have trouble answering that last statement, not only because it is a kind of back-handed flattery but because they feel similarly: that the "wrong" kind of people are producing offspring.) Probably the most inane of all the accusations is this one: "Where would *you* be if your parents had made the same decision?" An understandably angry woman from the Northwest who was confronted with such a remark told me only good manners prevented her from retorting: "Well, I certainly wouldn't be here listening to you ask stupid questions!"

The pressure to procreate, claims Jean Veevers, is greatest in the third, fourth, and fifth years of a marriage. During that time, she writes, the childless couple may be especially defensive, all too often provoking the very disapproval to which they object. Eventually they learn to deal more subtly with the issue, not revealing their feelings at all to some, being selective in what they say to others.[32] (One couple from New York, married twelve years and both in their mid-thirties, told me: "Our parents didn't exactly pry. They just asked very simple questions and we supplied simple but not quite on-target answers.") Reasons that are valid but not at the heart of the decision, like overpopulation, and pity-gaining ploys, like a troubled family background, might be emphasized.

When subjected to outside pressure, childless couples commonly say: "If we are sorry later, we can always adopt." In most cases this is a vague, generalized statement, not based on any actual investigation into the procedures and realities of adoption, but useful as a hedge against the eventual biological irreversibility of nonparenthood. Furthermore, because talk of adoption usually evokes approval from others, it becomes what Veevers refers to as a "passport to normalcy."[33] Some childless people, however, make it clear that they would never consider this option. Dave Craig of St. Louis voiced a comment I was to hear many times in one form or another: "I've taught long enough to see all the messed-up kids that are adopted. It's such a risk that I don't know if I could handle it."

There is a significant difference in the attitude toward childlessness depending on the geographic area of the country and whether it is urban or suburban. Twice as many childless people live in urban as in suburban and rural areas. Cities are particularly well suited to families of two. Needing less space than do parents, many of them find centrally located apartments to be compatible with their life styles and, on two salaries, affordable. The cultural and entertainment offerings of a city are a major attraction to people whose evenings are not centered around family life. Career opportunities for both husband and wife are greater. There is the likelihood of finding many other childless couples with whom to socialize. Conversely, the negative side of city life, including the high rates of crime, is not so crucial a consideration for nonparents.

Suburbia is structured with families in mind. (As a disgruntled character in John Updike's *Couples* complained: "Half the reason we live in this silly hick town is for the sake of the children.")[34] It is largely through their children's activities that adults become acquainted with each other in these areas. Nonparents, on the other hand, may feel isolated. One NAOP member told me she heard a childless suburbanite complaining to a local parent about the difficulty of forming friendships with her neighbors.

"Well," responded the well-meaning acquaintance. "Why don't you just get a baby carriage and promenade around the block with it?"

"What for? I don't have any babies to put in it," said the surprised nonparent.

"That doesn't matter. People will talk to you anyway."

Even with these difficulties, many childless couples prefer the cleaner air, the peace and quiet, the space, the green of suburbia, and have made a good life for themselves in the heartland of America's baby carriages. Their main problem, a few told me, is convincing others that the extra bedrooms are intended to be dens or studies—not children's playrooms.

As receptivity to voluntary childlessness increases throughout the nation, it becomes more difficult to pinpoint regional differences in attitude. Nonetheless, some generalizations can be made. A city which has a substantial proportion of young, mobile, and career-oriented residents, like New York or Washington, D.C., is likely to be a hospitable climate. People in the Northwest told me there is still a spirit of rugged individualism there and that nontraditional choices such as childlessness are appreciated rather than scorned. Chicago was one city in the Midwest described to me as receptive, while St. Louis seemed everybody's favorite example of hidebound conservatism. In the South, the qualities of reserve and gentility which prevent people from asking too many personal questions of others can be welcome to those without children, even though they may sense an underlying disapproval. (One voluntarily childless Georgia wife told me she and her husband don't even know why a certain couple—their best friends—are similarly childless. "You just don't talk about that kind of thing down here," she said.) Several New Englanders felt a comparable shrinking from subjects of an intimate nature on the part of natives, though cities like Boston have given substantial press publicity to voluntarily childlessness. California, especially Los Angeles, is characterized by a curiosity about and support of unconventional life styles, among which the childfree marriage by now appears downright humdrum.

In view of the significant percentage of couples who are electing not to have children, several researchers have attempted to study the personality characteristics of those who make that decision. Current findings suggest that as a group they are not dissimilar to parents in terms of mental health.

Two social psychologists at the University of Kansas, Linda Silka and Sara Kiesler, concluded that the voluntarily childless are no more materialistic than their parent peers and are equally interested in mankind; however, they show less desire to interact socially with others, having a preference for being alone and maintaining their privacy. In life satisfaction, maturity, and self-esteem, they appear not to be different from parents.[35]

Veevers summarizes the results of her massive research this way: ". . . at least some voluntarily childless couples *do* achieve high levels of personal, marital and social adjustment. Moreover . . . for many of the childless . . . the maintenance of sound mental health is not achieved in spite of being childless, but is predicated upon the continued avoidance of parenthood."[36]

Because childbearing and rearing are considered a more critical ingredient in the psychological health and social adjustment of women than of men, various studies focus specifically on nonmotherhood. Kathryn Welds, a New York psychologist, studied both mothers and nonmothers who were listed in *Who's Who of American Women.* She found no important differences in the emotional development of these highly competent women.[37]

Another psychologist, Judith Teicholz of Massachusetts General Hospital in Boston, has carried out some valuable research comparing voluntarily childless women with those who definitely planned to have children. The only area in which she found they differed significantly was in the measure of "psychological androgyny." "Non-mothers were more likely than the Future-mothers to be androgynous or, in other words, to give equal endorsement in themselves to both 'masculine' and 'feminine' personality characteristics; correspondingly, it was found that the Future-mothers were more likely than the Non-mothers to describe themselves in terms of exclusively feminine personality characteristics."[38] (Among typical feminine traits would be nurturing, sensitivity, and creativity, while masculine traits would include assertiveness and competitiveness.) Other researchers have noted the same tendency toward androgyny among voluntarily childless men. "They claim with relish female characteristics," Landa told me. "They say things like, 'I'm loving, gentle. I cry a lot.' "

Are the voluntarily childless this way all along or as the result of their nonparenthood? Evidence points to both. Those who choose such a life style tend from the beginning to have "open," egalitarian marriages with flexibility in roles and division of power and money. But other marriages start out this way and change when the children arrive, with the wife assuming all the expected maternal traits and the husband those of the father. Hence it may be that the reality of parenthood brings out traditional patterns of behavior even in nontraditional marriages, while nonparenthood is conducive to continued androgyny.

Another trait that has been observed among the childfree, especially women, is a drive toward perfection. Whereas those who elect to combine marriage, parenthood, and career generally expect that a certain amount of compromise will be necessary on all fronts, women who are childless by choice characteristically see parenthood and career as being mutually exclusive. Psychologist Margaret Baker told me that she once ran a discussion group at the National Alliance for Optional Parenthood in which "all of the women who were ambivalent about having children were invested in careers and felt that if they were to have a child they would have to give up their careers because they wouldn't be able to do a perfect job in parenting. It was the all or nothing assumption."

In keeping with this characteristic is a feeling many voluntarily childless women expressed to me: they believe, despite their nontraditional marriages, in traditional child care with the mother at home. Diane Elvenstar, the psychologist who runs a Los Angeles seminar, admits to sharing these sentiments personally even though she believes fully in the concept of outside child care. Fulfilled in marriage and career, she says: "I was raised in a supportive, loving family where my mother stayed home, and it was a very rewarding experience. I would want to give any children I had what I received myself. But, because of things like career, I cannot see myself taking time out for what I feel is the responsible approach to parenthood."

Of all the decisions people make in a lifetime, none is more crucial than the one to become a parent or remain childless. Unlike jobs, houses, and mates, you can't exchange one child for another. A child regretted is not returnable, and one desired too late will not be born.

The reasons for childlessness are many and fluid, evolving with time. And those who choose this life style are as varied as their reasons. Some approach it with an enthusiasm for the positives it offers, others more with relief at the pitfalls avoided. Both approaches are valid.

Among the people I interviewed were several who stated that their motives for childlessness differed somewhat from those of the mate; what counted, they said, was that they agreed in the decision. This is not an unusual circumstance. A study by P. E. Cooper, B. Cumber, and R. Hartner revealed that husbands and wives characteristically list their reasons for nonparenthood in differing order. Personal freedom heads the list for both, but while intimacy with spouse and career interests are next on the women's list, lack of interest in being a parent and the wish to limit their responsibilities are more important for men.[39]

In his novel *The Human Factor,* Graham Greene deals deftly with this subject. Describing the childless marriage of country gentleman spy Sir John Hargreaves, Greene writes: ". . . he

had never wanted a child nor had his wife; they were at one
in that, though perhaps for different reasons. He hadn't
wanted to add to his public responsibilities private responsibilities . . . and his wife . . . wished to guard her figure and
her independence. Their mutual indifference to children rein-
forced their love for each other.''[40]

One might expect, with all the positive publicity given the
childfree life in recent years, that those who choose that route
will be free of ambivalence or regret once the decision is
made. This, however, is asking too much. Some people are
fortunate: their feelings are so sure that hardly a moment is
spent in reflecting back and questioning. But many couples
endure short and even prolonged periods of doubt—and this
includes those who made their decision with great care. The
fact is, childlessness, like parenthood, is a long-term decision
made with only a short-term knowledge of life. Any number
of stimuli can bring out the ghost of the unborn child: the birth
of a friend's baby, loneliness around holidays, career disappointments, separation from or the death of the mate, the loss
of a parent.

Childless people may never fully resolve their conflicts because they cannot compare what they know (nonparenthood)
with what they do not know (parenthood). They cannot say
what kind of child they would have had or whether they
would have liked the child and been glad of his or her presence in their lives. There is no crystal ball to tell them what
happinesses and sorrows their offspring would have experienced. Hence they suffer from what author Elizabeth
Whelan refers to as a "nagging ambivalence."

Ambivalence does not mean a decision was wrong. After all,
life consists of many roads, and "the road not taken"—in
Robert Frost's phrase—will forever remain full of unanswered
questions and unfulfilled possibilities.

3

Sterilization:
The Active Decision

Lee Hernandez knew from early adolescence that he didn't want to have children of his own. He was, however, very interested in "special needs" children—those with physical or emotional handicaps—and he hoped someday to help them, perhaps through a career in medical research.

Of Spanish-Mexican descent on his father's side, Lee certainly was not typical of the *macho* philosophy that some of his relatives held to tenaciously. Fortunately, his parents were accepting and rather nontraditional (they'd had him circumcised as a baby, whereupon, he told me, "my aunt yelled and screamed that I would never be a man"). Still, when Lee at age fourteen informed his mother that he wanted to have a vasectomy—the surgical procedure that would forever terminate his fertility—she didn't quite believe it. Nor did she act on it.

Lee was married at twenty-one to a girl one year older whose lack of interest in motherhood equaled his in fatherhood. Laurel liked babies but not pregnancy or "the idea of walking around for months not being able to see my feet." The example of her sister, who she describes as "dropping children like a Chinese peasant—she loves having them but isn't so hot on raising them," didn't add to her enthusiasm. Yet pronatalist pressure from her family was far from subtle: "My father's belief is that women sour if they don't have children."

When they married, Lee and Laurel had a tough financial road ahead. Lee took on a job as a truck driver for a supermarket chain to help put money together for medical school.

Laurel worked at various jobs to save toward the goal of a five-year bachelor's and master's program in anthropology. Since having a family was not to be in either the short- or long-term Hernandez scenario, sterilization seemed a logical and simple choice. But it proved to be not so simple. From 1972 to 1975 the Hernandezes searched in vain for a physician who would perform the surgery on either one of them. "Not a doctor or a population control group would hear us out," Lee told me. "They would just hang up the phone."

This episode did not take place in rural Kentucky or Mormon Utah. It was Los Angeles, an area noted for its open-mindedness and receptivity to nontraditional life styles. And voluntary sterilization was no undercover basement matter. It was legal for "competent, consenting adults" in all fifty states —a safe, sure answer to just what the world needs: fewer people. Why, then, was nobody listening?

The answer is basically twofold. One is age: physicians and counselors responsible for approving sterilization fear that people as young as Laurel and Lee are too immature to make decisions of such a final nature. The second reason for all the turndowns was that the Hernandezes were childless. In the minds of quite a number of Americans it's quite all right to be vasectomized or to have your tubes tied so long as you've had a couple of children already. But to do it before you've proved yourself as a parent borders on the abnormal. This is not just an attitude; for quite a while it appeared in black and white. Up to 1969, for instance, the American Society of Obstetricians and Gynecologists had guidelines for recommending female sterilization, including the so-called "120 Rule": for a woman to qualify for a sterilization, her age multiplied by the number of children she'd already produced should equal 120.[1] (That meant a twenty-five-year-old would have had to give birth to five offspring, and a thirty-five-year-old, four; Laurel, at age twenty-two, wouldn't have been off the hook until her sixth.)

In any event, after a three-year search Lee Hernandez finally found a doctor who would both listen and act. "He talked to

me, said, 'This is permanent, don't count on its being reversible. Is it what you want?' " It was.

Lee and Laurel, now twenty-eight and twenty-nine, are satisfied with the vasectomy and the way their life is progressing.
When I met with them, Laurel was due to quit her bank job
as a senior judgment credit specialist and begin undergraduate
studies; medical school for Lee is still a good while off. There
was, however, an ironic little twist in the Hernandez story.

About a year ago a Los Angeles television station decided
to do a segment on voluntary childlessness. They contacted
the Hernandez couple—a natural choice: Laurel, fair-haired,
slim, with a breezy, cynical style, and Lee, dark, serious, articulate, his brooding manner relieved unexpectedly by a winning
smile.

The plan was to do part of the filming at the job and part
at home. Lee's trucking firm did not impose obstacles; Laurel's
bank did. When she approached management for permission,
she sensed an atmosphere of "panic." Finally the TV crew was
allowed in but, she says, management "insisted that everything with the bank logo be removed so that viewers couldn't
possibly figure out where this crazy person worked. The statio-
nery had to be face down. I had to put my bank telephone
directory in the drawer. They did the same with all the desks
around mine. When it came time for the filming, there were
me and twelve empty desks. All the other employees had to
stand out of camera range, so the entire office is sitting over
in a little corner giggling and waving at me."

The reaction of Laurel's co-workers to the show was not
positive. "One man said, 'Well, I have children. I can prove
I'm a man. Your husband can't.' And my boss told me Lee was
crazy to go out and have a vasectomy like that.

"Oddly enough, there is one woman vice president who
hasn't said three words to me in two years except to ask me
after the show if I knew a doctor who could sterilize her. And
at the next office Christmas party I was talking to my boss's
wife. She told me she'd had her tubes tied three months after
they were married."

However difficult a time the Hernandezes and other young childless couples may have had obtaining a vasectomy or the female counterpart, tubal ligation, voluntary sterilization is definitely "in" today. In fact it was dubbed "the contraceptive phenomenon of the 1970s," with roughly one million Americans opting for it each year. (The latest published figures date from 1979, when there was a slight dip, due mainly to reports, as yet unsubstantiated, linking male sterilization with atherosclerosis.) All told, twelve million individuals have been sterilized in our country, out of ninety million worldwide, during the past decade. It is the most popular contraceptive method here for couples married ten years or longer and among wives aged thirty and older; for couples aged twenty-five to twenty-nine it is second only to the birth-control pill.

Why do people choose such a drastic measure in the first place? In part, because the American public has become increasingly sophisticated in medical matters. The side effects of the pill, especially when it is taken for a prolonged period, can hardly be discounted, and the intrauterine device (IUD) is not entirely safe or sure for all women. Fairly reliable old methods like the condom and the diaphragm have been discarded by many simply because they find them a nuisance, and others, like the foams and jellies, have made involuntary parents of too many people. The same can be said for the rhythm method, which is referred to by cynics as "Vatican roulette."

In truth, we have become very demanding: when we don't want children we expect not to have them, and we're not about to shrug our shoulders philosophically when they appear (as the ancient Egyptians must have done when the prescribed contraceptive formula of honey, soda, and crocodile excrement[2] didn't work). Sterilization right now provides the greatest assurance possible; though it's not absolutely foolproof, reliability is very high, complications rare, risks to the patient minimal, and degree of satisfaction after the operation very high on the part of sterilized men and women and their partners.

What makes the change in our contraceptive preferences so interesting is that for decades the only sterilization was involuntary; hence there was a decidedly negative aura surrounding it. Introduced in the United States at the turn of the century and sanctioned by the Supreme Court in 1927, involuntary sterilization was seen as a way of dealing with "mental defectives" and was employed for such diverse malfeasances as alcoholism, syphilis, chicken stealing, and masturbation.[3] But gradually sterilization was recognized as a viable means of enabling people to limit their families by *choice.* (This acceptance was facilitated by the great progress made in surgery, especially anesthesia.)

It is largely due to the efforts of the Association for Voluntary Sterilization (AVS), an international organization with headquarters in New York City, that this operative technique has made the transition from stigma to normal procedure, with most of the legal, religious, and administrative restrictions against it having been lifted in 1970. Though the bulk of sterilizations are being requested by the well-educated, higher-income segment of our population, there also was a good response to an AVS pilot program in the economically depressed Appalachian area. An equally significant development is that people who *don't* want to be sterilized—the masturbators and chicken stealers among us as well as the genuinely mentally incompetent—are now adequately protected by law.

Female sterilization, known as salpingectomy, or tubal ligation, involves the cutting, cauterizing, and tying off of the fallopian tubes, which are the passageways down which the ovum works its way into the womb. A more complicated and expensive operation than the one for males, this until recently involved general anesthesia and a hospital stay of up to several days. However, techniques have improved significantly, including the development of the so-called minilaparotomy, which, frequently done under local anesthesia, is a technically simpler operation with easier recovery and lower cost.

Male sterilization or vasectomy remains the simplest of all the procedures, generally being performed in a doctor's office or a clinic and under local anesthesia. One or two incisions are made in the scrotum through which each sperm-carrying tube

(the vas deferens) can be lifted out, cut and closed, thus block-
ing the passage of sperm to the penis.

Vasectomy was by far the more popular of the two methods
a decade ago, when an estimated 80 percent of those sterilized
in this country were men. Aside from the ease and lower cost
of the vasectomy, some men were beginning to feel it was time
they played a bigger role in matters of birth control. But, as
methods of tubal ligation improved, the number of female
sterilizations increased greatly. By 1977 a striking reversal had
taken place, with approximately 60 percent of those voluntarily sterilized being women.

This change also reflected the impact of the women's movement. Pregnancy and childbirth are, after all, a female function, and child care has hardly reached a stage of equal sharing. If a woman does not want any children, or more children,
why depend on a man for protection against these functions?
Among the most ardent converts to sterilization are those who
don't want to live through—or already have endured and
don't want to repeat—the trauma of an abortion. (And that
includes men, who, according to one sociologist, Arthur B.
Shostak, suffer more than is realized from what he calls "fatherhood lost."[4]) Similarly, women who have experienced
pregnancy and birth followed by a severe postpartum depression are likely candidates for sterilization.

More and more, however, people are seeking what Betty
Gonzales, AVS deputy director for national programs, calls
"sterilization at your leisure": that is, sterilization carried out
before an unwanted pregnancy occurs, rather than after. Private patients simply approach a qualified physician who is
responsible for making a medical and psychological judgment
on the case, taking into consideration the requirements of the
facility where he or she operates. Those candidates on Medi-
caid must go through a more rigorous procedure, involving
counseling and a waiting period. In all cases, the person requesting the sterilization has to sign a consent form indicating
that he or she understands the nature of the operation and
desires the permanent sterility that will result. Spousal consent
is not an uncommon requirement. (Parental consent for a

mature adult *is* uncommon, but I found it in Chapel Hill, North Carolina. A sophisticated childless woman, now thirty-seven, who held a responsible position in psychological testing, told me that, when she had her tubes tied six years ago, not only her architect husband had to sign the consent form but her mother and father as well.)

Some knowledgeable people, including Miriam Ruben, who is public-relations director for the AVS, see the pendulum swinging in the direction of more conservatism in sterilization as in matters of reproduction generally (witness the messianic zeal of the Right-to-Life movement). Ruben cites recent laws in New York City and California requiring a thirty-day wait between the signing of the consent form and the operation. She says the amount of paperwork required of professionals who approve a sterilization is often so great that some are turned off, preferring to avoid the whole issue.

While researching this book, I encountered a good sampling of voluntarily childless couples among whom one or the other (or both) had been sterilized. Many held membership in the National Alliance for Optional Parenthood (NAOP)— a recognition of their need for emotional support in the face of familial and outside disapproval. I questioned them about their reasons for choosing to be sterilized, the difficulty of arranging for the procedure, and the results.

Elaine and Gary Burhop of Seattle, both in their mid-thirties, were married in 1968. Gary is youth director at a United Methodist church, and Elaine's field of expertise is children's recreational activities. Since their working lives were very rich in contact with young people, the Burhops did not feel the need or desire for children of their own.

Gary: "We were comfortable with our decision and lived with the idea of sterilization a couple of years before we actually went ahead with it. Elaine had been on the pill for ten years and was feeling more and more that she'd taken it long enough. I felt, She's right, it's my turn to take the responsibility. But I kept putting off the vasectomy because the idea of an operation didn't appeal to me. That was the only part we had to overcome—my insecurity about pain."

Elaine: "I was willing to be sterilized, but it cost $300 for a woman and $100 for a man and it was a simpler operation for him, so it made more sense." (Today some large insurance companies are covering sterilization, realizing that the fees are far less than those associated with pregnancy, childbirth, and children's medical care.)

The Burhops had trouble finding a physician; their own wouldn't do the surgery. Then, four years ago, they discovered a clinic in Seattle where the physician specialized in abortion on some days of the week and sterilization on others. His vasectomy charge was less for childless men than for parents —an unusual stance in an era when parents traditionally receive more financial benefits. Gary had the operation with no ill effects, his fears about excessive pain proving unfounded.

Severe physical distress does not commonly follow a vasectomy. I met only one man, a midwesterner in his fifties, who referred to "two weeks of exquisite pain" after the surgery. But with this kind of operation, like a hysterectomy, the fear of pain is complex, many-faceted, and inextricably tied up with one's sexuality. There is for some men an unconscious—if irrational—concern that "they'll cut in the wrong place and I'll be castrated." (Castration, the removal of the testicles, which are the body's sperm producers, was, in fact, a prevalent operation in the seventeenth and eighteenth centuries. It arose as a result of the Roman Catholic Church's ban on women singing in the religious service or on stage. By castrating boys before puberty—illegally and often without their consent— greedy impresarios were able to prevent a boy's voice from changing. The result was a physical eunuch with a soprano or contralto voice that frequently had extraordinary power, range, flexibility, and beauty.)

Such castration is, fortunately, a thing of the past, but because sterilization in men involves an external organ—the very source of male potency—they have a not unnatural fear of the operation. Miriam Ruben at AVS has seen this revealed in an amusing way: "I remember one meeting of male medical students which had a blackboard showing the male reproduc-

tive system with the flow of sperm before and after sterilization. Young medical students would come along and look at
it and then cross their legs; they didn't even know they were
doing it. In fact, whenever I talk about vasectomy to men,
whether they're sitting or standing, they cross their legs involuntarily. It's a protective device."

Ruben advises that men who consider having a vasectomy,
especially childless ones like Gary, give careful thought
beforehand to how they perceive themselves. "Many men still
suffer from what we call *machismo*. They see themselves in
terms of their ability to reproduce." (The same, of course, can
be applied to women: i.e., femininity is equated with pregnancy and childbearing.) Similarly, professionals try to weed
out couples with problems in their sexual relationship who
mistakenly think that once the fear of pregnancy is gone the
underlying sexual problem will disappear too. But for Gary
and many others no such confusion existed. Four years after
the surgery he says: "We are constantly reminded of how glad
we are we made that decision."

Bruce and Ellen, a highly motivated New Haven career
couple in their mid-thirties (she is a patent attorney and he a
public utilities official) also decided on a vasectomy. Like the
Burhops, they were anxious to discontinue the birth-control
pill for reasons of safety. Why was Bruce the one to be sterilized?

Ellen: "Because in our view the person who feels more
strongly about not having children should be the one to do it.
I was admittedly schizophrenic on the subject. We thought
about children for a long time, and we decided that, if we
ended up not wanting any, Bruce would be the one to be
sterilized. We knew that long before we made the final commitment not to have a family."

An intense, dark-haired man who tends to treat sensitive
subjects with a brash but disarming honesty, Bruce talked of
his own childhood, which his wife described as "horrid" and
he redefined as "tortured." "I was overweight, an only child,
Jewish, and with an IQ of 170 or 180, in a wholly gentile
neighborhood," he told me. "The bright, fatty schoolboy Jew

doesn't sit very well with the peers." All this led to his becoming an adult much before his chronological age. "He missed childhood, stepped right over it," says Ellen.

Bruce never thought very much about having children of his own but claims that "by the time I was aware of the question, I was aware of the answer." The answer was "No." Ellen, ambivalent on the subject but deeply committed to her profession and her marriage, had little problem going along with his wishes.

When it came time for the vasectomy, Bruce and Ellen talked with the rabbi at their local congregation. "We didn't ask him to bless the decision in any way," said Ellen. "We just wanted to be sure that what we were doing somehow fit within the scope of our religion. The rabbi was a very special man to us and, I think, understood the grappling we were going through."

Reassured by this discussion, Bruce went on to the surgery. Because it was not associated in his mind with diminished malehood, the vasectomy posed no threat.

Did it affect your sexual attitudes or responses at all, I asked.

Bruce: "Well, after the swelling died down, we decided to see if it still worked. And we tried it out, and I said, 'Look, it works! It still works!' And that's the end of the vasectomy story."

Ellen, laughing: "Except for the purple balls."

Bruce: "Yeah, you turn all sorts of bizarre colors down there."

There were people at work, he added, who asked him how he could possibly have done such a thing to himself. "I said 'Done what? Done *what?* Fifteen minutes. Snip snip cut cut.' And I really did not view it as a big deal at all."

The successful experiences of men like Bruce and Gary are in keeping with most scientific findings about vasectomies. One of the largest and most careful studies was done in 1969 by the Simon Population Trust; of the 1,000 vasectomized men studied, 99.4 percent said they had no regrets over the operation and 73 percent cited increased sexual pleasure as a result of it. That last figure is not surprising; once the fear of an unwanted pregnancy, of abortion, of the side effects of birth-control pills is removed, an initially good sexual relationship is likely to become even better, with intercourse more frequent.[5] (Critics tend to point out that the reported increased frequency of intercourse can just as easily indicate anxiety over potency as it can a heightened libido; this is an area that to date has not been studied extensively.)

Another study by Ronald H. Magarick and Robert A. Brown (1976), comparing vasectomized childless men with vasectomized parents, found no differences in overall social or emotional adjustment or marital satisfaction. They also determined that, although the childless men were typically better informed, more flexible, and more independent than the fathers, the former felt they were negatively stereotyped by society[6]—an attitude illustrated by Bruce's comment about the chilly reception he'd gotten at work.

Among the voluntarily childless wives I met who had undergone a tubal ligation was Rina Boodman, twenty-nine, a graphics artist married for four years. She and her husband, a self-employed carpenter, were college dropouts who belonged for a while to a commune and now live in a small town in North Carolina. Small, attractive in her jeans and long Afro hairdo, Rina told me that her husband had offered to have the operation but "I felt—and he disagreed with me—that if either of us was ever going to change our mind about children, it was more likely to be him." Rina likes her freedom, her job; she can't remember a time when she wanted children and feels she'd have made a poor mother: "impatient, intolerant, and inconsistent." She set the tubal date ahead to age thirty but, after a lot of birth-control problems, realized at twenty-seven that it was not wise to put it off any longer.

"Right when I made the appointment I felt some nervousness about it, and I thought, 'Am I having reservations that I'm not recognizing?' The main one was I didn't like having to admit that I'd come to a stage where some roads were closed to me, of making an irreversible decision. That bothered me, and so did the thought of looking ahead twenty years and not having an adult relationship with a son or daughter." (Like many voluntarily childless people, Rina would have wanted the grown child but not the growing one.) Still, she went through with the sterilization. Her parents were unusually supportive. So far Rina and her husband are both satisfied.

Suzanne Zumbrunnen, thirty-two, is from West Virginia and now lives in Atlanta, where she is an undergraduate at Emory University. The campus is, she says, something of "an intellectual oasis in the Deep South, with all its rigidity and set cultural standards." Blunt, strong, but warm in manner, she speaks more forthrightly than you might expect from someone with so southern an accent. (Indeed, that candor on television and radio talk shows about voluntary childlessness has brought Suzanne such unwelcome responses as bomb threats.)

The decision to remain childfree was not one that Suzanne or her husband John made lightly or easily. "We soul-searched for six agonizing months." Friends and relatives provided meager support, especially when the matter of sterilization came up, but finally John went ahead with a vasectomy. The marriage eventually began to fail for other reasons, at which point Suzanne decided: "I'm not going to deal with separation and fertility at the same time. So I went out at age twenty-six and got sterilized. Another partner is not going to make any difference in the way I feel about having children."

Now divorced, Suzanne analyzes the tubal ligation as a kind of "insurance that I won't be faced with that decision again. I think it would have been difficult if I met someone who wanted children while I still could have them." In effect, then, she was intentionally foiling whatever temptation came her way regarding parenthood. She remains happy with that choice today, though well aware of the trap any sterilized person can fall into. "You're going to try to justify your behavior, to say you don't want kids. Right now I feel fine about what I've done, but if I change my mind, I won't hesitate to adopt a child. An oriental child, maybe."

Sterilizations like Suzanne's which take place pending or after a divorce may sound bizarre but really are not. When an individual has thought long and hard about the parenthood

question and decided against children, he or she is often unwilling to go through it again with another mate. Such was the
case with NAOP staff member Dorothy Lohmann Wilson in
Washington, D.C. A pert and lively twenty-five-year-old with
a sturdy sense of self, Dotty was recently sterilized after being
separated from her husband for some months. She had been
thinking about having a tubal ligation for many years and
approached it with "excitement" as the realization of a long-
term goal.

Research on the effects of voluntary sterilization on childless females is more scanty than on males. Tubal ligation is,
according to Betty Gonzales of AVS, a very complex issue, for
all women experience some ambivalence about pregnancy,
childbearing, and the maternal role. Hence a sterilization is
likely to entail a certain amount of grieving over lost reproductive capacity; this, professionals feel, is normal. On the
other hand, she says, because most women reach their highest
level of sexual desire and fulfillment at a later age and continue
at that level for more years than men, they can benefit greatly
by a sterilization which relieves their minds of unwanted pregnancy, allowing full freedom of sexual expression.[7]

A study by Steven A. Leibo and Jennefer Santee at the
Laboratory of Behavior and Population in San Francisco compared childless couples who chose various methods of birth
control with those who turned to sterilization.[8] Their findings
were particularly interesting as regards the sterilized woman.
Characteristically, these women had had unhappy childhoods,
dominating mothers, and unstable family settings; as a result
the subjects doubted their ability to make good mothers and
had negative feelings about the day-to-day care of children.
Most said if the conditions in their family background had
been ideal they would have had children. The same women,
according to Leibo and Santee, felt very capable in the business world, and sterilization gave them a positive sense of self
and freedom, enabling them to set higher goals and achieve
more ego satisfaction. Another study, by physicians Nancy D.
Kaltreider and Alan G. Margolis in 1977, reported that tubal-
ligation candidates, as compared with women on nonperma-

nent methods of birth control, expressed fears that if they had a child they would be emotionally destroyed by him or her and that they would become like their own mothers. More than half said they did not like children. After sterilization, this group too responded very well.[9]

My interviews did not lend themselves to such measurements, but it is always tempting to compare personal observation with the controlled experimental results of others. Occasionally I found what appeared to be a clear exception to such results—like sterilized women whose childhoods had been basically happy, if not without the usual traumas of growing up. Yet I also encountered those whose feelings seemed to parallel with almost uncanny similarity those cited by Leibo and Santee and others.

Jerrie, for example, a curvaceous, honey-blond TV situation-comedy writer in Los Angeles. Her story had an intriguing twist: she didn't have to go through a sterilization, because she found, consciously or not, a husband who'd already done it for her.

At age thirty-three, Jerrie has a family background and personality not unlike television's legendary Rhoda, the brash yet lovable store-window dresser from the Bronx with a weight problem and a stereotypical Jewish mother. The humor that characterizes Jerrie's writing and conversation is self-directed, an armor against life's darts. We talked in her office—a colorful mélange of hanging rugs, velvet couches, toy mice, and lush spider plants which showed no intention of limiting their offspring.

"I always had this fantasy," Jerrie told me, "that if I got married, on the third day after we got back from our perfect honeymoon we'd be having breakfast at our cute little round table in our darling little apartment—and I would run out of funny stories. And that would be the end of the marriage. I didn't have a lot of good stuff going for me, which has to do with my childhood, which has to do with not wanting children. What I got from my mother was 'Anything you do, you will do wrong.' She perpetuated inadequacy. I developed my humor to steal my father from my mother, but then I finally realized they were perfect for each other."

At twenty-five Jerrie became pregnant despite the use of an IUD. "I was amazed. It was wonderful, the fact that it worked" ("it" meaning her body, not the IUD, which she refers to sarcastically as Jaws, "because it grabs you and makes you hostile"). During her brief pregnancy Jerrie daydreamed about carrying the fetus full term, about childbirth. Given her insecurities, the "womanliness" that she was experiencing was a joyous thing. "I hated to give up that nice feeling of knowing that everything worked, how pretty I looked with that glow, and the closeness it brought between me and my boyfriend, which I knew would change once I got 'depregnatized.' But of course it was all wrong, and I didn't want to deal with the child afterward." So Jerrie decided to have an abortion.

"I remember the main feeling of sadness was because I knew: 'This is the last time I'll become pregnant.' But I was quickly able to say to myself, 'Well, that's not sad because, clearly, if it's true, it will be out of choice.' Even today I'm kind of glad to have experienced the abortion, which is a selfish thing to admit. Here I'd gone through this horrible thing that everybody says is so devastating. Would you believe I had a very perfect abortion? Of course it was legal. I remember everybody in the hospital was so nice, and light was streaming in my room. It really feels special when people show you how much they can care."

After the abortion Jerrie broke up with her boyfriend and went back to her normal life with her career once more all-important and with the dreary old question: "Will I ever have a close relationship with a man again? There wasn't even a round table this time." And then she met Larry. "We felt immediately like we'd been together all our lives." Within five months, Jerrie was married. "The trick was I knew he'd had a vasectomy." (Larry was divorced with two children.) "That, I think, registered as 'good.' If I was ambivalent before about children, now I was off the fence. There was nothing I could do about it."

Jerrie claims to have been so surprised by her own decisive action that "I thought I'd just run it past my therapist. I asked her, 'Do you think I'm masking anything about children, because it just seems so clear.' And she said, 'No.' She thought my career had become my child.''

Double sterilization: the sterilization of both parties to a marriage. At first I found this very puzzling; it seemed like overkill. Then one very cogent explanation was given me: commitment to one's personal philosophy of not wanting children. Thus a sterilization becomes a statement about life goals even above and beyond a given marriage. It is a responsibility one takes on alone instead of depending on the mate. When the rationale for a dual sterilization becomes tinged with commitment to the partner ("You did it; I will, too"), this is a less healthy attitude, professionals suggest.

Another factor that is sometimes present, although couples tend to talk about it less, is that extramarital affairs are more easily carried out after the sterilization of both husband and wife. One midwestern couple, Bob and Fran, admitted to me that this entered into their decision. It is a second marriage for both, and there were no children (by choice) in either first marriage. Bob, a veterinarian now in his fifties, was sterilized shortly after marrying Fran. "I welcomed the vasectomy and have never had one moment of regret," he told me, "especially since, when I met Fran, she had been on the pill for five years, which, according to most doctors, is long enough."

As for Fran's sterilization, added Bob, "We hadn't placed a whole lot of restrictions on the marriage sexually, within limits, of course, and so it was only fair for us both to be protected."

Fran, in her mid-thirties and beginning a medical career, adds her views: "After Bob's sterilization and before my own, I began to realize that he had a freedom to play around while I was dealing with pregnancy as if I were eighteen again. Yet for me to be sterilized was a kind of admission that we were not going to be monogamous, and it was hard to make that statement. So it was sort of up in the air. Then we went to an NAOP meeting where a husband had been vasectomized, and shortly afterward the wife got pregnant from being gang-raped. That solidified it for me." Her tubal ligation followed shortly.

Fran had another pressing reason for not wanting to be pregnant: she already had been. "When I was nineteen I had an abortion. I was pregnant by my first husband before our marriage, and we did not want the child. I got blood poisoning and almost died from the black-market job. I have freak fits now whenever I hear them talking about making abortion illegal again. Those damn Right-to-Lifers don't know the sheer panic, don't know you'll do anything to get rid of the pregnancy. I tried lifting furniture. People said, 'You might die,' and I said, 'That's a risk I'm going to have to take.' The only regret I have had is that the abortion couldn't have been done openly, legally."

Bill and Marie Bernardy of St. Louis, both twenty-seven, are a well-spoken, highly attractive couple active in NAOP, Bill as president of the board of directors and Marie as vice president. Their two-sterilization marriage is a clear example of mutual commitment to nonparenthood. Married five years ago after a high school and college romance, both were aware early on of ecological and population concerns and found themselves increasingly attracted to the idea of the childfree life. This attitude was not in keeping with either their own Catholic familial background or the politically conservative, heavily Catholic climate of St. Louis (the city where, after a great stir, condoms were removed from open display in pharmacies). Eventually Bill and Marie left the church.

Marie was first to be sterilized, one year after their wedding. She had developed gallbladder disease and required surgery, at which point her physician informed her that she would no longer be able to take the birth-control pill. If she intended not to have children, would she want to be sterilized at the same time? Marie welcomed the suggestion.

I asked her what her feelings were at the time. "I really felt certain of the decision. But I did have a sense of aloneness, a lack of support from people I considered to be friends, even professionals." (She was working then at a marital sex clinic.) "I also was sad that I would be missing out on pregnancy and childbirth. Yet, when Bill and I talked, I felt very comfortable. I was excited about it, because it was something we were sharing and because we weren't taking chances anymore. We knew where our life was going."

Six months later Bill had his vasectomy. "For each of us," he says, "being sterilized was acting individually on our own feelings." Having dealt with so many vasectomy clients while associated with the St. Louis office of Planned Parenthood, Bill found no surprises or problems in the procedure. Nor does he feel different today. In fact, he is working toward a Ph.D. in counseling psychology and intends to remain professionally as well as personally involved in the field.

Family reaction has not been supportive. Last year the Bernardys were invited along with other NAOP members to be interviewed by Phil Donahue for a segment on voluntary childlessness which would be aired on the *Today* show. "When I told my mother," Marie recalls, "she kept saying, 'My God, it's your decision, it's your decision. But please don't say it on TV.' I told her that if Donahue asked me about the sterilization I wasn't going to lie. She said, 'I always thought we'd be grandparents.' I said, 'Well, what have we been telling you all this time?'" (The Bernardys claim that psychiatrist Robert E. Gould, who is a national authority on voluntary childlessness, compares sterilization with homosexuality in that the parents are the last ones to face it, and when they finally do they tell the errant offspring to "keep it in the closet.")

"Anyway, at the taping," continued Marie, "the first question Donahue asks is, 'Is it permanent?' I said, 'Yes, it's permanent.' He says, 'Does that mean you've been sterilized?' I said, 'Yes.' I called my mother right afterward and when I told her what had happened, her reaction was, 'Well, I'm not going to tell any of the neighbors.' And she didn't. She didn't tell anyone. I didn't hear from her for three weeks.

"Finally, I called her again and said, 'Did you see the show? What did you think of it?' She said, 'Your aunt called and I couldn't watch.' At eight-thirty in the morning? I said, 'You could have left the phone. I mean, it's all of seven minutes long. How many times am I going to be on national TV, whatever the topic?' And it's never come up since. Finally, she said, 'I guess I'll have to tell your father.' I said, 'Please, don't make it a replay of *Playhouse 90*. Just tell him like a fact, like we bought a car.' "

It's not only the nongrandparents that take a dim view of sterilization among the childfree. New Yorker Sherry Barnes, who had a long professional association with Planned Parenthood, witnessed a similar reaction among TV and other media people. "They make a lot of requests for couples to interview who are voluntarily childless," she told me. "Those who do the interviewing often start with the viewpoint 'Well, if you're serious about not having children, why haven't you been sterilized?' Then, when they find out the people *have* been sterilized, they take an almost perverse interest in them. 'How *could* you have done that?' "

This attitude infuriates many young childless couples who have chosen to be sterilized. After all, as several of them complained to me, they are harming no one by this action but, in fact, have done something that should be applauded in view of world overpopulation. Particularly they resent society's harsh view of sterilization in comparison with its lenient and romantic attitude toward pregnancy. "You can be eighteen years old with no money to raise a kid and not the slightest inkling of what childrearing is all about, but when people hear you're pregnant their response is: 'Great! What are you going to name it?' " complained one vasectomized male.

The Association for Voluntary Sterilization makes the same points. It is particularly supportive of childless young people who wish to be sterilized, feeling they are often better candidates than parents. The reason for this, according to Betty Gonzales, is that parents tend to think of their own children when contemplating a sterilization; if they go through with the operation, they may well feel a sense of grief and guilt.

It is no easy job to be a counselor or physician responsible for granting or turning down a procedure that will critically affect the future of the person requesting it. I talked with social worker Phyllis Hyman, now a Boston resident, who was formerly associated with a sterilization clinic of Planned Parenthood in the Midwest. Hyman, in her twenties, married, and thus far childless, said that at first she had trouble personally in giving approval to childless people who wanted to be sterilized at a young age. Knowing how *she* had changed and is still changing, she feared they might regret the sterilization at a later date. However, she eventually separated out her own feelings, concluding that people have a right to make decisions for themselves and to live with the consequences, even if these prove to be unsatisfactory. The men and women she saw were, almost without exception, serious and thoughtful; they had given much consideration to career, spousal relationship, and their own values.

In fact, the only person that Hyman ever turned down was a young man of twenty-two whose fiancée was nineteen. They had never had intercourse. "As it turned out, he wanted the vasectomy only because *she* wanted him to have it. She definitely didn't want children; he wasn't sure. Through his bringing up the issues with me, it became clear that there was a real power play going on in their relationship. She would not use any method of birth control because she had no faith in their reliability. If she had become pregnant, she would have had an abortion. And he couldn't have handled that—he was morally opposed to abortion."

Why, I asked, wouldn't she consider her own sterilization —did she want to foist all the responsibility onto him?

"Right. And so I denied the vasectomy. I worked and worked with him, shared my feelings with him. He didn't see it the way I did or at least he didn't acknowledge that he saw it. I told him I couldn't approve him, that I had to live with myself too. I referred him to a private urologist, which was our policy when we turned someone down. I don't know what happened. It really tore me apart."

I talked also with two psychiatrists who have had many years of clinical experience with marital issues. One was Martin Goldberg at the Institute of Pennsylvania Hospital in Philadelphia. "I respect fully the choice by some young people to remain childless and I don't think we should cop out and say there is some underlying psychological reason for their decision. They may well have thought things out and arrived at an intelligent, conscious choice at a young age. However, there is no guarantee that these people might not change their minds about this or anything else. So, if a permanent sterilization is done, that can be unfortunate. Hence I almost never *recommend* sterilization. And when a person wants it who is subject to changing moods and volatile judgments, I do raise an objection."

Psychiatrist Robert Gould, of New York Medical College, told me he approaches the issue this way: "I would discourage a sterilization at twenty just as I would discourage a marriage at twenty, though some people are mature enough to make either decision at that age. In any event, at any age, I would most likely explore in great detail the reasons for desiring the sterilization. If the couple seem to have a life script that is convincing and rational (such as long-term career plans) and if they are in a stable relationship, then I would be inclined to trust the decision. I think age twenty-five is 'iffy' and thirty for sure is all right, though once again there are differences. A twenty-five-year-old, happily married for five years, is usually more stable than a twenty-five-year-old who has never been married. But the main point is when something is irreversible you ought to take great care before approving it."

What about all this talk of reversibility? It is true that a limited percentage of both male and female sterilizations are reversible, meaning that the operation can be "undone" and fertility restored. But the fees are large and there are no guarantees. In women, the greater the length of tube that was destroyed during the sterilization, the lower the chance of a successful reversal; in men, the longer the time that has elapsed since the vasectomy, the less likelihood of a reversal.

In any event, almost all physicians and counselors as well as the AVS are quick to advise against a sterilization for any person who comes in for it because it is the "in" thing or with the attitude that if it doesn't prove satisfactory it can simply be reversed; such thinking reveals both ambivalence regarding the operation and a lack of knowledge about what it entails. The same response goes for the man who comes up with the idea of depositing his sperm in a sperm bank before the vasectomy "just in case"; in fact, frozen sperm decreases in potency with time.

Sherman J. Silber, urologist and microsurgeon at the Ballas-Parkway Medical Center in St. Louis has earned a national reputation for work in vasectomy reversals. A large number of the requests he receives are from men with children who divorce and remarry, then wish to start a new family. But Silber also has expressed serious doubt about the wisdom of sterilization for childless men. Because this sentiment was at variance with many of the reports I had read about vasectomy, I asked him for a clarification.

Silber: "I have just met so many men who said they never wanted children at all—twenty-one-, twenty-five-year-old men who were absolutely against the concept of children, and then five or ten years later for reasons that I don't understand (and they can't articulate it very well either), they come back wanting to have children. I say to them, 'Well, now, why did you have that vasectomy done?' And they can't explain it. Their views on family life just seem to mellow."

In contrast, Silber has found that a much smaller proportion of women are changing their minds and asking for a tubal reversal. "My impression is that when women have their tubes tied they are usually more mature, more thoughtful about their decision, and they have a much more realistic view of what having children is all about. Those women who *have* changed their minds generally had their sterilizations under extremely emotional circumstances, like a terrible marriage or an abortion."

In all, Silber has performed about 1,200 vasectomy reversals as compared with 35 tubal reversals—a striking imbalance. Still, and Silber himself mentions this, for all the unhappy male cases he sees there are millions of vasectomized men whom he and other microsurgeons *don't* see for precisely the reason that they remain happy with their sterilization.

Looking to the future, the big hope is in the direction of

techniques that will bring about temporary sterilization. One method being tested at present is a female procedure using silicone injections which harden and form plugs in the fallopian tubes; the same substance might also be appropriate for men, implanted in the vas deferens. It is not a surgical procedure and presumably would be quite readily reversible, though surgery might be required for that.

But for now tubal ligation and vasectomy are the only viable means of sterilization. Their popularity is unquestioned, and their combined features of safety plus reliability make them superior to other methods of birth control. The big question is how sterilized people will feel not only years but decades later, about that choice. In that long-range sense sterilization is still in its infancy.

A number of voluntarily childless couples admitted to me that they have avoided sterilization precisely because of such doubts. Joyce, a New York City fundraiser in her thirties, says: "Like many others, I grew up assuming I'd have kids, then married and made the decision with my husband after a lot of thought that I'd rather remain childfree. Frankly, I can't see us going back on that decision, but I did change my mind once. So why have an operation that is so final?"

And Gordon Palmer, California urban planner in his late twenties, also quite assuredly childfree, says: "If I were sterilized, I would have to justify to myself and my wife that I didn't want kids, which doesn't allow for free growth. As it is now, I am responsible for that decision intellectually at any point in my life."

Childless people who *have* been sterilized and remain satisfied with that step analyze matters quite differently. They say when one door is closed that allows other doors to be opened. They feel liberated from fear of pregnancy, from their own ambivalence, and hence are able actively to pursue long-term goals. They are certain that what they are doing is right for them now and in the foreseeable future. Life, they say, requires hard decisions, not all of which are reversible. After all, a child who proves to be unwanted is the least reversible decision of all.

4

Infertility: Those
Who Can't Have Children

The bride at thirty-eight was red-haired, shrunken, yellow-faced, ill, and old-looking. Her twenty-seven-year-old groom, a widower, was handsome and coldly dignified, a man of unflappable serenity. She was in love with him, he not at all with her (the marriage took place under orders from his father). Still, as befitted his station in life, the young man was attired in garments that "glittered like starlight."[1]

The year was 1554. The bride was Mary Tudor, queen of England and Ireland; the groom was her cousin King Philip II of Spain. By this union, if it was blessed by the subsequent birth of a child, Spain was expected to achieve almost world domination.

Mary, joyful in her new wifely role, frequently opened her prayerbook to the blessing for women in confinement. Philip, though he wasn't around much, performed his husbandly duty toward that end.

A few months after the marriage Mary announced that she was with child, and later she wrote her cousin that the baby had leapt in her womb. On April 20, 1555, the queen went into seclusion to await the birth. Nurses and cradle rockers were at hand, while bishops and priests chanted litanies; when the labor pangs seemed to have begun, bells were rung, bonfires lit, and feasting prepared. But no child was born. In fact there had been no conception. Mary had dropsy, a disease which results in a great accumulation of fluid in the body. Desperately eager for motherhood, Mary had fooled herself and her court into accepting a pregnant appearance as pregnancy.

Up to then a gentle and charitable lady, Mary, who was Catholic, became convinced that God was delaying the birth as punishment for certain acts, such as her clemency toward heretics (Protestants). To assuage His anger and bring on labor, she ordered the heretics engulfed in fire, earning herself history's enduring nickname of "Bloody Mary." But still no infant came. Gradually the cradle rockers, the nurses left.

Once again, a few years later, Mary thought she had conceived and the whole macabre scene replayed itself. But this time it ended even more sadly: with Mary's death.

England now had a new and brilliant ruler, Mary's half sister, Elizabeth I, the "Virgin Queen." She was a Protestant. Because of one woman's infertility, history would take an entirely different course.

Mary Tudor was one among many for whom infertility constituted not only a great personal deprivation but a threat to the future of a nation. Even today, some rulers with cold practicality divorce wives who fail to reproduce in the expected fashion. The recently deceased Shah of Iran, for instance, wanting a male heir to inherit his now meaningless throne, disposed of Wife Number One for producing only a daughter and Wife Number Two for being barren.

Our own country, which from its earliest days was governed by elected leaders rather than monarchical succession, has taken a gentler approach to infertility. George Washington, who at age twenty-seven married a twenty-eight-year-old widow with two children, was probably our nation's most famous nonfather, though he loved children and, in fact, adopted two of Martha's grandsons. History has never passed a sure judgment on whether or not he was infertile, but contemporaries referred to our first president fondly as "the father only of his country."[2]

Even in the United States, however, fertility remains, as it has been through recorded time, a subject of tremendous concern and even obsession. We may not worship fertility gods or perform exotic rites to bring on conception, but many of the words and phrases we use in daily conversation—a fertile mind," "fruitful enterprise," "pregnant with hope"— reveal our ingrained attitudes just as do their antonyms: a "sterile approach," "barren soil," "fruitless labors." And, though we have reached the stage where we must limit births in order to achieve a decent world standard of living, still we think of fertility as something which is our right. Even those who decide against having children don't like the idea of being *unable* physiologically to reproduce. And, for those who do intensely want children, to be denied them is a major life disappointment.

Infertility is generally defined as the inability to achieve a pregnancy after a year or more of regular sexual activity without contraception, or the inability to carry a pregnancy to a live birth. (The word "sterility" is reserved for those cases which are determined to be permanent and incurable.) It is estimated that about ten million people in the United States from age eighteen to forty experience some difficulty in this area. Of that number a diagnosis can be established for 80 percent; half of those can eventually, with competent medical help, achieve a pregnancy and carry it to term. Even though this relatively new science still has a long way to go, progress has been great, with breakthroughs such as the 1978 birth of English baby Louise Brown—conceived in a test tube and implanted in her mother's womb—bordering on science fiction.

By tradition infertility has been considered a female problem, and some men even today refuse to undergo tests that would show where the fault—if, indeed, it be a fault—really lies. Among those cases in which men and women seek help and a diagnosis is reached, one-half of the problems are attributable to the wife, 30 percent to the husband, and the rest to both as a couple (among the latter are some relatively slight malfunctions which, with another mate, might not interfere with pregnancy).

Among the leading causes of female infertility are blockage

of the fallopian tubes and endocrine disorders that affect the hormonal balance. Male infertility, which is less well understood, can be caused by inadequate production of sperm, perhaps as the result of fever or exposure to chemicals, or low motility, another common condition, meaning that the movement of the sperm is not sufficient to reach and fertilize the ovum. One example of combined male-female infertility is incompatibility between the sperm and cervical secretions.

In the past, physicians put a heavy emphasis on psychological factors as causing infertility. Miriam D. Mazor, M.D., a psychotherapist associated with the Harvard Medical School, described in *Psychology Today* various elaborate but unsubstantiated theories, such as "rejection of the maternal role." Though emotional factors may, indeed, be at work in some cases of impotence or failure to ovulate, wrote Mazor, the accurate diagnosis of medically caused problems has undermined many of those theories.[3] Still, old wives' tales die hard, and one hears often in conversation of a relative or acquaintance who "can't get pregnant because she is uptight"—an accusation that angers the "infertiles" (a name they call themselves). Who wouldn't be "uptight," they say, after all the "workups" (another trade word, used to signify fertility tests and treatment) they've been through in order to achieve what is supposed to come naturally?

As mentioned in Chapter 1, despite significant medical advances of recent years infertility is thought to be on the rise. It is believed that one of six couples of childbearing age is experiencing this condition now as compared with one out of ten three decades ago. There are several reasons for this. One is the intentional postponement of childbearing into the thirties and forties, when fertility decreases—not only in women but, more gradually, in men. Another is the epidemic rise in venereal disease. A third is birth control itself; certain methods, like the pill and IUD, can cause all kinds of problems resulting in infertility. Abortions sometimes cause damage to the cervix; in a later pregnancy such damage may result in miscarriage. Dr. Ralph Dougherty, a professor of chemistry at Florida State University, goes so far as to claim that the sperm count of males in our country has gone down sharply, possibly as the result of toxic chemicals in the environment.

Fortunately, infertility is no longer a taboo subject. People talk about it and seek help instead of burning heretics as Mary I did or hiding in the closet in the style of King Louis XVI of France. (Louis's problem was actually one of impotence. Because he had an impediment under the foreskin of his royal penis, he was unable for seven years to consummate his marriage to that pleasure-loving queen Marie Antoinette; finally his brother-in-law talked him into an operation which was such a success that Louis ended up a father four times over.)[4]

Many infertile couples, in fact, become so knowledgeable about their reproductive systems that their medical vocabulary is well-nigh incomprehensible to the uninitiated. One cannot, however, minimize the physical pain and emotional indignities that these people go through to determine and treat their condition: from postcoital examination of the woman to biopsies of her uterine lining; from masturbation into a glass jar by a man (so his sperm may be tested) to repair of a varicose vein in his testicle.

Why do they go through it all with less than a fifty-fifty chance of success and with the risk that some treatments may end up worsening, rather than ameliorating, the condition? Because they want to have babies for all the reasons, healthy and neurotic, that fertile people want to have babies. Because they are angry at the removal of choice (we are a very choice-oriented society, whether the subject be clothes, friendships, mates, or number of children). And so they go on, spending years and large sums of money, sometimes forgetting in the process why they wanted children in the first place, whether they'd make good parents, and what facets of their present childless life might be downright pleasant were it not for their focusing on what is missing.

"The quest for a child becomes an obsession," wrote Dena Kleiman in a recent *New York Times Magazine* article. "Vacations are postponed, employment opportunities rejected, business trips synchronized with doctors' appointments and ovulation schedules. Many couples say that if only they knew for certain that they could never have a child, they would give up and get on with their lives. But as long as there is one more doctor, one more possible remedy, even the most unlikely straw to clutch at, they continue."[5]

One individual who has done an admirable job in helping infertiles cope with life is thirty-eight-year-old Barbara Eck Menning, founder and executive director of the nonprofit organization Resolve. Menning, who was trained as an R.N. and holds a master's degree in maternal and child health, started Resolve in the spring of 1973, right at the time she learned that her own infertility—despite years of exhaustive workup—was permanent (she is now divorced and has three adopted children).

I spoke with Menning at Resolve's headquarters in Belmont, Massachusetts. She told me that the organization had evolved out of a conference concerned with "issues of the childless couple." This really meant infertility; however, that word was at the time too straightforward for most tastes. Menning objected to the half truth ("It's like calling alcoholism a wee bit too much to drink") but took part anyway. So responsive was the audience that she put together a support group which later was incorporated.

The first organization of its kind in the nation, Resolve presently has thirty-six chapters and, in 1978, received a three-year HEW grant to expand its work. Its members come for counseling, referral to medical specialists, and contact with other infertiles. Some have been trying for a pregnancy for just months, while others have endured years and years of disappointment. The first goal is to help them overcome the physical infertility, if possible. A second and concurrent goal is to enable them to feel better about themselves individually and as couples, especially if they don't achieve pregnancies in the end.

"There is a kind of suspended animation that infertile couples fall into," Menning told me. "At Resolve we try to get them past that, working through painful feelings so they can somehow get on with life." She cited certain stages that sterile individuals characteristically experience. These are, not necessarily in prescribed order except for the last one: surprise, denial, isolation, anger, guilt and unworthiness, depression, and, finally, grief. Facing each stage, believes Menning, is vital to the healing process.

But before that healing occurs all kinds of self-deprecating behavior and attitudes can be observed. Psychiatrist Mazor described several patients whose image of themselves was harshly critical: one female called herself "The Sterile Cuckoo" and several males referred to intercourse as "shooting blanks."[6] The longer the infertility workup drags on, the greater its likely toll on the couple, especially in the area of sex, where intimacy and spontaneity fast disappear along with self-confidence.

"The act of sex," according to Barbara Menning, "really takes a beating because for at least a portion of the diagnostic work and most attempted treatments, the couple must have intercourse on a schedule. Initially the stress is minor and, in fact, the situation can even be humorous, but that wears down pretty quickly. I have known couples to become so stressed that the whole sexual act becomes abhorrent and the man may experience bouts of impotence.

"When definitive sterility is determined, there is a great deal of sadness and even futility connected with sex. It may feel rapelike and invasive just like all the tests. Also, the teachings of some religions, which justify sexual pleasure only through reproduction, add guilt to an already heavy burden.

"Often there is a sort of moratorium after the final news, when sex doesn't happen at all for a while. In my own case there were several months when I just needed to rest; I didn't want to be reminded of that awful sadness. It's a real process to get back to sex for its own sake when you have been wounded in your sexuality."

The loss of sexual self-esteem is frequently accompanied by a lowered sense of worth in many areas of life: career, physical appearance, personality, intelligence. Relationships with parents, especially those who make no secret of their grandparent longings, can become strained, and the presence of siblings who reproduce with rabbitlike ease adds further tension. Well-meaning friends who show their concern by constantly inquiring about temperature charts and sperm motility sometimes incur anger instead of gratitude. Acquaintances who cite interminable cases of those who got pregnant on vacation or just as they were about to adopt heighten anxiety. Brothers-in-law who kiddingly offer their own children because they're such a nuisance aren't found to be amusing. Physicians—often the very ones who are trying to overcome the problem—can become a target for the infertile person's anger.

Some infertiles seek self-affirmation through extramarital affairs, others through their work. Some, writes Mazor, try "extra hard to be extra-good to atone for whatever real or imagined sins they feel may have caused their infertility. . . . They may bargain magically with God, offering to suffer in return for a baby." The infertility workup itself, being so painful, can serve as a form of expiation, she adds.[7]

I asked Menning about the usual scenario when one party is found to be the sterile one. "The fertile person often feels initially that he or she must be loving and supportive to the infertile person and not cast blame. That 'no matter what, I will stick by you' attitude doesn't rest well with the infertile person, who feels a lot of guilt in tying the partner into a marriage where that partner has no chance for genetic continuity.

"I can speak from my own experience. There were beautiful nieces and nephews in the Menning family from my ex-husband's sisters, and I felt he had a right to his own children. His professions of undying love which came to me in support didn't help because in my secret heart I feared abandonment. We all do, those of us who are infertile. So it's almost a relief when some anger and resentment are expressed by our partners." (Mazor believes that even worse than the fear of abandonment is fear that the fertile partner will remain in the relationship resentfully; some infertiles make offers of divorce to test their mates.)[8]

At Resolve, time is spent in helping fertile individuals face and express the anger they feel toward the infertile mate.

"We've usually been able to identify that the person isn't angry at the partner," says Menning, "but at the situation, and that's legitimate. We've also realized that anger is not the antithesis of love—apathy is."

Sometimes the tension brought about by long-term infertility proves to be so great that the partners cannot repair their marriage but are able to move on to new and happier relationships. One infertile divorcée told me that she is now involved with a man who, unlike her ex-husband, does not want children. His attitude has helped make for the fullest sexual relationship she ever had. "We are simply together because we love each other, and sex is for its own sake."

A similar reaction has been experienced by George, a witty and attractive linguistics professor in his forties, divorced and remarried after a childless first marriage.

George's ex-wife Marina, not having achieved any measure of professional success, felt that having children was the one thing in life left for her to do. She saw motherhood, George told me, "as a biological, God-given right." For reasons that were never determined, Marina was unable to conceive, except for one tubal pregnancy, from which she nearly died. Her response to nonmotherhood was increasing hostility to George.

"When it came to the point where the doctor said, 'Do this and do that, do it on such and such a day,' it began to get worse and worse." The marriage became so strained that Marina did not even tell George she was taking fertility pills, which, he now feels, led to her tubal pregnancy. "After that was over she was left with the most ghastly scar I have ever seen from her navel down. Then she started to pull the on-again off-again switch sexually, until it got to the point, to call a spade a spade, where it reduced me to 80 or 90 percent impotency. At which point she began to accuse me of being homosexual. If there had been a chance of conception in all that horror, it would have been the biggest surprise of all. Finally I said something in the best of faith and it had absolutely the reverse effect. I said, 'Wouldn't artificial insemination maybe work better?'

thinking, 'God, if all you need is to be fertilized, don't keep at me this way,' because the thought of sex had become absolutely a nightmare. Anyway, Marina took my suggestion as if I was sending her out on the streets as a prostitute."

(It takes an especially good marriage to deal with artificial insemination by donor (AID). George may have *thought* he could cope with it, but he was speaking out of a sense of defeat; had Marina taken him up on the offer, this further blow to his self-esteem might have been enormous. AID is a technique whereby at the time of ovulation the supposedly fertile wife has injected into her vagina the fresh sperm of a healthy anonymous donor. The great advantage is that it allows the wife to experience pregnancy and childbirth and assures genetic continuity on the one side.)

Continues George, "The effect of all this on my self-respect was the worst thing of all, even worse than what was happening at the university." At that time he was undergoing a great deal of pressure in his teaching job. Despite this, he'd managed somehow to produce an award-winning piece of research. "I'm sure that an awful lot of the drive I got for the book was sublimated energy due to the frustration I felt. Also, it provided me with an excuse for not having sex. Time and again I would say, 'I'm tired,' and it was the truth. On the other hand, I was blessedly tired.

"I'll tell you something else. This is so painful I have to root around in my memory to see where it comes from, but I got to the point where I'd think of friends, particularly men, and I'd say, 'This man is a father; he has a family.' Eventually I could not be in the presence of people who had children. One of the worst nights I ever had in my life was when the phone rang and it was friends announcing that they were expecting a first child. Marina got off some flippant remark. It was one of the most agonizing times I've ever had in terms of psychological nightmares. I didn't sleep a wink that night. I realize now something that was totally in my subconscious then: the thing I will never, never, never forgive Marina for was annihilating my masculinity."

"She didn't annihilate it," corrects George's new wife

fondly. "She just put it temporarily in the deep freeze."

Clearly, George's first marriage had not been secure for years before the breakup, but even good relationships are sometimes shaken beyond repair by infertility. Kleiman writes: "The psychological trauma can devastate individual self-esteem and erode even the most secure marriage."[9]

Still, many authorities are of the opinion that how the marriage ends up depends very much on the couple's overall relationship. Martin Goldberg, Philadelphia psychiatrist, described his clinical experience to me: "If the couple is a conflicted one and if they are looking for a place to fight the conflict out, here's one area where a great deal of hurt can be inflicted. On the other hand, if they are reasonably harmonious, it can be quite a different story. After all, it is the pain that we endure together, just as much as the joys, that bring us closer. I've seen it go both ways." And Miriam Mazor has found that her patients react to infertility much as they do to other aspects of life: "Those who are aggressive and optimistic tend to approach the infertility crisis that way; those who view life as an insurmountable struggle and themselves as failures will tend to see infertility as a confirmation of that."[10]

One couple I met who had dealt very gracefully with infertility were Bobby and June, New Jersey residents in their late thirties, married for twelve years and working together now as co-managers of a small appliance store. Bobby had been married before and divorced. He was very close to his ten-year-old daughter from that marriage, Veronica, and plans were being made for her to live with him and June when suddenly the child was killed in an automobile accident. Shortly afterward June learned that she was infertile.

"I think it was just assumed that Bobby and I would have children," June told me, "since I come from a family of fifteen brothers and sisters. But after the doctor told me I couldn't have children, it wasn't one of those questions of how am I going to tell my husband. It was so easy to talk to him and he didn't make me feel that I was less of a woman like I've heard so many other women say. He made me feel like, 'I married you for *you*.' "

Bobby's mother, claims June, was equally supportive. "She's a great mother-in-law, not the interfering type. When I shared the problem with her, she said, 'Honey, with all the problems raising kids, there's not much happiness in it. You'll probably live longer and have a happier life without them.' It was so ironic, I mean she doesn't understand all the medical terms and I was telling her, 'My tubes are blocked.' She said, 'Honey, you just let the block stay right there!' "

Today Bobby and June have a very intimate marriage, and each admits to being "spoiled rotten" by the other. Bobby says: "We are each other's best friend. We don't need kids to fulfill our marriage."

There are other specific conditions associated with infertility which can be expected to seriously undermine self-esteem. One is hysterectomy, the surgical removal of the uterus, and sometimes the ovaries and fallopian tubes as well. Upsetting even for women who do not want children, the operation brings particular anguish to those who do. To help them over the hurdle, Resolve organizes special support groups for hysterectomized women. Barbara Menning told me that characteristically they see themselves as "defective," "empty," as being incapable of genuine sexual pleasure (a kind of "why bother?" attitude). They fear how their husbands will respond to them; they imagine premature aging. If they are single, they worry about entering a relationship, explaining the situation, and feeling "devalued" as women; they may even choose to marry similarly sterile men. In a book she wrote on infertility, Menning states: "The uterus, though not necessary to life . . . symbolizes femininity and fertility. Even though it is internal and invisible, the uterus is not a silent organ like the liver or spleen . . . but waxes and wanes with hormonal tides."[11]

Particularly upsetting in connection with infertility problems is the use by a physician of terminology that reveals an insensitivity to what the patient is going through. Mazor cites one such term, "hostile vagina," which, though it sounds downright accusatory, merely means that the vaginal secretions are unfavorable to the survival of sperm. Equally distasteful are "blighted ovum" and "incompetent cervix."[12]

A childless woman on the editorial staff of a major eastern newspaper who tried to conceive unsuccessfully for several years, then had a hysterectomy at age thirty-eight, described to me her own physician's unfelicitous choice of words:

"I'd had fibroid tumors for five years. Before the operation the doctor told me, 'Maybe we'll just take out the tumors and keep the uterus, maybe not; you've been married eighteen years and you don't have children so we may as well take out the whole thing.' I said I didn't want it all out, just the fibroids. I wanted the uterus. Not particularly to have children anymore, but to function as a woman. It didn't bother me to have periods every month and I didn't like the idea of not being complete.

"But when he did the operation he had to take out the uterus because I had one tumor the size of a grapefruit and another the size of an orange. I had forty tumors all around the uterus and they were of different sizes. There was a whole fruit salad in there. It upset me terribly when he told me the largest fibroid was the size of a baby's head. I'm sure they do it on purpose. Doctors have a mean streak. He also told me my uterus was the size of a four-and-one-half-month pregnancy. I was quite depressed by the whole thing. Here was my chance to have a child gone. I mean, nobody knows it from looking at you, but *you* do, and the scar is awful—it's nine inches long. Still, what can you do? I'm lucky I didn't have cancer."

Acknowledged to be two of the most acutely painful among infertility problems are miscarriage, or spontaneous abortion, the inability to carry a pregnancy to term, and stillbirth, the birth of a dead baby at or near full term. Both these conditions occur with more frequency among women who have experienced difficulty in conceiving.

Miscarriage—terrifying, painful, often totally unexpected and even potentially dangerous—can be over in minutes or it can drag on for weeks. Having planned happily for the birth, a couple normally undergo an enormous letdown after a miscarriage, and comments made by well-meaning friends that the fetus was probably defective, even if true, do not necessarily help. Stillbirth carries with it an even greater agony in that an entire pregnancy has been lived through, probably without a hint of this tragic outcome. Yet, paradoxically, because with stillbirth there is an actual baby which the parents can mourn and bury, the recovery process is sometimes facilitated. Indeed, one of the most perplexing and difficult aspects of those cases of infertility which never lead to pregnancy is that people feel they are mourning an unknown, an intangible, a nothing.

Women who have been through a miscarriage or stillbirth sometimes continue to become pregnant beyond the point of medical wisdom because, knowing they can at least conceive, they go on summoning up hope that the next time they will carry to term and deliver a healthy baby. Sometimes this happens; sometimes not. If not, they eventually have to decide how much agony is too much.

I met Al and Janet at a dinner party in Chicago. An intense couple in their thirties, they were vibrantly alive—Al with a thick, curly round of black hair fringed in gray, Janet with green eyes, the facial contours of a *Vogue* model, and a slightly aquiline nose that added character to her otherwise perfect features.

They married young with the idea that they would eventually have children after career and self-identity were established. Janet became a social worker. Though she vacillated along the way about children, she reached a point where she felt deeply, beyond the mere rational recognition, the desire for motherhood. She was then twenty-seven.

Al, a psychologist specializing in sex education, had been traveling a different mental route without Janet's knowing. "I came to like and value our life style without children. Also, I had a lot of fears that I would not make a good parent. I was concerned that many things that had shown up in my clinical practice with parents would repeat themselves in my own case, and I wanted to spare a child that kind of unpleasantness. Being a professional in family counseling, I knew it really is hard for people to change their child-rearing patterns from those they experienced while growing up."

A crisis between husband and wife developed. Janet recalls that rough time: "I didn't realize Al had made up his mind negatively until we started talking about it finally and it came out. I became quite upset and so did he, and we went round and round."

Al decided to go into therapy with this problem as the focus. The result was a happy one: "I did a lot of reviewing of my feelings about my own upbringing and parents, and somehow through that I was able to come to terms with certain of the issues and to feel much better about a decision to have a child."

But that was five years ago. There are still no children and the marriage is twelve years old. The problem now is not psychological in origin; it is physical. Janet has had three miscarriages.

"It's one thing to choose to be childless; it's another if the decision is made for you," she told me with some bitterness.

Adoption? No. They don't have the gut-level desire, and both claim that professionally they have seen many family problems made worse with adoption. Being much in tune with the times, they are aware of the career and financial benefits as well as the freedom that come of being childless; Janet, in fact, is about to enter a new career, having just obtained a master's degree in business administration. But both remain determined to try one more pregnancy before giving up.

Why? I couldn't fathom at first what kept motivating them. One miscarriage, perhaps, or two. But three? And now the possibility of a fourth?

Janet: "I don't know. I really want a child and it's not at a level that I can explain."

Al: "I think there's something that's been added in the last couple of years that wasn't there before."

Janet: "No, it was always there. But the realization has been added."

Janet is Jewish, the only child of a couple who survived a World War II concentration camp. Al, born in America, had a Jewish education in a New York yeshiva (parochial school), where he associated with many children of Holocaust survivors. Today they keep a kosher home and are involved with the Second Generation, a group whose backgrounds are similar.

"A lot of what comes out in the meetings," Al told me, "is the need we feel to prove that it was not all in vain. Somehow that people survived the Holocaust should not have been for nothing. It is important for people like Janet's parents to have grandchildren, for the survivors' children to have children. Our ethnic Judaism has become very meaningful to us. And that, I think, accounts in large part for our persistence."

When infertility stands in the way of so deep an emotional need, it is no wonder that people persist.

Assuming that a childless couple has reached the stage where infertility is accepted and the grieving for the unborn child less intense, they must decide, individually and together, how best to fulfill their lives. Adoption is an obvious next step for some, though reaching this stage is neither easy nor automatic. According to one study cited in the *New York Times Magazine* by Dr. Jacqueline Horner Plumez, one out of four infertile couples in the United States tries to adopt.[13]

Why do the other three not wish to become adoptive parents? The answers are many and complex.

Barbara Menning has an interesting theory that "there are some people for whom the pregnancy and childbirth experience as well as genetic continuity are extremely important for whatever reasons, and if this is denied them they don't want a child in any other way. Others find the parenting to be the larger thing. I was a maternity nurse, and though I grieved at the sadness of not being able to make my own children, parenting was the overriding need for me.

"I'm not making judgments here. In fact, I think it's wise when people understand their needs and do not adopt if the childbirth and genetic considerations are that strong because then an adopted child would be a living reminder of their own infertility and would end up receiving all kinds of direct and indirect abuse. Parenting is hard work and one should never get into the situation of being responsible for a child he or she can't love. We don't have any bias here at Resolve that everyone has to have children." (There is, incidentally, a subtle but serious form of pronatalism in our society which maintains that the infertile person who is unwilling to adopt doesn't deserve to have a child of his or her own; a corollary to that is the thesis "If you *really* wanted a child you'd be ready to adopt," which implies that the infertile's maternal/paternal instincts are suspect. Such accusations have about as much validity as the "selfish" label pinned on the voluntarily childless.)

The subject of genetics is admittedly a touchy one because it can be used to mean not just continuity but superiority. The most radical example of this today may well be the recently opened Repository for Germinal Choice in San Diego, to which several Nobel Prize recipients donated their sperm. The plan is to artificially inseminate women of supposedly similar intellectual merit with the end result of genetically exceptional children. Whether or not such children will result remains to be seen. Many authorities point out that even the most outstanding of humans carry poor genes which might produce a seriously defective child. Dr. Hope Punnett, head of the genetics laboratory at St. Christopher's Hospital for Children in Philadelphia, told me that statistically the tendency is for people at both extremes of overall intelligence—high and low—as well as people who are average, to have children whose intelligence level comes out somewhere in the middle. Highly gifted offspring *can* be born to parents of similar ability but they also can result from the mating of two average people. The whole thing is a gamble. "You can't produce children exactly like yourself unless you get cloned," says Punnett. "And even then the children would grow up in a different environment and hence be different." (This view probably would not have been well received by dancer Isadora Duncan, who, according to a well-known if apocryphal story, suggested to that acerbic—and childless—man of letters George Bernard Shaw: "As you have the greatest brain in the world and I the most beautiful body, we ought to produce the most perfect child."[14] Shaw, it is said, responded:

"But, my dear woman, what if the child had *my* body and *your* brain?" Unfortunately for science, no child was conceived to settle the matter.)

Science and humanitarian principles aside, the fact remains that those who want children are usually quite willing to take a chance on the genetic product that would be the result of their breeding with a chosen mate. When it comes to adoption, they are not so sure. Time and again I heard infertile couples express an unwillingness to consider adoption because of all the cases they know personally or have heard of where it just didn't work out. Valid or not, as Menning says, adoption with a negative attitude surely would not bode well for the child.

There are other factors at work, too, in the infertile couple's decision to forgo adoption. Social worker Eleanor Lavin, an adoptive parent who is professionally associated with Love the Children, an agency in Quakertown, Pennsylvania, expressed one theory: "Adoption is the final disappointment. It's the last level of realizing you're never going to have your own baby. Some people can face that. Others, especially those from traditional families—say, an old-fashioned Catholic upbringing where everybody has babies—cannot."

Assuming that an infertile couple does sincerely want to adopt, opportunities are becoming fewer and fewer. What has happened in the last decade to make healthy babies such a rare commodity? Several things. Birth control has prevented unwanted pregnancies, and legal abortion has ended them. Though the illegitimacy rate has soared, far fewer mothers are giving up their babies.

There are so few infants around, in fact, that you're lucky if an agency, even of your own racial, religious, and ethnic persuasion, will sign you up for what characteristically is a five-year wait. (As for adopted infants of other backgrounds, this too is next to impossible, since the various communities —Lutheran or Jewish or black—exert pressure to keep their own.) And, because the nation's 1,800 adoption agencies have so few bundles of joy for adoption, they can make judgments on everything from the prospective parents' ages, weights, and financial situation to their motivation and marital stability. I asked Eleanor Lavin what kinds of people would be turned down by her agency as being emotionally unfit.

"First on our list would be those who are prejudiced against an adopted child. Number two is those who are on the verge of divorce. I see it happening in front of my eyes—the hostility between partners."

Are they on the verge of divorce because they can't have children of their own?

"Not necessarily. Because of any reason or reasons, and they're coming to us to cement the marriage."

Whom else do you turn down?

"Those for whom adoption was not the real motivation but a means to another end, like raising their status in the community. Those who see adoption as a second-rate deal. Those who are emotionally sick and don't know it.

"Considering all the divorce today," adds Lavin, "some agencies are beginning to feel that single people who have never been married are more stable as adoptive parents."

What with all the obstacles, some couples give up entirely. Some pay exorbitant rates ($20,000 and $30,000 are not uncommon) for the illegal purchase of a baby from a doctor or lawyer. Others try adopting children of relatives. Quite popular today is adoption from the developing world, like Vietnam, Korea, and Latin America. This is legal and financially reasonable, though getting through the red tape can be frightful and the supply of these babies too is shrinking. Easier to obtain but harder to cope with are the older special-needs children in our own country who are physically or mentally handicapped and/or had an unhappy history in terms of former placements.

You can't help admiring those who are willing to face the huge mountain that adoption presents. But some are much more ready for the reality than others. During my interviews I met two infertile couples who were contemplating adoption. One seemed truly ready for that large step, the other still weighing, agonizing, grieving.

My telephone interview with Betty, a governmental liaison officer, was a sad conversation, magnified by the inanimate nature of the faceless black instrument through which we communicated. Betty told me that she suffers from endometriosis, the growth of uterine tissue in abnormal locations, such as on the ovaries. Despite this condition some women become pregnant but, at thirty-eight, Betty has not yet been among the lucky ones.

"I was married when I had just turned thirty-one and I tried getting pregnant about six months later. I went through all kinds of tests and one miscarriage.

"There's been a lot of emotional pain in the last six years and sometimes I am resentful that this nonexistent thing, this thing that I don't know, is making me so unhappy. My husband and I have both cried many times together. He is very concerned about my depression and my obsessing on the subject, and of course it has interfered with our relationship a great deal. But his whole orientation is that he not lose me in the process.

"I remember this past spring I was at the end of some treatment and I was kind of saying goodbye to doctors for a while. I got into this thing of 'I'm not going to have children, I don't want children,' and I felt so good about that. It was such a relief. My husband didn't think it was real because it was too fast. He was right. But it was delightful while it lasted. You know, three weeks of just incredible energy and euphoria and saying, 'Oh boy, I don't have to think about this anymore; we've made a decision and I'm going on to new things.'

"Somewhere along the line," said Betty, "Hal and I signed up for adoption with the best agency in town. It's difficult because the list is endless. And with me being thirty-eight and Hal forty-two, we're at the upper limit, which is a combined age of eighty. I keep wondering if they will ever call us.

"Of course the initial thing for me was that I wanted my husband's child. I think that is something very basic. You choose a mate to breed with—you want that person's child. So it's very difficult to reorient your thinking.

"My husband has come around to the idea of adoption, but

for him that does take away the whole creative element, something that we have produced. He feels you have to face that and not lay it on the child.

"I think a lot of people want an adopted child to look like they do. I admit to this myself, but our chances of that are slight because we're both very light-skinned and there are so few babies available who resemble our coloring. This kind of thing bothers me because it's like everyone will know my handicap immediately. They will know I was infertile, they will know the child is not mine."

I asked Betty if she and her husband felt they could lead a fulfilling life without children. "My husband thinks it is very possible. Having children doesn't seem to be quite as important to him. Also, I think men can lose themselves more in their work. Their self-image is not quite as shattered. Hal is a very creative person. I don't feel I am that creative. What I think of children is a relationship of love, and there aren't any substitutes for that . . . for me."

A different scenario seems in the offing for Tom and Doris Grabowski of Philadelphia. Though they were still childless at the time of our meeting, they appeared to have come that full route about which Menning talked and which is so necessary to a happy adoption.

Tom, twenty-nine, is a self-employed electrician and Doris, thirty, a homemaker. From the beginning of their marriage six years ago, they wanted a family. Life without children, in their view, can be described in one word: empty. When after a time Doris did not conceive, Tom assumed the infertility was on her side. "I guess I felt it was the woman's problem—you know, *macho*," he admits readily.

A few years were wasted with incompetent physicians. Then the Grabowskis found an excellent fertility specialist who determined that Tom was the infertile one; his sperm count and motility were both low. Hoping this could be overcome, Tom submitted to tests and an operation, gave himself needles, even took female fertility pills. Nothing worked. Despite all their efforts and a total expenditure of $5,000, the Grabowskis finally reached a point where there was no hope.

During all the years of workup, friends, one after another, had begun to have families. "You feel different," says Doris, "like a freak. It's hard to relate to your friends. They're into having children and you're into the trying and it really separated us. Even our parents were afraid to tell us when Tom's sister got pregnant—we were the last to know."

Joining Resolve helped because they found so many couples in the same boat. Thanks to that organization and a generally changing philosophy, Tom feels that male infertility is now more admissible, with the *macho* image fading. Still, he told me, many men he met at Resolve resolutely refused even to see a specialist, finding it easier not to face the possibility of their own infertility.

Tom also learned that just because *he* had come out of the closet didn't mean that others would necessarily respond to him appropriately. "When you tell people you have a low sperm count, they think you can't perform." He and Doris recently took a cruise to Bermuda, which inspired one well-meaning neighbor to say before their departure, "Hey, that's great—I hear when you go to Bermuda you come back pregnant!" On the ship Tom met a woman who worked with children professionally. "She was very talkative and was always asking us questions about kids, so I told her I was infertile, that I had a low sperm count. She just looked at me, her mouth dropped, and she didn't say anything for five minutes. I really felt out of place."

Doris was ready to adopt early on. Tom came to that desire more slowly. She feels that had the fertility problem been hers rather than his, Tom might have been able to accept adoption sooner. But somehow it was easier for him to keep hoping that his own infertility could be overcome. "She blames me sometimes," Tom admitted, "saying that I don't face reality. Usually I have to work seven days a week to build up my business, and when I come home at night there's paperwork to do. Then I eat and go to bed. I guess she's right. I bury myself in my work. She can't." Doris adds: "I'm a person who likes to face things head on."

When the Grabowskis began to consider adoption seriously, they hoped for a child of their own background. But then they calculated the difficulties, including the probable years of waiting and the individual agency requirements (Tom, who hardly appears to be overweight, says he would have been turned down by Catholic Services for precisely that reason), and so they gave up this plan.

Instead they focused on adopting a Latin American baby— or rather two babies simultaneously—probably from Colombia. One reason for choosing this racial background instead of, say, Korean, is that they feel the child will encounter less prejudice. "I lived in the city all my life," says Tom, "and it's rough. If anybody was different, you made fun of him. I don't care if someone says something to *me* about having foreign children, but I don't want my kids feeling badly."

How did the marriage survive in seemingly fine shape the six years of false hopes and painful, expensive tests? Doris says it's because Tom was so willing to do everything to help them have children. She also feels that, although they wanted babies from the beginning, their marriage is stronger for their having been alone together, learning about each other and sharing a special and private grief. Both Tom and Doris look forward to the day when that quiet nursery up on the second floor isn't so quiet anymore.

Infertile people, like anyone still hurting, are sensitive, especially in the early years. They react with particular anger to child abuse, Barbara Menning told me. "We also take offense at those who tell all the gory details of, 'Oh God, I'm pregnant again, even though I'm on this method or that one.' "

As for abortion: "I don't think you'll find infertiles are any more in the 'Right-to-Life' movement or any more generally politicized than the general population. But, yes, it hurts us to know babies are aborted when we may be desperate to have a child." "Still," adds Menning, "I don't have the right to ask any woman to bear a child for me."

(Though it's still something of a curiosity, infertile wives now have a new option—hiring fertile women to be artificially inseminated with their husbands' sperm and give birth for them. Fees for this have been as high as $25,000. One recent arrangement had an unexpected dénouement when the pregnant woman's physician announced that the purchasers would be receiving a bonus: twins. Less felicitous is the story of the infertile wife who was suddenly informed that the surrogate mother, a divorcée, had decided to keep the child herself; the case is at present in court.)

The sensitivity of the sterile population may be aroused over even a celebration. "There was a time," Menning recalls, "when I couldn't go to baby showers. I remember turning one down and the woman having it said, 'Well, why don't you send your gift along with Sue; she lives near you.' I said, 'I am not sending a gift; you tell that woman her baby *is* her gift.' Now it's a very pained person who would say something like that, and I realized later that it was quite petty of me. Right now I could easily go to baby showers, only nobody's giving them!"

In view of the wide breach in philosophy and experience that often separates the voluntarily from the involuntarily childless, it is not surprising that—even though their life styles might be fairly similar—feelings toward each other are sometimes downright hostile, especially in the childbearing years. The voluntarily childless person sees his or her life as full and rich without children and goes about making the most of it. The individual who is involuntarily childless feels his or her life lacks something vital and focuses on what is missing rather than what is present. The childless-by-choice couple get bored with conversation about fertility tests and newborns, while the infertile couple feel the voluntarily childless neighbor is insensitive.

In later years a mellowing may well occur on both sides as each learns more objectively the advantages and disadvantages of life without children. As time passes they will face certain of the same situations: a renegotiation of the relationship with their own parents, for instance, so that they can interact as adult to adult, rather than adult to child. The death of their parents may be particularly hard to accept without children of their own to provide direct generational continuity. Childless couples will also face many of the same questions: To whom shall I leave my china? Who will come to see me in my old age?

One psychologist, Anita Landa of Lesley College, goes so far as to say she has found that infertile childless couples who choose not to adopt fit many of the same personality patterns as the voluntarily childless. Kleiman, in her article on infertility, reports another interesting sidelight: that infertile couples, wanting to put an end forever to the ambiguity of their situation or to avoid the agony of further miscarriages or stillbirths, sometimes choose to be sterilized.

In any event, the growing acceptance during the 1970s of marriage without children has made the burden of the infertiles less heavy. People don't quite so automatically feel sorry for them because it is possible they *chose* this childless life, and friends with children may actually envy them. The progress of the women's movement has had a strong influence, too. Whereas most wives of twenty years back had only limited opportunities outside the home, today there is a great variety of satisfying endeavors in which they can focus their talents. This, in turn, can lead to a more vital marriage with both partners realizing their potential and sharing the rewards.

The fact is, an infertile couple needn't lead a sterile life. Whether they choose to adopt or to channel their creativity and nurturing gifts elsewhere, they can find some measure of fulfillment, even though they may be unable ever to entirely cease mourning for the baby that never was.

5

Careers and Childlessness

Stan is holding a meeting of stamp collectors in the living room while, downstairs in the den, Denise and I talk. Periodically he rushes down to answer my questions, then heads back to his fellow philatelists.

"If you start like two and a half weeks ago," says Stan, "Denise was in Rhode Island on business, came back on a Thursday. Saturday morning we went for a one-week cruise to the Caribbean, returned home the next Saturday. The following Monday she was off to Rhode Island again, I went to Chicago to give a lecture, she came back and then . . ." My head spins as the tape recorder turns, and I marvel that I was able to find them in the same place at the same time.

"You have to understand that travel is part of our jobs and our personal lives, too," explains Denise, a financial planning officer. "I work for a corporation where travel is a way of life, but added to that we are both practically professional speakers; we do volunteer career counseling for young people on both the local and national level."

And that's not all. Denise for a few years was president of a national organization in her field which consumed about twenty extra hours per week. Somehow she also earned a master's degree in business administration at night while Stan, an actuary with an insurance company (he is trained in the mathematics of risk), took an advanced degree in his field. This frenetic activity has been going on almost since the marriage began. "We are an upwardly mobile couple," says Denise.

When they were first married, Denise leaned toward parenthood; Stan did not. "I never wanted kids," he says emphatically. Denise remembers that "When things didn't go right in my office, I'd say, 'Well, I'd like to have children.' Stan would answer, 'You don't want to be a mother; you just want to escape. It's a convenient out.' And when I thought about it, I said, 'You know, you're right!' " Eventually she felt sufficiently sure about these feelings so that it posed no problem when Stan decided to have a vasectomy.

Stan and Denise, now in their mid-thirties, say the childfree life is well suited to their personalities because it gives them the opportunity to do things on the spur of the moment. "Coming home once," recalls Stan, "I'd heard of a real airplane deal. I said to Denise, 'Hi, want to go to Copenhagen next week?' So the next week we went to Copenhagen." They have a lot of friends, both with and without children; much of their leisure time is spent with a neighboring couple whose interests are similar and whose children are grown. And they have each other. They are very close.

"We are scared of being apart; we don't like being apart," says Denise. "I go through a separation trauma when Stan goes off on business. I don't mind *my* going so much because I'm so busy there's no time to think."

Do they have any sense of one competing with the other? Denise: "Stan and I are very pleased not to be in the same field, not to work for the same company. We are both ambitious and it would be damaging if we competed directly with each other. As it is, we have a friendly sort of rivalry as to who is primary breadwinner. This year I am, next year he is. And in a way that's a positive force."

"Over the years I've come to know that I have a much stronger career drive than Stan, and I'm beginning to realize that what I seek out of my career is not money but recognition, prestige. Of course, being a successful two-career couple without children, we have a very comfortable life style. We're not wealthy by any means, but we *are* comfortable."

That fact is obvious to the visitor in their home. Stan and Denise own a spacious and expensively furnished house with a large plot of land near Columbus, Ohio. Though both enjoy their present work and the suburban life style, they would be interested in relocating if that meant a career boost. However, they have strict guidelines. Denise specifies: "If one of us had a job offer that was really outstanding in another city and the other had an offer that was at least as good as the job he or she now has, we would make the move." If these criteria could not be met, neither would be interested. And they've turned down a couple of top positions for precisely that reason.

Stan: "Our relationship comes first, before anything. Period. We have something going that we think is sort of special. We've been married for eleven years, and one year ago on our anniversary we got married again. We had a rabbi, a ceremony, exchanged new rings, had twenty-nine people, siblings and very close friends. Even the license. And we intend to do it again for the twenty-fifth and once more for the fiftieth."

Any worries? "So long as we have each other we won't be lonely," says Denise. "There's no question in my mind about that. But if a tragedy should befall one of us and not the other, then life would be extremely difficult because even though we are very independent people, we are also very dependent on each other. And that is my biggest fear."

The two-career couple: a phenomenon which took root in the 1970s and which, at the start of the 1980s, shows distinct signs of mushrooming. It is nothing new in American history to see large numbers of women in the work force—this was common especially during times of hostilities such as the Civil War and World Wars I and II when the men fought and the wives took their place on the job—but it *is* new in character. Now women are working for many reasons: economic need spurred by inflation, the desire to maintain a life style to which they became accustomed in easier financial times and, very significantly, the urge for self-fulfillment and independence. With over 50 percent of American women now employed outside the home, great changes have occurred in the marital relationship and family life as a whole. For those like Stan and

Denise who want to focus their energies on career while still maintaining a close marital relationship, voluntary childlessness can prove a wise course.

An important distinction should be made here: between a job and a career. While some voluntarily childless couples look upon their work as a job and nothing beyond that, more typically they are career-oriented. Margaret Baker, Ph.D., chief psychologist at the Center for the Study of Adult Development in Philadelphia, who specializes in counseling two-career couples, told me she distinguishes this way between the concepts: "Unlike a job, a career tends to get more complicated and demands greater responsibility and expertise as it evolves. It requires a long-term personal commitment, is an integral part of one's life, carries status and prestige, and generally pays well." (Obviously, there is not always a clear separation between the two. A job may be transformed by an ambitious employee into a career, while a professional position of much responsibility may be viewed as simply a day's work.)

The fact that a childless couple is invested in career does not necessarily mean that career was a major reason for the childlessness. Some people feel careers and children to be compatible but for different, unrelated reasons decide against parenthood. There are others for whom an active career is the result of, rather than the reason for, the childlessness—for instance, the infertile man or woman who, deprived of parenthood, focuses upon profession as an alternative means of fulfillment.

Characteristically, however, committed career couples who *choose* to be childless usually do so for reasons which relate rather intimately to the way they spend their weekday hours. This comment was made by Connie Matthews of Bunker Hill, Illinois, a law student in her thirties who is married and child-free: "I think I was as young as sixteen when I realized I didn't know one woman who had a good marriage and a good career and was a good mother. So I decided that children would be the prong that I would forgo. I would rather be happily married and happily involved in my job."

Connie's attitude homes in on one of the greatest dilemmas faced by young women today: how to juggle it all. Speaking at Loyola College in 1979, nationally syndicated columnist Ellen Goodman, who is a divorced mother, vividly depicted America's hypothetical wonderwoman: "She wakes up her 2.6 children. Feeds them a Grade-A nutritionally sound breakfast . . . puts on her $450 Anne Klein suit and goes off to her $35,000-a-year job which is socially useful. She comes home and in one hour whips up a Julia Child dinner, spends a really good hour with her children, because as we all know it's not the quantity of time, it's the quality that counts. Then she makes love till midnight."[1]

Connie Matthews is one among many women who will not buy that image. In its 1980 poll for Virginia Slims regarding the attitudes of American women, the Roper Organization, Inc., concluded: "Working women see no inconsistency between maintaining a career and marriage, but many are uncertain about the compatibility between a career and motherhood."[2]

What specific advantages do two-career couples feel derive from their childlessness? A major one is professional growth. Women, in particular, gain in this sphere. Without the responsibility for child care which, even in the most egalitarian of marriages, usually falls largely upon the mother, they can do what men do to get ahead: stay late at work, socialize after hours, take on extra training and responsibility, and generally prove that they are "serious" about their career. Unlike mothers, who characteristically—and often willingly—stop at a level below their potential for reasons of family responsibility, nonmothers can reach to the limits of their capability.

Sociologist Jean Veevers determined that one-half of the wives she interviewed were committed to a demanding profession. Among them, she found childlessness to be a critical factor in "facilitating career involvement." Ambition was extremely high. A woman with this degree of commitment, Veevers concluded, tends to think about having children only when her career hits a snag[3]; parenthood is thus the kind of "out" to which Denise referred in our conversation. Such women see having a baby as a substitute for the degree not received, the book not published, the promotion not won.

Financial security is increasingly being considered by women to be a necessary ingredient of a good marriage—as well as a critical factor in the event of a divorce. Yet the average American woman earns only 59 percent of what a man would earn in a similar position. When a couple remains childless, the woman has a much better chance to lessen that disparity. In Veevers's Canadian-based study, the two-career, voluntarily childless couples showed almost equal earnings, with husbands averaging 55 percent of the combined income and the wives 45 percent. This, in turn, facilitated the potential for "negotiating equal partnerships" in other aspects of life, as contrasted with marriages in which the husband as "senior partner" had more authority than the wife as "junior partner."[4]

Writing in *USA Today,* Kent State sociologist Denzel E. Benson claims that because childless women are able to make that all-important extra effort in career, they achieve "a disproportionate share of highly prestigious executive positions." Benson goes so far as to predict: "Given the mores of America, it is quite likely that the first woman President of the U.S. will be married, but voluntarily childless."[5]

It is natural to focus on the unusual woman, that future President, in contemplating childless career women. But what about those with fewer gifts and/or limited energy and motivation? Veevers makes the observation that nonmotherhood is of even more positive significance to them, freeing them for maximum growth.[6]

The man in a two-career childless marriage characteristically derives somewhat different advantages. Not being in the conventional role of breadwinner, responsible for support of wife and children, he is less likely to fall into the all-too-familiar "job trap": holding on to a position he does not like simply because it is secure and pays well. Though voluntarily childless men, as well as women, are judged on the whole to be strongly motivated and ambitious, they also, according to Veevers. show a high degree of "job satisfaction" as differentiated from "job success." In other words, they become involved in work they enjoy, even though that work may not be judged by conventional standards (power, prestige, money) to be desirable. Though very few men in her study had been unemployed for extended periods, they felt it important that they could quit a job if they wanted to.[7]

Typically, Veevers's couples were involved in different but related fields, though occasionally they worked together.[8] Being active in the career development of the mate is quite common among the childfree, I found, largely because not having children allows time and energy for this. Here are the words of Katie, forty-five, a journalist whose husband is a political analyst:

"Our life is a succession of page proofs and our home is carpeted in discarded drafts of manuscripts. We practically live at the Xerox place down the street. And we enjoy it. Each of us has different skills—I add some dash to Tim's writing, which tends to get turgid, and he catches me up on loose grammar and statements that I can't verify. Sometimes we get edgy over each other's criticism, but basically we're constructive. I suppose this kind of life would drive others nuts, but we are happy doing it. Also, we get to travel together a lot because of each other's research assignments. And we have a very well-trained dog to keep us company—she's learned that chewing up manuscripts is frowned upon here."

Others find that degree of involvement to be undesirable. Juditha Bullock is a Pennsylvania resident who is responsible for community and government affairs in a petroleum-products company. She attends many social functions in connection with this work, and it can be very helpful for her to have her husband Whitney attend them as well. However, she is highly selective as to his degree of participation in her work, not only because he has a demanding career of his own in middle management of a national financial and banking service, but because she likes to keep career and marriage separate. "If you start making them into one thing, you've got problems," says Juditha. "There are differences in our careers too, since Whitney is in an exact science—he's very much into numbers and taxes, which I don't have any understanding of.

But I admire and respect him for *his* ability to comprehend all that, and I feel secure at having him there. I can go out and be involved in all my humanitarian efforts, but I know I have this real solid base at home."

Given the tendency today for people to switch careers in midstream for varied reasons (boredom, low pay, the shortage of jobs in certain professions), the childless couple has the special advantage of being able to manage more easily on one salary than can parents. Will, thirty-eight years old, is a Philadelphia-based special-education teacher who told me that the chronically low income caused by insufficient state financial support for schools like his made the profession less satisfying as the years passed.

"Besides, I invested so much of myself emotionally in the kids that I simply ran out of steam," he said. "It's the kind of work that is so wearing that after five or ten years most people need a total switch. So I decided to quit and get into something entirely new. I made a careful study of my own skills and the job market and learned that I'd be wise to think about computer technology. I've been at school for about a year now and am about ready to start the job search. We've been living on my wife's income as a commercial photographer. She does okay financially but she doesn't take in big money. Can you imagine how tough it would be if I tried this career switch with two kids?"

"When we decided six or eight years ago not to have children it wasn't for this reason," he added. "We had no idea back then the difficulties that lay ahead jobwise. But it certainly has been a nice advantage to have only the two of us to support. And, once I'm established, I can return the favor. If Sue decides she wants to be—I don't know—an interior designer or a restaurant manager, well, it'll be my turn to carry the burden."

There is a certain amount of risk taking in Will's career change, but he has every expectation that in the long run it will prove worthwhile. Other childless people with whom I talked had taken bigger gambles. One couple packed up their bags, rented out their house, and moved to Europe to assume a glamorous but temporary (two-year) position which they had been offered jointly. She had to resign from her U.S. job and he to settle for a rather tenuous leave of absence from his college post. It worked out well on all fronts. But both doubt that they ever could have taken such a chance had they been parents.

One word that was frequently used by the two-career couples I interviewed as being an advantage of their childlessness was "time." Time is a precious commodity today when our lives seem so fragmented. A study of two-career couples by Rebecca and Jeff Bryson and Marilyn F. Johnson revealed that dissatisfaction with the amount of time available for all activities—whether related to occupation, family, recreation, or whatever—increased in both men and women with the number of children. Similarly, husbands and wives felt less freedom to pursue long-range job goals as family size increased.[9]

Two-career couples without children, on the other hand, have a greater number of unallotted hours per day to use as they will, be this in overtime at the office or in avocations, hobbies, or entertainment. Especially if their work is highly demanding, nonparents take pleasure in the peace and quiet of their home life. Many couples told me they feel their marriage is stronger for having this time alone together, free of the noise, distractions, and problems of children. These are a few of the comments I heard:

A builder, male, from New England: "Sometimes I can't get home until nine o'clock in the evening, even midnight. And I'm too exhausted to do more than turn on the TV. But I don't feel any pressure from my wife. It's great. We are very undemanding of each other. We don't *have* to be demanding because there is not a child's education or emotional development at stake."

A female gift shop manager from Portland: "The pace of life is slower with just two people. We sit down and enjoy the fireplace together. I don't have to be upstairs bathing a child or worrying about planning nutritious home meals every night. I can just say, 'Hey, I'm beat,' and he'll say, 'Let's go out and have some spare ribs.'"

A Seattle social worker, female: "If you have a career that takes a lot of extra hours like mine does, there's no way you can devote enough time to that and your marriage and your children too. I think not having children has helped our relationship to be as good as it is."

That same added time can be used for simply having fun. A Cleveland paramedic, male, said to me: "We're out on the tiles as much as we can be, given our limited incomes."

I asked a number of two-career couples about the division of household chores. Most said that because there was less housekeeping without children, assigning responsibility was not difficult. If one partner's job was at the moment particularly taxing, the other tended to take on the greater burden in the home; if one partner's prediliction was for dishwashing and the other's for gardening, that too was taken into consideration.

"We don't go by a 'this is the man's role and this is the woman's' approach," said a botanist, female. "Whoever has the time and isn't too tired does it, whether it's the laundry, food shopping, or taking the cat to the vet."

Some childless couples whose marriage is more traditional maintain more traditional roles in the division of housework. A fabric designer who works independently from home told me that, although she considers her career to be vital to her well-being, she devotes less time to it than her dentist husband does to his work and brings in far less money. Hence she feels responsible for doing more of the daily chores and does not resent this at all.

It is too simple a formula to say that some careers mesh well with parenthood while others do not. The situation depends much on such factors as individual personality, energy level, the status of each career, and the nature of the relationship between husband and wife. But unquestionably certain professions pose special problems for parents, particularly for the woman as primary parent, and hence are rather well suited to childlessness.

Take, for instance, those careers in which unpredictability

is a way of life: medicine, an editor's job on a daily newspaper, legal work involving long hours in court, and the like. This characteristic, while not harmful to a two-adult relationship, can spell trouble with a child or children involved—especially if the mate's career is similarly structured so that he or she cannot fill in with child care during such times.

Other careers that tend not to mesh well with parenthood, especially with motherhood, are those in which one moves up the ladder fast. Caroline Bird writes in her book *The Two-Paycheck Marriage:* "The more promising a career, the more likely it is to lead straight to the top, the more a woman has to lose by taking time out for a baby. If you step off the ladder in any rewarding, advancing field you not only lose your place, but may never get back on it again. This is true of highly paid executive and technical jobs in fast-moving fields such as health care, research, fashion, communications, and entertainment."[10] Even fields that at first glimpse seem ideally suited to parenthood can present problems. Consider, for instance, an academic with a flexible schedule during the school year who has adequate time for child care. What about the summer months when, in order to maintain or better his or her position, it is necessary to travel—perhaps even to go abroad—for three months of intensive research?

Women in fields that once were considered the domain of men (like law, medicine, and politics) frequently experience obstacles in the early years of practice. Remaining childless enables them to devote their full efforts to career in that crucial period. A recently graduated female lawyer who was sterilized after her marriage a few years ago, told me she likes potential employers to know that she definitely will not be having children because this is a boost to her candidacy; yet she can't quite see bringing up so intimate a subject as a salpingectomy in job interviews. "So if they ask me whether I have a family I say, 'No, and there *won't* be.' I let it go at that and hope they'll know I won't be asking for pregnancy leave in the middle of a big trial!"

Architecture is another field that women are entering in large numbers. A graduate student in Seattle, Washington, married and in her early thirties, told me that she had embarked on this course after giving up an unrewarding job as technical writer; she will not be licensed to practice architecture until age thirty-five. "The first few years after that are a real push to get started. I can't see taking time off to have kids even though I must admit I sometimes think I would like to have a daughter and raise her to be a good, solid, producing woman!" A well-known woman architect in her fifties from the same city, divorced and childless, feels that such a decision is wise.

"I know a number of women who had children and tried to practice architecture from their homes," she said. "They do small projects, remodeling and so forth. It's very limiting. I do not think you can maintain any kind of practice beyond that of any consequence." As a partner in a prestigious firm, she still works hard to maintain her position. "I'm down here Saturdays, Sundays, evenings too. How can you do that with a family?"

Travel, as we have seen, is a major inducement for childlessness in the opinion of many couples; this may be of either a business or recreational nature, or both. Business travel as a couple is less common, but that kind of life can be very rewarding for partners who work well together.

Linda Caldwell, age thirty, is married to a thirty-three-year-old employee of the U.S. Foreign Service. Early in their marriage ten years ago, they decided to remain childless, largely because the constant uprooting in this career makes for what Linda described to me as "an exciting but not exactly stable existence."

. When assigned to certain areas of political unrest, it is not uncommon for Foreign Service employees to be prevented from bringing in dependents, including mates. When I spoke with Linda, she had been barred from Lebanon, though her husband remained there. She was planning to take an apartment in Cyprus to which he would fly once a month until a reassignment would bring them together. This situation is hard enough to face alone; with children it would have been worse. Even in locales of relative stability, Linda told me,

Foreign Service employees often find education to be inferior and choose to send their children to school back in the United States—not an ideal situation for family closeness.

Linda has her own career—something she can take with her anywhere in the world—as a professional belly dancer and teacher. "Though being a belly dancer is certainly not the reason we didn't have kids," she adds, "it sure is nice in my profession not to have stretch marks!"

Another career that some couples without children have found to be particularly rewarding is as Peace Corps volunteers overseas. Because of harsh living conditions in many areas and because children involve added expenses, the Peace Corps gives preferential consideration to nonparents. The National Alliance for Optional Parenthood chose as its 1978 Non-Parents of the Year a few couples engaged in such work. Among them Mary Kay Johnson was serving as nutritionist for an orphanage in Costa Rica and also as a teacher of mental health and nutrition in the rural areas of that country. Her husband, David, a psychologist, was head of a leadership training program at a Costa Rican YMCA.[11] Cases like these prove once again that people need not be parents to care about the lot of children.

In recent years an increasing number of two-career couples have joined the ranks of so-called "long-distance marriages"; that is, they work in two different geographic locations hundreds or even thousands of miles apart, maintaining two residences. This is a natural development at a time when jobs are in short supply and when it could be extremely unwise for either husband or wife to pass up an excellent career opportunity, even if it does mean a long commute. Obviously such an arrangement poses problems, especially for parents, who must face such issues as increased need for child-care services as well as insufficient time with their children. Some childless couples as well feel a resistance to this concept. Stan and Denise, the actuary and financial planner whose travels take them from one end of America to the other, would not consider a commuting marriage. And they are not in the minority.

The same 1980 survey by the Roper Organization[12] referred to earlier revealed very traditional attitudes on this subject by a cross-section of Americans. The question posed was: "Suppose both husband and wife work and the husband is offered a very good job in another city. Assuming no children, which one of these solutions do you think they should seriously consider?" Fully 77 percent of the women and 68 percent of the men said the wife should quit her job, relocate with the husband, and try to obtain a new job; only 4 percent, both male and female, felt the best solution would be for the husband to take the new job and move, the wife to keep her job, and the couple to live together whenever they could. (It is revealing that this questionnaire did not pose the reverse possibility: if the *wife* were offered the "very good job in another city," what should the husband do?)

Despite such reservations, many childless couples are finding that a long-distance marriage need not be an unhappy one. One well-known individual leading this peripatetic existence is Charlotte Curtis, editor of the Op-Ed page of the *New York Times,* who is married to a neurosurgeon in Ohio; they maintain separate residences in each city and fly back and forth weekends to be together. Curtis claimed in an interview with Leslie Bennetts that one of the reasons the marriage works well is that she and her husband maintain independent and busy lives. "With many couples somebody makes a terrible sacrifice to live in the same city, and usually it's the wife," she said. "I just don't believe in that."[13]

Joyce and Alex are an attractive, easygoing couple with whom I talked. They have been married for fourteen years; he is thirty-seven, she thirty-four. Manhattan residents, they took on a long-distance marriage one year ago, when Alex was transferred by his company, which specializes in environmental law, to Washington, D.C.; Joyce continued her fund-raising career in New York. It was not a difficult decision. Both liked their jobs and didn't want to give them up. They also enjoyed living in New York and didn't want to give that up. Each weekend they are together in a cluttered but very comfortable Manhattan apartment, Alex also maintaining a room in Washington near his job.

Joyce: "We don't think much in terms of being separated all week. We feel we *are* together whether we're physically in the same place or not. Three or four mornings a week at six-thirty we talk on the phone, and we write sometimes." Because she is busy week nights with her own volunteer activities, as is Alex, and because the two have always led independent but complementary lives, the adjustment has not been traumatic. Joyce does admit: "I don't mean to act like it's the easiest thing in the world, because when you get used to many years of having someone with you every night to talk about things, debrief from the day, let off steam, you really miss that. Sometimes it doesn't seem quite right to come home and find nobody there, but basically I feel we need to be able to live on our own to be happy anyway, so I look on this as a growth experience."

Joyce and Alex feel they would not have taken this chance with children in their lives. But with just the two of them (and they are quite sure they will remain childfree) it has worked out nicely. The problem is, rather, the reaction of other people.

Alex: "My co-workers still keep saying, 'Well, when is she moving down here?' Some of them sort of look oddly at me, and I get the feeling they're thinking, 'Well, it's too bad you don't have a wife and you don't have kids and don't you want to come over for supper sometime and have some real good home cooking?' There's always the sense that they're expecting you to get divorced."

Joyce adds: "I mentioned to Alex's mother that it takes a strong marriage to be able to do this. She said, 'Well, you know, you could both find someone else if you continue living like this.' But being apart some of the time doesn't necessarily lead to that."

Alex agrees: "You can live together, you don't spend one day apart—and you *still* get divorced."

How long will this commuting life go on? They don't know. Says Joyce: "Maybe two months, maybe the rest of our lives."

Are there stresses and dangers peculiar to two-career marriages without children? Psychologist Margaret Baker feels there are. "Most people have a lot of energy beyond what is necessary for a productive career, and much of that energy goes into children. It seems to me that if you *don't* have children, you have to find other ways to meaningfully invest emotional energy and commitment."

Baker also feels that in a childless marriage there is not the necessity to interact on a personal plane which being a parent entails. "The husband goes off on his career and the wife on hers. They get extremely busy and forget about issues of intimacy, sharing, really talking to each other, though they may talk constantly on a professional level. In other words, their life style helps them to ignore unresolved issues, and these can lie dormant for years. But with a child there has to be a lot of interaction and cooperation."

Baker described for me one client, a voluntarily childless man of forty-five, now divorced, who had put all his energy into his career as physicist, professing no interest in children. In truth, he felt himself to be a failure as a human being and not sufficiently competent for fatherhood. Though his career did, ironically, succeed in precisely the fashion he had hoped, it did not bring the expected happiness. Recognizing his underlying problems too late, with his wife beyond childbearing age, he watched helplessly as the marriage itself crumbled.

"Just by definition," said Baker, "that individual's career was going to fail him because it was not the answer to what had damaged him. . . . Professional success seemed to be something that was going to give him a sense of definition about himself and make him feel okay, but in my mind there is no way of compensating for a perceived and felt damage except by undoing it, by accepting and experiencing the pain and disappointment and root causes. Hopefully, in doing that he can now go on and be freer to be truly successful because he doesn't have such an ego tie to his career."

Several of the two-career couples with whom I spoke said they were aware of the danger of preoccupation in career. Denise, the financial planning officer, approached this subject with particular insight: "I have resisted the temptation to fall into my career, although I am so close to that I have to watch out. I know that when I go fully into anything I become depersonalized. You have to keep a sense of humor, that personal side of you, even with a job—in fact, it is an essential part of the job. I feel this very keenly. I know that if I don't take an evening off or a weekend, I won't be able to do anything well. So there is a real balance necessary. I think for a lot of people children provide that balance, and I commend them for their ability to turn off the office, get in with their children, play hard, and love hard."

In the main, the voluntarily childless couples to whom I spoke felt that they were not using career to hide other lacks in their life. They also seemed quite sure that not having children allowed for precisely the energy they needed to devote to marriage and career and that if they had chosen to become parents they would have ended up exhausted. Excess energy does not seem to be a commodity that is in great supply these days.

As regards the avoidance of intimacy through nonparenthood, this too seemed at variance with the life goals expressed to me by childfree couples. They want *more* marital intimacy, not less, and they see childlessness as helping them achieve that. Psychiatrist Martin Goldberg of the Institute of Pennsylvania Hospital in Philadelphia points out the reverse side of that coin: parents not infrequently turn to their children to find the intimacy lacking in the marriage, he says.

Another subject that is being studied with great interest today is career competition between husband and wife, a factor that can be deadly to a marriage or, if dealt with appropriately, a positive force. Are childless couples more competitive in a negative sense than parents? Goldberg says no. He sees more potential for problems when there *are* children, because children complicate life and can cause each mate to feel resentment over the inability to devote sufficient time and energy to career. Childless couples, according to Goldberg, "can just go on and do their own thing."

Problems sometimes occur in the two-career marriage when the woman's career is more successful than her mate's. (Caroline Bird writes: "For traditional couples, there's a struggle when she goes to work. For contemporary couples the struggle occurs when her career moves ahead faster than his.")[14] One can hypothesize that since the voluntarily childless marriage is on the whole considered to be egalitarian in nature, with the husband characteristically not wanting to dominate his wife, there is less likelihood that such a situation would cause tensions. Still, it is not easy for a man in a society accustomed to male domination to be less successful and to make less money than his wife.

I talked with a female weaver whose work is beginning to achieve some local renown, surpassing that of her sculptor husband, and she is frankly worried about how he will react if this continues. "I keep thinking that maybe if I had had children I could have invested some of my dreams in them," she said, "allowing my husband to have the edge careerwise —he so much seems to need that."

Other couples do quite well in the same situation. Speaking at a NOW conference in New York in 1979, author Nancy Friday, who is voluntarily childless, referred to career competition with her husband, William Manville, also an author. "Fortunately," she said, "I was the one who had a best seller. If Bill had, I wouldn't have coped so well. When it comes to success in my work, he is terrific. He gets more excited over my writing than I do."

A Manhattan couple, also childless by choice, told me that they feel fortunate as regards competition because each is ahead in a different sense. Corinne is a well-known banker with a prestigious financial institution; her salary is good but not remarkable. Jonathan is a shipping-company executive; his work, he admits, cannot compare with hers in prestige. "When we go to a party, she's the one everybody knows," he says. However, Jon is bringing in a hefty income, which Corinne can't begin to match, and he takes pleasure in using that money to provide her with everything from diamond earrings to skiing at Chamonix. There is a decidedly protective tone in Jon's attitude toward Corinne, and one senses that she leans on him in matters apart from banking. Others may not respond well to the traditionalism inherent in this marriage—but for Jon and Corinne it works.

"Somewhere, deep within me, I was never interested in having children," said Hungarian-born artist Sari Dienes. "Of course, I consider my work, all my pieces of work, as my children. So, instead of having one, two, five, ten children, I have thousands. Also, I find it very interesting that little children love me and I love them. I always say that I would like to pickle them, to keep them. In fact, a work of mine is called 'Pickled Babies'!"

Sari Dienes is eighty-two years old. Her extraordinary artistic output, in materials ranging from pine cones to mirrors, hawks' wings to rubber scraps, has earned her thirty-two solo shows and an enviable position in the vanguard of modern art.

We met in New York's Soho district, where Dienes, working with a group of young people, has made of a crumbling old longshoreman's bar an artist's haven, with crayons piled on every paper tablecloth for drawing. Dienes, on the chilly, drizzling day of our meeting, was supervising the production of homemade borscht and chili. She is as vibrant in manner as is her art, full-faced, with gentle, laughing eyes and a halo of irrepressible golden-white hair.

The artist told me that her late husband, a renowned mathematician who had two children from a previous marriage, wanted very much to be father to her unborn children (as, indeed, had a number of other men) but she turned down the role of mother. And she has never felt any regret.

"I think that's a great achievement, to do or not do something you feel totally natural about," said Dienes. "I don't know what explains my not wanting children. Maybe it's because I didn't like myself enough in those years to reproduce myself."

She does, however, enjoy a close relationship with many

young artists. "They look up to me and take me as a sort of example and love me—not the way a mother is loved just because she is a mother."

Would her art have been less successful with motherhood? "I don't know. Sometimes when you are overburdened with this or that it makes you even richer, even more fertile, more productive. So I don't know.

"But, nonetheless, at this age I still do not wish I had had children. It never occurs to me. Never. Not in my dreams. You know, when I consider it intellectually, I think 'Oh, my, I could have had wonderful children!' But emotionally it doesn't upset me. I think I've fulfilled myself. I've done more than most mothers have done.

"I've reached a level of serenity where I can do anything, be anything, accept anything."

Dienes's feeling that her works *are* her children is not uncommon among creative artists. But she is perhaps unusual in that she never had any desire to be a mother. Hence she did not feel she was making a sacrifice in choosing a life devoted to art. Many other women struggle much more than she did over the issue.

The contemporary American author Tillie Olsen has written a book, *Silences,* about the circumstances that hinder creative activity. In it she deals extensively with gifted women who face the question of whether they can combine motherhood with dedication to their art. The great works of humanity, posits Olsen, have come almost entirely from individuals able to surrender their lives wholly. Rarely have women been free to do this, for they are "traditionally trained to place others' needs first." For centuries, she contends, women had to choose between fulfillment as artists or as women; society would not allow them to have both. Even in our own century, writes Olsen, until very recently most literary women of achievement did not marry; if they did, they remained childless (Edith Wharton, Katherine Mansfield, Lillian Hellman, and Dorothy Parker, among them). Though, during the last two decades, women have been assuming their rights in both the family and the creative realm, she finds "the fundamental situation remains unchanged": only by sacrificing the opportunity to do their best work can women bear and raise children.[15]

Because their medium is words, women writers have expressed with special poignancy their changing emotions regarding childlessness, especially as this relates to their work. British novelist, short story writer, and critic Virginia Woolf, who recognized that her own emotional fragility would make motherhood unwise, was one. At thirty-eight she cried out: "Why is life so tragic; so like a little strip of pavement over an abyss? . . . It's having no children, living away from friends, failing to write well."[16] Biographer Quentin Bell, in fact, claimed that not having children was for Woolf a "permanent source of grief."[17] Yet, at forty-eight, surveying her finished book *The Waves,* Virginia Woolf could write joyously: "A day of intoxication . . . when I sat surveying the whole book . . . felt the pressure of the form—the splendor, the greatness. . . . Children are nothing to this."[18]

Sara Teasdale, a lyric poet and contemporary of Woolf, professed a genuine desire for motherhood, according to a recent biography by William Drake, but realized a child would consume her limited energies. Hence, when she became pregnant, she had an abortion. This action so repelled her that she flagellated herself later in a poem called "Duty": "Fool . . . the wrong is done, the seed is sown,/The evil stands." All that was left for her was to create "Out of the web of wrong," from "ill-woven deeds" her "thread of song."[19]

The loss of her only child, stillborn at six months, was described by French-born novelist Anaïs Nin, whose many-volumed diary is one of the most vivid chronicles about modern woman: "A dead creation . . . my first dead creation . . . The failure of my motherhood." Even more horrible than the loss, however, was the recognition that, while the fetus had still been alive in her body, she had wanted it to die "because in this world there are no real fathers." (Nin's own father, a famous Spanish composer-pianist, had deserted the family.) "I love man as creator, lover, husband, friend," she wrote, "but man the father I do not trust . . . when I wished this child to die, it was because I felt it would experience the same lack."[20]

Oriana Fallaci, the well-known Italian journalist who is also childless, dealt with a similar theme in her novella *Letter to a Child Never Born*. Told in the first person, the story is of a pregnant woman, unmarried, whose fetus dies within her body; afterward she undergoes a fantasy trial in which she is accused of having caused the death through indifference and selfishness. Forgiven at the end of the trial by the fetus, she convicts herself: "Splendid words, Child, but only words. All the sperm and all the ova on earth united in all single possible combinations could never create a new you, what you were and what you might have been. You'll never be reborn."[21]

Through their own personal struggle, their nonmotherhood, such women as these four have enriched our literature and our understanding.

The male creative artist is in a somewhat different position with different problems. Composer Irwin ("Buddy") Bazelon is one such individual.

Bazelon is a dominating presence, with graying steel-wool hair, thick brows, and intense eyes which confront the world from beneath a heavily creased forehead. His studio, located in a spacious Manhattan apartment, is rich in colors and textures: a Mexican piñata, zebra-striped chair, bright red eating apples on a silver tray, and, over the sofa, a large oval painting in muted colors featuring a number of delicate white eggs— the work of his artist wife Cecile. On the desk are two stands of razor-sharp pencils, points turned upward, ready for action. Bazelon's musical script is clear, firm, no-nonsense, much like his personality. At fifty-eight, he is a highly successful composer of orchestral and chamber works as well as documentaries and art films.

Married to his wife for twenty years after three earlier, short marriages, Bazelon never really wanted children but was prepared to take on fatherhood for Cecile's sake. She did not conceive, however, because of a chronic problem with fibroid tumors, which eventually necessitated a hysterectomy.

"Cecile wanted kids and I indulged her," Bazelon told me.

"But I didn't care one way or the other. If it happened, fine; if not, that was all right, too. I probably would have made a fairly decent father.

"However, I think that having a child would have had a tremendous effect on me because my wife is somewhat old-fashioned in spite of her women's lib views, and she thinks that man is supposed to take care of woman. And, if you have a child, the financial responsibility also belongs to the man.

"The position of the artist in having children is somewhat different in many respects from the businessman, whose primary interest is to make a good living. Most artists do not make money; they make a living if they can. And if they manage that out of their work like I can, they're extremely lucky.

"Children cause other kinds of responsibility too, other kinds of pressure, and it would be extremely difficult for someone like myself to be able to put together creatively the things I have in my mind—which demands an enormous amount of concentration and selfishness—and still at the same time support a child and be a good father. I'm not saying I couldn't do it but it certainly would have changed my life. I probably would have had to go back to Hollywood and into the motion-picture rat race. God only knows, most likely I wouldn't even be married to Cecile at this time.

"As two people who are both professional and creative persons, Cecile and I don't have very many hours to spend with each other. The time we *do* have together becomes infinitely more intense and more pleasurable and more important in our lives than it probably does to other people for that reason. If we had children, the day would dwindle away to nothing.

"I suspect that not having children has helped this marriage to survive. On the other hand, I suppose being a father would have speeded up my growing-up process. I would have had to face the fact that the world doesn't owe me a living.

"Most artists are children, you know. I'm twelve and my wife is ten, and we get along fine."

I spoke on another occasion with Bazelon's wife, Cecile,

petite, knowing, assuredly feminine. She is a woman who very much wanted children, yet carved out a rich creative life for herself when this was denied her. "Buddy and I are very self-involved people," she reflected. "Perhaps I would have resented a child. Maybe I would have grown less as a painter or even ended up not painting seriously at all. But certainly at this stage of our lives when finances are tight and New York so expensive, and being in professions that are not remunerative, it is better for us not having children. Our life revolves around our serious work activity.

"In many ways Buddy is my child. He is a very little boy. That is also very much of his charm. Matter of fact, he is marvelous with students, he is one of them. Our house is a mecca for young people and there are always happy vibrations here, even if Buddy and I are fighting.

"Anyway, we *did* have a child—for eighteen years. Clem was our child. He was a Yorkshire terrier, and we got him on our honeymoon. He smiled—not just any time, only when you normally would smile. It cracked us up."

It is tempting, in talking with creative people like the Bazelons, to hypothesize on what superior offspring they might have given to the world. But such romanticization causes one to forget that the individual possessed by a vision, a goal—be it scientific, political, artistic, humanitarian—may not have the time or desire, let alone the talent, for parenthood. Psychiatrist Robert Gould has devoted much of his writing to this subject and is thoroughly annoyed by the idea that unusually gifted people are doing the world a disservice by not reproducing themselves.

"There are outstanding men and women in all professions who have failed miserably at the task of raising their children well," wrote Gould in a *New York Times Magazine* article about the wrong reasons for parenthood.[22] "The same ambition and dedication necessary to succeed at a demanding career are also necessary to succeed as a parent."

The two-career marriage without children, though certainly not new, is also not an established American life style. Only time will tell whether most couples who choose that route will, on looking back several decades later, find it to have been a happy decision. Some need not wait that long; they decide in mid-career that something is missing. That something may or may not be children.

Gail Sheehy, who did a study for *Redbook* on the factors that make people happy, wrote this: "When given to career-committed women or men, my questionnaire consistently turns up evidence that a sense of stagnation in work first catches up with them at about the time they turn thirty. Unless they rattle a few doors, if only to test whether or not they truly want to recommit themselves to the original career path, the sense of stagnation often creeps into home life and, if left unchecked, begins to weaken the whole foundation of middle adulthood."[23] Though Sheehy does not claim that children are *the* answer to such stagnation, the clear implication is that parenthood is one important option, another being to seriously alter career course.

Rachel and Howard are a childless couple who are moving in the direction of that first option. "My work has become a career," said Rachel, thirty-four, a high school math teacher, "yet I'm not totally committed to a career goal." She is attractive, large-boned, with fair skin and a vibrant manner. Howard, a tall, lanky man, more reserved than his wife, says he is "straddling thirty-six and not very comfortable about it." His position is as a social scientist at a major Ivy League college.

"I'm very involved in my work and it takes a lot out of me," Rachel continued. "I'm relatively perfectionistic. Recently I was offered the chairmanship of my department at school, but I'm not sure that's the direction I want to go in."

Why? "Because our attitude about what is of value in life has changed over time. We've been married twelve years. We've done our traveling and other things that we wanted to do, and as time passed we found ourselves asking, 'What is the purpose of life on this planet? Why are we here? How can we best make a contribution?'

"I've given teaching my best shot, and while I'm not eager to bail out of it for psychological as well as financial reasons, it's not enough. We both realize that these are very hard times, a hard culture to raise a child in, and neither of us is a risk taker. But not to take a risk is to remain on the career path, which I think for me is a somewhat sterile, dead-end path. What appears to be a very comfortable nook can become an upholstered cell. And one thing I have seen among a lot of voluntarily childless couples which I do not like is an emphasis on hedonism, whether it is material possessions, careers, pets, travel, or even causes."

Rachel feels that only if she were doing work that contributed to the betterment of society (and she does not look upon her teaching as accomplishing that) would she consider continued childlessness an acceptable, lifelong state. Howard, on the other hand, though he certainly is supportive of her wishes and willing to assume his responsibilities as a father, receives a good deal more gratification from his career. Hence he feels less pressing a need to restructure his life. "In an abstract way through some research I've done," Howard said to me, "I can point to contributions that pay off somewhere along the line in terms of helping people. For me, having children isn't the thing I most want to do. But I don't think that means my motivation isn't adequate to cope with the rough spots that inevitably will occur."

When I met her, Rachel was hoping to become pregnant within a few months. But there were still a number of unanswered questions: "After my one year's leave of absence do I go back to full-time teaching and leave the child in day care which I am not pleased about, or do I try to work part time, which has problems of seniority and all kinds of other horrible things? And what kind of division of labor do we work out? I get antagonistic about that because I'm so afraid I'll end up with all the burden. Howard says, 'Well, you've no reason to feel I won't do my part,' and it's true, but I don't have any reason to believe he *will* do his part either except that in other areas he's very responsible. Still, I see child care as coming much more out of *my* hide, since he's clearly got a greater income, and he's got long-term career goals."

There are other nagging worries for Rachel. Is the marriage

strong enough so that she can risk not earning her own way for a couple of years? Will becoming a mother give her life that new meaning she so much desires? Could she be subconsciously evading the issue by not losing the excess twenty-five pounds that are significant to a pregnancy at her age? And if, for whatever reason, she does not become pregnant, what kind of personal or career change will enhance her life and Howard's? Rachel is seeking answers to all these questions. So are many others.

Feminist Betty Friedan is among those who feel that our society is poorly structured for career women who would like to become mothers. She sees a childlessness today which is akin to that of the Depression: women having to work because their financial contribution is needed and unable to be mothers because there is not an adequate support system in the form of day care, flexible working hours, and maternal and/or paternal leave. (*Newsweek* reported in May 1980 in an article titled "The Superwoman Squeeze" that the United States has fewer day-care slots available now than it did in 1945.)[24] Friedan also claims that women are falling into the same obsession with career that used to be characteristic of men, while men are desirous of a return to the traditional family—traditional in terms of spouse and children giving meaning and focus to life but not in a paternalistic (father as "head of the family") sense.[25]

Even though many men today wish to take on a fair share of responsibility for the day-to-day care of their children, society prevents them from doing so. In the same article mentioned above, *Newsweek* reported: "Employees who request time off for a PTA meeting often risk a step down the company ladder—especially if they're male."[26] The childless too can pose a threat to parents in their careers. One professional woman with a child who was interviewed for the book *Up Against the Clock* complained that childless women in positions of power expect that competent help will allow a female colleague with children to leave all her maternal responsibilities and worries at home. "Women who do not have children just can't understand the feelings of those who do," she says.[27]

In some ways our country is actually better structured for those who remain childless. But how can one know if career dedication, to the extent of eschewing parenthood, will mean fulfillment or emptiness in the long run? We cannot be certain, of course. But we *can* make considered judgments. A major factor is the meaning of career in a person's life. Is it an aspect —albeit an important one—or is it the very essence?

Here are the words of Addie Herder, New York artist, fifty-nine, divorced and childless. Her intricate collages have appeared at the Guggenheim, among other fine museums.

"From the time I was five I knew I wanted to draw or paint or something like that. Other things have interfered, like marriage and the exigencies of serving that institution. If I had had children—and at one time I really wanted them but I just didn't conceive—that probably would have interfered, too. My purpose in life was determined long before the question of children or no children. It was clear from the first time I could pick up a pencil. The purpose of my life has always been art. And, when I lost the thread for a time because of some intellectual problems I was having about the meaning of art and my own dealing with it, that was probably the worst time of my life, worse even than when I left my husband. Then the bottom of my life really dropped out."

A differing viewpoint was expressed by a highly successful female urban planner, European-born and now practicing in the Northwest; she is in her fifties and married. Her childlessness, she says, is really neither voluntary nor involuntary; she simply put off thinking about motherhood until it was too late.

"I have a sort of frenzy about doing very meaningful work that I can leave behind me, that speaks for me. My work is a physical extension of my body. In a sense it might be considered my children. I could never imagine my life without doing it, though I am not terribly satisfied with my progress. Sometimes I feel I am a failure.

"I have invested everything in my career, and I think the rewards are not as much as they should be. I see other people managing to raise children and to have more serene lives than I do and also to do some work. As I watch my parents growing very old, I am thinking increasingly about the fact that suddenly—or so it seems to me—youth has ended. I have to take stock and see what it is that I can still do.

"That sense of mortality enters the picture, I think, as you get older. You feel you could have left a legacy to someone, that someone could have continued your work. I find myself thinking, To whom am I going to leave my books? I am looking in the ranks of my alumni to see who can continue my work, because I am getting wornout.

"If I had it to do over, I think I would have devoted more time to myself and not so much to being overwhelmed with the intricacies of my chosen profession. To have children would have been a kind of duty, a human duty, in a well-knit marriage. And actually it might all have worked out quite realistically—you take a little chip off career but you are enriched."

Juditha and Whitney Bullock, whom I mentioned earlier in this chapter as being very interested in but not involved in each other's career, have been married for five years and are voluntarily childless. They have their own approach for dealing with what they feel will be an eventual career letdown in later years.

Juditha, forty, handles community and government affairs for Sun Petroleum Products Company in Philadelphia. It is a sensitive and challenging position: she acts as a social barometer regarding her company's obligations to the community in which it retains an industrial residency. Her husband, Whitney, is director of tax systems world-wide for the American Express Company in New York. They live in rural Pennsylvania, commuting to work in opposite directions. Both are studying toward master's degrees, she in communications and he in taxation.

Juditha, a woman of proud carriage and effortless style, was among the eldest of fifteen children from a poor Virginia family. As an infant, she was sent to live with a childless aunt and uncle in Connecticut, returning home at age seven. When she was back in Virginia, everything puzzled her: the assortment of relatives, their southern accents, and the clear racial lines that restricted their freedom of activity. And new babies kept coming. "I cannot remember my mother ever being not pregnant, only then I thought she was just fat. And because she was always attended by a midwife, I thought the babies came out of the midwife's little black bag."

Life in Virginia, though rich in love and wholesome farm food, was burdened with endless household and sibling responsibilities in assembly-line fashion. "We were taught independence and survival early on—and we hated it." Juditha describes her wardrobe as consisting of "hand-me-down dresses, hand-me-down shoes, hand-me-down hand-me-downs." Her big goal in life back then was "to have matching underwear, color coordinated." She also wanted to live alone and have a car.

Later, when she saw the marriages of her sisters taking place, assuming new forms as the children arrived, and all too often crumbling, this frightened her. "It was a kind of reinforcement of my fear of responsibility. I think I made the decision at that time that I did not want to have children and would have to find the kind of mate who would agree with me or I would remain single." Juditha was also learning through her career: "I was very people-oriented and I had a lot to give to them—but I wanted to give on my own terms."

Whitney, now in his late thirties, is a man of informal, easy manner who looks at life with little sentiment. His childhood was similarly burdened with heavy responsibilities since his father, a fruit and produce huckster, deserted the family when Whitney was thirteen. That left him as head of the household with care for a much younger brother and the necessity of working a full shift at night through junior and senior high school and college. By the time he was twenty-one he had already purchased a house for his family. But graduation was much longer in coming. While his fellow students were in the class of 1960 or '62 or '64, Whitney, with his heavy work schedule, was just hoping to make it from one week to the next. He did eventually graduate, then was drafted into the Army for two years, after which he finally began the career climb that took him from an accounting firm to his present association with American Express. By the time he could think of having children, Whitney was convinced that the world he would be bringing them into was one of regression rather than progress, that the middle class would soon disappear with only the poor and the wealthy remaining. "I would hate to have a child point a finger at me and say, 'You brought me into this?' "

Juditha and Whitney Bullock are living very comfortably now. When I met them they were preparing to move into a large new home in an affluent suburb. This is their second home purchase, and they have done it on their own without financial help. Careers absorb their time and their energies. They are happy in their jobs and, through their employment, have reached out in other directions, Whitney having done volunteer tax work in Harlem, Juditha serving as the first black woman on a prestigious committee of the Philadelphia Orchestra. But what about the future?

Juditha explains: "We are very pleased with our progress, but at some point, you know, materialistic accomplishments like the house are no longer going to bring us great satisfaction. You no sooner gratify one desire than you have another. So what are we going to do? There will be a void. There have to be ways you can share and give love to others—a dog, a cat, other people.

"Whitney and I are very futuristic in our thinking, and we talk things over from A to Z. We predicted about four years ago that the extended-family concept is coming back because of economic conditions. When we bought this house we chose a very large one. Yes, we bought it for ourselves because we wanted that kind of enjoyment and pleasure, but we feel at some point we're going to have not only us but maybe Whitney's brother, maybe his mother, maybe my parents.

"We are also very receptive to becoming adoptive or foster parents. Whitney's cousin elected not to have children and adopted three instead. To see the look on their faces change from fear that this would be just one more stop along the way to the joy of being really accepted as part of the family was beautiful. As Whitney says, why bring someone into the world who doesn't have to be here, but that homeless eight-year-old who's already here—what are you going to do? kill him?

"I have a number of godchildren but I'm especially close to one fifteen-year-old, and judging by that experience I don't think I can continue to pass through life untouched by children.

"There's something else, and that's putting that maternal instinct to use. I see my husband acting as my child and me acting as his mother. I don't like that.

"The future is still unclear. I don't know where all these ideas are going to take us. But I do know that we are prepared to nurture others."

6

The Middle Years

"Being together was enough for us twenty-nine years ago when we got married and it still is today," says Frank, a fifty-eight-year-old purchasing agent. Betty, his wife, fifty-one, agrees. They are an example of an American minority: the voluntarily childless couple who made their decision in the heart of the baby boom.

Was it a hard decision? "We were lucky," answers Frank, a trim and good-looking man whose rather conservative appearance belies an underlying lightness of spirit, a roll-with-the-punches mentality. "Betty and I never discussed having a family before we were married like most of our contemporaries did—you know, the three-and-a-half kids and two-car garage. We found out later that neither of us wanted children."

Betty, a substantial blonde woman with a pretty, happy face and a rollicking laugh, explains that, although she was never enthusiastic about motherhood, it took her ten years fully to face and admit this. From then on it was easy. There was no parental pressure and little criticism from others. "I think a lot of people back in those years considered it indelicate to ask questions and didn't discuss it."

The two live in a tastefully furnished apartment in Bridgeport, Connecticut, with softwood paneling and their own artwork—Frank's oils and Betty's needlepoint—adding a personal touch. One senses quickly in their relationship an easy intimacy with breathing space for both, a genuine interest in what the other is saying. Frank is the funny man behind the serious face, Betty the appreciative audience in her zebra-print hostess gown.

That their voluntary nonparenthood was highly unconventional in post–World War II America did not bother Betty and Frank. "We just were not child-oriented," recalls Betty. "We wanted to enjoy ourselves. Neither of us was career-oriented either, though we knew we had to earn a living." Her own work was in merchandising and bookkeeping for a department store.

Life had been far from easy when they were children. Both grew up in the Depression years. Theirs was a hand-to-mouth existence, especially Frank's. "When Betty and I met, I used to drive her around town and show her all the places where I'd lived as a kid. She couldn't believe it. Stupid me. I didn't realize my parents were so poor they used to sneak out because they couldn't pay the rent. They would pick me up at eleven o'clock at night, put me in the car, and drive me somewhere six blocks away. I didn't know the truth until I was forty! But, since I didn't realize any of that when I was a kid, I had a nice childhood."

Nice but with plenty of adult responsibilities, like extensive care for his divorced sister's two children. Frank's one big personal goal in his teen years was to be an actor, but when that didn't work out he took on whatever work he could find. If he lost a job—and he has held many, from art dealer to underwear manufacturer—he would sit down and play cards instead of worrying.

Betty was raised in a home where her mother did not know a day of leisure. "She worked very hard from the time she was a small girl and was the mainstay of our family." As a result Betty determined early on to extract whatever pleasures she could out of life and to be free of all but necessary responsibilities. Children for her fell in the unnecessary category.

Betty's and Frank's needs and life styles meshed from the beginning. Frank explains: "We weren't the type of people who ever set a purpose or goal the way young people do nowadays. We lived almost day to day. Our whole life has been that way. We do things on the spur of the moment."

Not having children made things a lot easier because whenever a job didn't work out or Frank felt like picking up stakes and starting over, he could do it.

"I got very upset at my boss and just quit one day and decided I'd like to go to California. I said to Betty, 'Let's get away for a while,' and she said, 'Fine.' We just packed up our suitcases and went. When you think about it, people with children can't do that."

Have there been regrets in the twenty-eight years? Betty says no. "You make choices in life. It's like two doors and you go through one. You never know what the other door could have led to. None of us ever knows that. All I can say is I don't feel any less happy or less fulfilled as a person because I chose not to have children. And I don't regret it.

"In fact, it's just the opposite. The older I get, the surer I've been that what we did was for us—for me, at least; I won't speak for Frank—a good decision. And it's not that we don't like children because we really do. Just because you don't have your own doesn't mean you're cut off from their society. In fact, I think you enjoy them more." Both are close as friends and confidants to the three children of Betty's cousin; they describe them as "super kids" and say they delight in watching them grow up.

Their only big fear is the prospect of one of them being left alone as a widow or widower with the problems of medical care and money. "But," says Betty, "as you get older you begin to realize that all relationships are temporary anyway. We're all in transit always, and I think maybe you come to terms with that. First Frank's mother died, then mine, then his father and mine. You don't become accustomed to death but you start thinking about it more, preparing for it."

She and Frank have talked about what possessions they will earmark for younger relatives and have already started giving items away. Frank says, "I'd rather see people enjoying my things while I'm still alive."

"Aren't you going to ask what we do on Thanksgiving?" Betty asks as I prepare to leave. What *do* you do? I respond.

She doubles up with laughter. "Some gal from *Sixty Minutes* called once and asked me that. I said: 'I eat too much. I drink too much. I do what the rest of America does!' "

What other thoughts would you like to add? I ask.

Frank: "That you can have a happy married life without children. That people should think maybe the marriage is first and children come second."

I was not surprised that the voluntarily childless couples of middle age I interviewed on the whole remain satisfied with their decision to be nonparents. After all, this was a courageous route to take in the 1950s and 1960s, and if one did, in fact, remain childless (not at all a surety given the less-than-reliable methods of birth control) you might assume that their convictions were strong enough to be valid years later.

What *did* surprise me was the substantial number of middle-aged people I met with who, unable to have children because of fertility problems, in the majority are quite nicely adjusted now and sometimes even relieved not to be parents.

Take Sally and John, a Delaware couple married almost forty years ago when they were barely out of their teens. Their early time together was financially very difficult, she working for $10 a week as a domestic, he for $20 as a truck driver. Though they had virtually no savings and even though there were many children on both sides of the family for them to love, they wanted to have their own babies. But after Sally had one dangerous tubal pregnancy, they were advised that another attempt would be unwise. Instead, they tried to adopt the child of a relative, an effort which fell through at the last moment when the mother decided to keep her baby. Having missed their turn to adopt through an agency, Sally and John decided not to reapply.

During the first ten years or so of the marriage, the thought of being permanently childless was hard on both. But gradually they began to make adjustments in their life style, to do things that would not have been possible with a family. Sally, whose education had been cut off at age sixteen, went to night school, earned her diploma, and then took courses toward a college degree; she also became an expert seamstress. John was able to start his own trucking business ("I got sick of being in companies where blacks were the last to be hired and the first to be fired"). Eventually they bought a lovely home in the suburbs, where they now live, traveling a lot and enjoying their hobbies and each other. They are very close. "If anything is ever wrong with Sally," says John, "if she stops . . . everything stops."

He is philosophical about not being a father, though he readily admits his choice still would have been otherwise. "I wanted kids when we got married. But, when we didn't have luck, I didn't worry too much about it. If the good Lord had wanted me to be a father, I would have been one."

Sally adds: "In my early years I thought not having children would be a real hindrance as I got older, but now that we *are* older we are just as content or more so than our friends who are parents. It seems like they are built-in baby sitters for the grandchildren and their kids depend on them too much financially so that they are always broke. Also, the relationship between the husbands and wives is just not as good as ours.

"We have lots of nieces and nephews and three godchildren. They don't take the place of your own, but we have our life now and we are happy just the way we are. I can't look back and regret it or have thoughts that we should have done differently."

What enables people like Sally and John to adjust so well to a condition that they did not choose? Is it because they, like all of us, have a vested interest in being happy with whatever life situation is meted out to us? Is it that the human capacity for adapting is greater than we sometimes realize? Are the middle years easier for infertile people because, if the marriage has withstood the trauma of the infertility itself, characteristically it becomes stronger?

Probably the answers are yes, yes, and yes. Barbara Menning, head of the national organization of infertile people called Resolve, told me that she has been struck by the dramatic and positive growth that occurs, particularly in women, after the adjustment to childlessness is made.

"The person who changes most significantly is usually the

woman," she says. "Men, I think, still tend to form their identity around their work, so not having children is less difficult for them. Women who learn they will not bear children generally mark time for a while. They have to adjust to the fact that the years they may have set aside for childbearing and rearing will not be used that way. Some of these women already have had fine careers but maybe it was a career chosen because it dovetailed nicely with children. Frequently, after coming to grips with their childlessness, they go back to school, embark on a new employment goal, do something they may have wanted to do years ago."

I asked Robert Gould, professor of psychiatry at New York Medical College, his views about the involuntarily childless couple in middle age.

"If someone who wants a child very much can't have one and is able to adjust easily, of course that is awfully good, but I would say such a change in adaptation is not possible for everyone. It demands a well-adjusted couple and a flexible one. Sometimes people who adapt to childlessness with particular ease are those who made a mistake in the first place—they didn't really want children as much as they thought they did and are fortunate not to have had them. Or perhaps their life situation has changed, their values are sufficiently altered that they see they are better off without children. Another possibility is that these couples are so strong and such creatively fulfilled people that they make up for children in other ways and hence do not feel the lack so much.

"On the other hand," continues Gould, "couples who allow their lives to be ruined because they are unable to have children are limited, inflexible people. You know, life is full of turns and if you can't have something one way there should be enough to do in a number of other ways. It may not be exactly as good; having a child is a very special thing, granted, but there *are* other possibilities for fulfillment. If you don't want to adopt, you can work as a teacher or in day-care centers or in other activities that involve children and where your help is needed and appreciated."

In the framework of Gould's analysis, Sally (who had the

tubal pregnancy) and her husband John would seem to be
among the well-adjusted and flexible couples who did genuinely want children but, being unable to have them, learned
to maximize the advantages of childlessness. Another couple
to whom I talked, Lucille and Neal of Syracuse, New York,
found that working with children daily was of great help in
coping with nonparenthood. A private-school teacher and administrator, now in her fifties, Lucille says: "I would have
liked six children, I would have settled for one, and I am sorry
not to have any. In the early years I was so sensitive about my
inability to conceive that when Neal suggested that I buy a
shopping cart to carry my groceries I wouldn't do it because
I refused to lug around anything that looked like a baby carriage. But I learned not to make a tragedy of it all. If you really
like children, you can be with them in many ways other than
having your own."

Neal, a professor of art and portrait painter, adds: "I'm not
one of those people who maintains that their work *is* their
children. But I do feel that I somehow have the responsiblity
of a poet or seer who in every age hands down this sacred writ,
this marvelous knowledge that he's accumulated. I feel that
continuity, that responsibility to the next generation very
strongly, and working with students has been deeply satisfying
to me."

For Sylvia Kauders the rapid adjustment to infertility was
quite different: a signal that children would have been a mistake and that her real purpose lay elsewhere. As special-events
director for the city of Philadelphia for many years, Sylvia is
a well-known career woman who, in what little spare time she
has, also juggles a host of supplementary activities, including
acting, TV producing and moderating, and the position of
assistant director of the Philadelphia area council of tourism.

Married to an engineer, Randle Kauders, in the 1940s,
Sylvia assumed, without really giving the matter much
thought, that she would have children. "In my generation you
were married about a year before you tried to get pregnant
so that people wouldn't start counting on their fingers!" she
says.

Now Sylvia looks back with a sense of amusement and almost disbelief at the years when, having not been able to conceive, she went through one painful test and treatment after another for her infertility. Finally she went to the biggest specialist in the city. "I told him, 'You're the Supreme Court. If you say, "No kids," I'll start programming that in my head.' " He came up with the same tests, the same diagnosis (low estrogen level) and the same results (no conception). "Frankly," admits Sylvia, "I was very relieved that the decision had been taken out of my hands.

"So I started looking for my fulfillment elsewhere. Fortunately this happened at a time when I was growing in my professional life and I was working in a job for which I was exquisitely suited. During those childbearing years my work fulfilled something important in my life. The truth is I never missed being a parent."

Neither did or does her husband. "Society expected you to have kids," he says, "and that expectation particularly conditioned the women in our generation."

Sylvia's assessment of the kind of parents she and Randy would have made is a harsh one: "If we'd had a kid and it wasn't a good mathematician, Randy would have disowned it. As for me, I would have been a lousy mother. I'm glad I never had the chance to foist some of the psychological abuse on a child that my mother foisted on me."

A brilliant woman "who could not realize her great potential because of the times and situation in which she lived," Sylvia's mother had been widowed at a young age and supported the family by managing a small delicatessen—a task she carried out with great acumen. "But she never should have had children. She never had any pleasure from us. Her tragedy was when she lived. Today she probably would have been president of a stock exchange." In her potential for achievement, if not her maternal qualities, "my mother," says Sylvia, "was definitely my role model."

Only rarely does Sylvia Kauders think of children wistfully today and that is merely to "fantasize on what an offspring of Randy's and mine would be like, what abilities and talents we might have invested in another human being. That's as far as it's gone. And when I see some of the kids my friends have turned out, well, if that's their immortality, it's unfortunate."

So if you had it to do over again, I ask Sylvia, you'd be voluntarily rather than involuntarily childless?

"Put it this way: I think if my mother had it to do over again, *she* would have been voluntarily childless and so I wouldn't have been on earth to make that decision."

Middle age. So much has been written about its satisfactions and miseries, potential and pitfalls, the differences between men and women at this stage.

Though generalizations invite exceptions, it seems fair to say that for the childless of middle age there are some clear improvements over the early years of a marriage. The voluntarily childless have made their decision about parenthood, and the years of turmoil, weighing pros and cons, are past. For the infertiles, the painful, demoralizing tests are over and thoughts are focused upon different aspects of life. Pronatalism is directed at others now: the younger set; that can be a relief both to those who are childless by choice and to the involuntarily childless, who were victims of the "if you would just try less" (or more, or take a vacation, or go to a psychiatrist, etc.) mentality.

Finances are likely to be on a sounder footing than those of parents, most of whom are struggling with diminishing energy and increasing burdens, like college educations. As one childless male from Connecticut, now sixty-one, told me: "I plan to retire next year. Imagine if we had kids going to Cornell Medical Center. We could never do it. Most of our parent friends don't have a dime saved. When they have to take care of both their own aging parents and their children, there is nothing left for themselves. We see this all the time. They are the ham in the sandwich, squeezed in between two generations."

Childless people are often pleasantly surprised to find that the parent friends with whom they may have lost contact are once again socially available and interested in their company.

This relates to the "empty-nest syndrome": with grown children starting to move out of the house, parents have more time and energy for other adults and frequently are eager to learn from their childless friends about life as a family of two. Particularly helpful to mothers who have been out of the job market for years are the insights of childless working women.

Another pleasure of the middle years is the long-term relationships that many nonparents establish with young people, which serve not only to enrich their lives but to provide a link with the next generation that may otherwise be lacking. "In a way I've had a vicarious way of looking at my sister's children as my own," said an editor for an eastern newspaper who is in her late forties. "I'm awfully close to my sister, too, so when there's any problem with the kids she calls me. I've helped bring up four little babies. And I've helped send them to private school. One of them went to Paris last year, which I paid for. I like to see the children growing. It's like a flowering, getting bigger and stronger, or a tree with branches. I get a lot of pleasure from them. They come to visit us weekends in New York and out to our house in the country. I see the world through their eyes. So what I've missed personally I haven't missed in my life."

The negative side of the childless life style in middle age cannot be discounted. It can be frightening to recognize that, with the opportunity to have children behind one, the potential for fulfillment has narrowed in scope. Discontent may be particularly great when career goals are not realized or when professional success does not result in the expected sense of satisfaction. Jenny, an educational consultant, married eight years, is dealing with that now:

"Here I am at forty. I've got this portion of my life that I'm going to live, but what am I going to do with it? I don't know whether it's part of my upbringing, but I always have it in the back of my head that somehow I've got to make a contribution to the world, that there's got to be a mark that I've been here. A child would accomplish that because you do imprint a lot of yourself in a child, for better or worse. But we decided against children. In another sense, your work passes on a part of you. You meet people, you nurture them. Hopefully, because of the work I've done, some people's lives are different and better."

However, Jenny's career is no longer challenging or satisfying to her. She is experiencing a sense of upheaval, of being without direction. If she returns to school for training in a new field, her husband will be saddled with a long-term financial responsibility, while she will feel a heavy dependency on him and the marriage that is contrary to her independent ways. If she takes on part-time work so as to devote more time to their relationship, she will feel cheated professionally. And, if she makes a wrong choice at forty, will she be able to rectify it at fifty?

Psychologist Anita Landa told me her research has shown cases like Jennie's to be common among the voluntarily childless. "Characteristically they are highly creative people, keenly aware of their own mortality. They want to make things that will outlast them. Creativity is their hedge against death." Landa has found this trait to be most prevalent among people of around Jennie's age. Further on into mid-life, "they feel more that they are a part of humanity."

The desire to pass on what we are to others, be they our children, our larger circle, or future generations, is universal. Typically, the middle years are characterized not only by the recognition of such a need but by a reassessment of how we can achieve it. When they do not have children, people in mid-life tend to look upon career success as the only way they can leave—to use Jenny's words—a mark that they've been here. But there are other, more basic ways. "A constructive, useful life, good works, and good relationships are as valid as writing poetry or inventing a machine," says Robert Gould. "Anything that one does well and obtains satisfaction from is a good enough reason for living. To be a decent human being that people like and feel better for knowing is enough."

Among the crises that most people in mid-life face is the death of one or both parents. For those who do not have their own children (and grandchildren) this loss can be especially traumatic, producing a feeling of deep, if passing, regret that there is no younger generation following behind to represent the continuity of life. Intimately associated with this is the fear of one's own old age.

As a parent one tends to live with the hope that in old age the children will provide emotional and perhaps concrete support and add meaning to one's life. This may or may not become reality. But the childless have no such expectations: they know they will have to look elsewhere—to other relatives, friends, neighbors, community groups, and above all their own inner resources. How well they deal in mid-life with approaching old age will determine in large measure how rich or, conversely, how impoverished those final years will be.

Among the middle-aged people I interviewed there was a great diversity in how they were planning (or not planning) for their old age. Some couples were closing in on each other in a kind of strangling dependency—an "exclusive twosome," one woman called it. Others were maintaining, and even broadening, their base of friends. "I run my household as if there were ten of us here," a vibrant fifty-one-year-old woman artist told me. "We have all the strays during the holidays— divorced, never married, widowed, young, old, gay, straight, people who do not comprise big family units."

Some middle-aged childless people avoid the aged and places where they live. Others seek them out, hoping that someone will do the same for them one day. A southern woman in her late forties told me that among her entire circle she is the only one who does volunteer work at local nursing homes. "My friends think it's depressing," she said. "It may have something to do with my seeing we're all going to end up like that someday, whereas they don't—or won't—see it because they have children."

> My body knows it will never bear children.
> What can I say to my body now,
> this used violin?
> Every night it cries out desolately
> from its secret cave.

> Old body, old friend,
> why are you so unforgiving?

These words, taken from the poem "Waiting" by Jane Cooper, express poignantly the grief women feel when their childbearing years are over. Cooper wrote the poem when she was forty-seven; she had never married.[1]

Even those women who have the desired number of children commonly find the onset of menopause to be unexpectedly difficult. For those who have not borne children there are special problems to cope with. The sterile woman may find it necessary to mourn her unborn child a final time, and voluntarily childless women sometimes go through what psychotherapist Miriam Mazor refers to as "grieving for a part of themselves never to be realized."[2] Some few look to this stage with relief. One woman who is in her mid-fifties and childless by choice told me bluntly she was delighted at the onset of menopause because she was rid of the menstrual period, which had had no practical purpose in her life.

Hysterectomy, common in the middle years, often takes a severe and unanticipated toll on the voluntarily childless. Colleen, a sleek, slim blonde who has enjoyed a successful career as a model in New York, is among them. Her childlessness had more than one cause: fear of childbirth and immersion in career on her part, along with a decided indifference to children on the part of her husband, whose childhood had been quite unhappy. Ambivalence and indecision regarding parenthood characterized the fifteen-year marriage, though Colleen persisted in keeping options open. When her husband, Len, learned he would have to undergo a prostate operation (known to sometimes reduce sperm count), she talked him into contributing a semen sample for freezing so that she could be artificially inseminated at a later date. He acquiesced. But that date never came. At forty-two Colleen had a hysterectomy.

"When I was going into the hospital to have the operation, I was very nervous and kept trying to tell myself that I didn't care what it meant about having children, but I found that I kept trying to hold back tears. I was scared, I thought I was going to die. They made me sign this paper stating I clearly understood that as a result of the operation I would be sterile. The aide who came in to shave me that night started to talk to me about her children and how she adored them. She had six and she asked if I had any. I said, 'No.' She said, 'For you this is a very special operation and I will pray for you.' That just unglued me.

"The next day while I was coming out of the anesthesia one of the nurses came up to me and held my hand and said, 'Now, dear, hurry up and get well so you can go back home to your children.' The day after that I felt very unwell and started to scream and cry at what I thought was a pain under my breastbone. They did all kinds of tests and nothing showed up. But later that day my minister and his wife came in and they stood at the foot of the bed. The minute I saw them I burst into tears and told them what the nurse had said. I told them, 'This is a terrible operation for me because I don't have any children.'

"After the hysterectomy I felt a terrible resentment toward Len, thinking he was the one who hadn't wanted children all along and that I had been denied my birthright."

Colleen is over the anger and the suffering now. She recognizes that even had she not needed the operation she most likely would still be childless today, still paying $40 a month to the sperm bank, and doing nothing about motherhood until the decision was taken from her in the next stage—menopause.

The finality of her childlessness has affected Colleen in another positive way: she has embarked on a new and successful career as an interior designer. In a sense she is experiencing what anthropologist Margaret Mead observed in her autobiography as being characteristic of some women who learn they are unable to have any—or any more—children. "Suddenly, their whole energy is released—they paint or write as never before or they throw themselves into academic work with enthusiasm, where before they had only half a mind to spare for it."[3]

Most women who are middle-aged today and have had abortions had them illegally. The operation was generally carried out under covert and downright dangerous conditions. For those who were unmarried, the stigma of the abortion itself could only be exceeded by the stigma of giving birth to and keeping the baby. How do the women who had abortions, then married, and remained childless feel now?

Belle is a New Jersey native, retired to Florida. She had three abortions (performed by a man whose clients were, like her, mostly showgirls). When she married, Belle was beyond the childbearing years. Since motherhood never had any particular appeal for her, she does not look back at the abortions with any regrets—except for the degrading conditions under which they were carried out.

For Melanie it is a quite different story. She is an actress now living in Los Angeles, well known for her work on Broadway and in television soap operas. In her sixties, she is a stunning woman with aristocratic features, severely cropped, graying hair, and a slim, proud carriage. Extremely unconventional by her own admission, Melanie was already playing the role of an Amazon on stage by the time she was sixteen. Her private life was equally nontraditional. A first abortion was performed while she was still in her teens and unmarried, a second as the result of an extramarital affair during her first marriage, and a third after she was divorced. It is the third abortion she will always regret.

"I wanted the child very badly but the man wouldn't marry me. And I was at that point just conventional enough not to want to have the child outside of marriage. So I had an abortion. I regretted it terribly. In fact, I went through hell over it and left him because of it. He was beside himself; he practically had a nervous breakdown. He hadn't realized I wanted a child that badly. I will regret all my life not having that child. Had times been different, I might have had the guts to do it outside of marriage, but I'm talking about a long time ago—at least twenty-five years.

"For the last eighteen years I've been married, and respectably so. At the time I got married to Norman [now retired, he was a leading man on Broadway] there was a point when I thought for a few weeks that I was pregnant. Oh God, I was ecstatic. It seemed like heaven had been good and kind to me. But I wasn't pregnant—I was going through change of life."

I asked Melanie if, given a career that took her from coast to coast on whirlwind tours, she might have found motherhood too much to handle. "I never thought for a minute that I had to choose between motherhood and career," she responded. "I always felt I could do both, and I still think I could have. And I would have been better off if I had. You become very selfish without children, I think. You become totally self-interested and that is very dangerous for a woman even if you are happily married or in a happy love affair."

Melanie says that she did not focus on the absence of children in her life until recently. "It's only been the last few years that I've consistently missed having a child and grandchild and a family to think about and worry about. Funnily enough, I am a very motherly kind of person. I rented out our little guest house recently, and it's all I can do to keep from mothering the man I rented it to. It's all I can do to control myself from washing his sheets for him."

Melanie feels her husband's recent decline in health is one reason for her fresh regret, and another is that she is between acting assignments. "If I haven't got Norman, I've nobody. I have nothing. It's a horrible feeling to grow older because you know damn well you are going to die.

"I love kids and I love to have them around, so it's hard for me as I get older to remember that I don't have any. I just have to keep reminding myself that I haven't got any kids. But I *should.*"

Melanie is one among a large group of women; she is neither voluntarily childless nor involuntarily so, according to the usual definition of infertility. Rather, she is childless by a quirk of fate: man, timing, social climate were wrong and motherhood proved an impossibility.

I talked with another woman, Donna, a forty-five-year-old Californian, whose abortion at twenty-two (on her mother's insistence) was followed in six weeks by the sudden death of her lover. Later, very desirous of motherhood, she married a man who, because he had had several children from a previous marriage, kept putting her off until, disgusted, she divorced him. Good fortune seemed within grasp when she met her present husband, who *did* want children, but two months into the relationship she was diagnosed as having cervical cancer and in need of an immediate hysterectomy. Now healthy and happy in her marriage some six years later, Donna is philosophical about it all: "I believe in reincarnation. I feel I must have goofed somewhere and that in this life I have to learn to do for others who are not necessarily as close to me as my own children. In another life, who knows? I always tell my husband next time around we're going to meet young and have a nice family."

Until fairly recently the problems faced by men as they come into mid-life were largely ignored because they do not undergo the unmistakable physiological changes that mark women's entry into the same stage. But that men do go through a parallel and often serious psychological crisis is now recognized.

Daniel J. Levinson of Yale University, in his pathbreaking work *The Seasons of a Man's Life,* [4] refers to "mid-life transition," which occurs in men between ages forty and forty-five, and to "middle adulthood" which is a longer period, encompassing the years forty to sixty-five.

"No matter how well or poorly he has done with the ambitions of his thirties, he is likely to experience a letdown in the Mid-life Transition," writes Levinson. ". . . It is no longer crucial to climb another rung on the ladder—to write another book, get another promotion, earn more of the rewards that meant so much in the past."

Coming to terms with his own death and mortality, the man in Mid-life Transition wants "to give his life a meaning that will live after his death. . . . He wants to leave a trace, however small, on the course of mankind. . . . He comes to grasp more clearly the flow of generations and the continuity of the human species. . . . He feels more responsibility for the generations that will follow his own."

Levinson maintains that men differ greatly in their views about what constitutes their legacy to the future. For some it is material possessions handed down, for others charitable contributions or work or raising children and maintaining tribal continuity. But whatever his kind of legacy, the man in this middle stage, recognizing that his death is not far off, wants to reaffirm life for himself and future generations. A major way of achieving this for some men is through what Levinson calls "mentoring": helping young people to develop their skills and potential by offering them one's own knowledge and mature guidance.

Levinson also talks about the well-known phenomenon of men who "fly the coop" in middle adulthood; this usually takes the form of a new relationship with a much younger woman. "It reflects a man's struggles with the Young/Old polarity: he is asserting his youthful vitality at a time when he fears that the Young in him is being crushed by the dry, dying Old."

The characteristics cited by Levinson are applicable to men with and without children. A disillusioned fifty-year-old male with three children can leave his menopausal wife to seek new fatherhood with a young woman just as the childless husband can. The man with no children, however, may be particularly vulnerable to the appeal of first-time fatherhood if he views his life as having had no real meaning, as offering no legacy to the future. Such men feel what Los Angeles writer Patricia E. Raley (cited in the book *Up Against the Clock* by Fabe and Wikler) refers to as the "dynastic imperative."[5] They are suddenly aware that there is no one around to carry on their name and provide the sense of immortality they now sorely miss. If the desire to establish this "dynasty" occurs after the wife is past her childbearing years, the story can take many directions —from mere fantasizing to an abrupt departure from the now barren wife.

I talked with Grace, an urban planner from Denver who did

not have children with her husband Arnold because both had been scarred by unhappy childhoods in broken homes. "At age forty," she told me, "Arnold decided he didn't need me anymore, so he started off on the usual thing men do at that age: he had found this marvelous person who wanted a family and wanted to settle down in the suburbs—all the things he had absolutely detested previously. We had never had a very satisfactory sex life and this girl was practically a nymphomaniac . . . it's typical, a pattern, I swear it, among people I know. She really did want kids, and I think he was pretending to himself that he did, too. He'd say to me, 'You're too old now—you can't have children.' It wasn't true at the time. Anyhow, he left me and went around with her for three years, though he didn't marry her. And he never became a father and he couldn't stay away from me. He had to come back to mama."

Thus began a pattern of one girl after another, during which period Grace divorced him but kept taking him back into her home between women. And there he remains now, along with his mother, though he and Grace, who is at present fifty-one, have not remarried. "Basically, he wants to be the child," she says, "and I am the only person who will treat him that way."

Such behavior is not typical of childless men who reach mid-life. Says psychiatrist Robert Gould: "The man who is in love with his wife at middle age and who is happy with what he is doing may have no more thoughts of having children now than he did at twenty-five when he made the commitment to nonparenthood."

Victor, a successful classical pianist, fifty-nine, is such a man. "Doris is no longer capable of having children," he said of his artist wife. "But I still am. What would happen if I suddenly decided at my age that, yes, I'd like to have a child? I'm then in a very, very strong dilemma. I can go out and find someone who will have a baby with me or else I can adopt or I can divorce my wife and have another marriage. I have a lot of options, none of which I intend to execute. Part of that is because marriage to Doris is the best of the options, and another part is that I'm no longer an old fool. I think that over several decades of growing up I have learned a few things. One of them is you don't start playing the twenties game at sixty."

Being creatively fulfilled by his music, Victor does not feel that gnawing lack of a legacy; he *is* passing on something of himself through performances and recordings. Other childless men leave their mark on the world through good works—for instance, money put to an important social purpose. One of the more prominent examples of this kind was industrialist Milton Hershey, inventor of the nation's first milk chocolate bar. Hershey, married to a beautiful young Irishwoman when he was forty-one, never became a father but founded a school for orphan boys when he was fifty-two. The school absorbed more and more of his time, especially after his wife's death, and eventually it was made beneficiary of his vast personal estate. It exists today with some five hundred students, all of whom live and work in a familylike atmosphere on a rural campus. In the main building there stands a statue of Milton Hershey with his arm around one of the students. "My boys," he used to call them.

Some professions lend themselves to Levinson's mentoring particularly well. A professor in his early forties, childless in both his first and second marriages, explained his views to me: "I would imagine that a man who is without children and works on an automobile assembly line wouldn't develop all that much of a personal relationship with his work mates—and certainly not with the auto bodies that go past. But I think couples in academic life have it a little easier in that they have so many surrogate families through the people they teach. I don't mean that a teacher is always in a paternal role, but there is an element of that. Also, if you have graduate students who hopefully are maturing under your guidance, you have a continuing relationship with them after they leave, so that is a help. An academic like me is fortunate, too, in that at sixty-five I probably will not be so completely severed as others from my place of work, my occupation of the last forty years. Most of us can go on teaching for a while; we can go on researching and writing and being with young people."

Many childless men who do not have this easy opportunity for relating to young people find other imaginative ways to give of themselves. One man in his fifties, a journalist, told me that his mid-life replacement for children has been participation in a variety of local organizations of a religious, historic, and artistic orientation. "It helps me feel I'm part of societal relationships," he said. "You might describe it as a community sensitivity."

"Are you glad or sorry you didn't have children?" I asked this of a friend in his late fifties who has been divorced for many years after a brief marriage.

"Depends when you ask me," Lou answered. "Like Wednesday I might be glad, Thursday maybe not."

I laughed.

"No, I'm serious," Lou continued. "Sometimes I think all this talk about having children or not having them isn't so smart. Maybe it's just better not to think about it. You know, do your thing in the evening or whenever you like it and see what happens. Take what fate has to offer you. That's the way it was way back. Choices are relatively new, I think."

One may not agree with Lou's philosophy, but there is truth in what he says about choices. We are, at the beginning of the 1980s, a society accustomed to decision making, establishing priorities and planning five, ten, and more years ahead. This going after what we want can be a positive, energizing force; on the other hand, it can make us inflexible, unable to cope with situations which arise unexpectedly and are not to our liking. Those who, like Lou, were raised during the Depression, who, like him, fought in or had close relatives involved in World War II, were not so demanding, for choices were available only to the privileged few. Even people like Betty and Frank (the couple we met at the beginning of this chapter), who were quite clear about their preference for nonparenthood, continue to approach their daily lives with a sense of fatalism.

Edith, a striking-looking and gifted children's photographer, married at age forty-five and now in her sixties, expressed succinctly the attitude of her contemporaries:

"You see, I come from a different generation. I come from a generation where if somebody made a decision about what they were going to do and how they were going to do it, they were pretty unusual. The tide just carried us, and whatever happened happened. If we were fortunate enough to get in a field of work that we liked, that was great. It was just pure luck. Now you plan. It's not that I didn't have the guts to do things—I was just completely and totally unaware.

"Most of the children back then were accidental. I don't think children were planned. Most people didn't know anything about precautions. When I was young, girls left it up to the men, and they wore 'rubbers.' We were lucky, a lot of us, that we weren't pregnant more than we were. And we *were* pregnant. I had two abortions."

Couples now in their twenties and thirties, raised in a very different world, characteristically bemoan the lack of role models. Especially if they are seriously considering nonparenthood, they look in vain for voluntarily childless people of middle age who feel similarly about life and who really understand what they, the younger generation, are all about.

I met one such role model in Irma Holland, an artist. We talked in her airy studio above the din of Manhattan traffic. On the floor was a very large sixteen-frame oil portrait of a young woman which Irma had created from photographs; each of the frames showed the subject in a slightly different mood, the total effect being of an arresting sensitivity.

Irma, fifty-seven and married for twenty-eight years, has a softly elegant beauty which is in rather startling contrast to her New York–accented speech and feisty manner. Her graying hair was pulled back in a long braid; she wore tan boots and a rose wool skirt, with a crocheted mohair stole over her shoulders.

For her generation, Irma's life and feelings were hardly traditional. To begin with, she lived with her future husband, a psychologist, for several years before marrying him. Furthermore, her career was not just a hobby but of primary importance to her. And, finally, she just didn't want children. ·

"When I was young, I thought why couldn't I be conventional, enjoy the Jewish holidays, get married with the wedding and the white gown and have four kids? But I had all these ideas that were way out in those days, and everybody thought, 'She's mad.' But I believed in them, and I lived by them. Like I never could make any sense out of the unequal treatment of women. It made me furious at a young age."

When finally Irma did marry, the relationship did not settle into one of easy domesticity. Rather, there were many ups and downs and even a period of separation. Irma's husband, she says, was no more ideally suited to parenthood than she was, being ambivalent about the subject, involved in his own emotional problems, and totally absorbed in his career. Children were surely not the answer to their life together as husband and wife and as professionals, but advice came in—unsolicited and heavy.

"My husband's friends were all psychoanalysts and psychiatrists, and all of them were telling everybody to go have kids. If you really were a woman, you had children, you took care of the family. There was a stage in my own analysis where I almost got taken in. I thought I should do it because it was an 'experience' and I figured maybe there was something terribly wrong with me. But then I would fight with all the analysts. I'd say, 'I have a vagina—*that* makes me a woman—and you have balls, and that makes you a man, and I don't want to hear any more about penis envy.' I said, 'I know a couple of analysts who got big bellies when their wives were pregnant and they never lost those bellies either—you want to write a theory about that?'

"A lot of creative women my age capitulated and most of them became child indulgers. God forbid you tried to talk straight to a child. I found that my friends who were working and who didn't have children were much more interesting. The mothers turned into a pack of ninnies. They had a way of putting me down that was very boring. They'd say, 'You don't know what it's like,' and 'Well, you should have finished your analysis.' But they *had* to put me down because they were all so miserable. These were college-educated women. And when the kids were finally grown, they had their faces lifted and went back to their little jobs and said, 'Isn't it nice, I'm out of the house again!'

"It makes me laugh—those people who said, 'Oh, you'll be sorry when you get older.' I'm still waiting to be sorry. What's a kid gonna do to help my future? I'll be an old lady and just get on his or her nerves.

"But I like young people and I love to be with them. I teach them yoga. And for years I worked as a children's illustrator. Everybody thought I had twenty kids. All of us who do that kind of work have the little child in us. It's probably the nicest part of any individual if you can tame it.

"I think it's great today because young kids have validation from the outside. You can be anything and do anything. But at the same time young people are struggling because they have too many alternatives. Suddenly they've got these major decisions to make—what do I want to do? what do I want to give up?

"I get the feeling that a lot of women will postpone having kids until the zero hour and have them then. But that's okay because I think they may really want them by then and have their careers well on the road. But those who don't really want children have to stop listening to everybody telling them they'll be sorry. *I'm* not sorry. I find a lot of young girls like to meet women like me who say, 'It's okay. Just take your chances. You take chances either way.'

"We have to get over this business of being Superwomen 'cause then we don't do anything well. My feeling always was that women have to decide. They can't have it all. You give up something to get something else. I think women have to learn to put their energies to their major love—children or career. Well, maybe if they're rich enough they can have both.

"A woman is a woman whether or not she has children."

7

Alone Again: Divorced, Widowed...Remarried

Vernon Matthews, a man of fifty-one with longish, graying hair and a gentle manner, reclines on the living-room sofa of his home in Bunker Hill, Illinois, looking out over forty acres of woods. Bushy the cat comes to him for a body rub, and out on the balcony fat squirrels scurry back and forth. Surrounded as he is by Mother Nature, Vern, a biologist, is very much in his element.

Eleven years ago Vern became a widower after a long and happy marriage. He and his wife had been voluntarily childless, mainly because there was so much else they wanted to do with their lives and secondarily because Vern was deeply concerned with overpopulation and the environment. Now he talks to me in that quiet, mesmerizing voice that makes me wish I could have learned about amoebas and frogs and Darwin from him back in ninth grade.

"The one time I really questioned the wisdom of our decision not to have children was when my wife died. I loved her so and I was shattered, I was just killed, but I was breathing. And I asked myself often how would I feel right then, when I was hurting so, if I had a child that she had borne? What I finally sifted out was that I would have grabbed at any little part, any little thing, in an attempt at regaining what I had lost. It would have been a selfish kind of holding-on which really wouldn't have been a holding-on at all. And, when I backed off and really looked at it, I thought, all that pain doesn't mean we were wrong in our decision about children; it simply means that I am hurting like hell now and questioning everything.

"As it turned out, the choice was right, the choice was okay for me, because I was far more free to rebuild my life as one single human being, which I had to do. I was able to abandon everything I had held dear and start over with nothing carried over.

"Recognizing the immediacy of happiness, more than anything else, was helpful and satisfying to me. I learned to take a moment and really squeeze it. My wife and I used to—oh, God—we used to have such big plans, and I did a lot of living in the future. But when she was gone, I realized you have to take hold of the here and now and learn to live with yourself, by yourself.

"I think if you can't be alone there's a deficiency in you that you're not going to cover up with a number of kids or friends or husband or wife or whatever. I've spent enough time here alone that I can do that. I don't have to look outside myself for a whole lot of fulfillment.

"Losing my wife was the worst thing that will ever happen to me, but it gave me some perspective on joy and pain. Now I've rebuilt my life. And it's good, and I've had good years. I'm probably as happy as anybody I know."

Seven years ago Vern was married again to a vivacious self-assured divorcée, twenty-one years his junior, who was similarly childless by choice. Today Vern is the head of the science department in the school where he teaches, and his second wife, Connie, is a law school student with clearly defined goals. Both see their future together as combining career with marriage; children are no more a part of the package now than they were in their previous marriages.

In his quiet but full life Vernon Matthews has more than sufficient children for any man: his students. They seem to spill naturally from his classroom to his home. While I am there, two students chop wood and then join us for brunch.

"I've spent my working life—twenty-five, twenty-six years —with students," Vern tells me later. "I do it out of choice and at an age level that I find absolutely fascinating; older teenagers. I'm sometimes inundated with them—it's totally kids, my whole focus, everything that I've done that's con-

structive that hasn't been for myself and for Connie or my first
wife. I think that's what allows me to maintain my philosophy.
I spend so much time with students it's as if I have children
of my own."

Whether one is childless or not, young or old, happily married or unhappily, facing widowhood is one of the most difficult experiences one can expect to go through in a lifetime.
According to a famous 1967 "social readjustment rating
scale" by T. H. Holmes and R. H. Rahe, the death of a spouse
requires the greatest readjustment, with divorce and marital
separation running second and third.[1] No wonder some people in these situations undergo the kind of painful self-ques-
tioning that Vern did over the long-ago decision not to have
children.

Of all the negative feelings experienced by those who are
divorced or widowed, none is more common than loneliness,
described by psychiatrist Robert S. Weiss as being caused "not
by being alone but by being without some definite needed
relationship." Weiss, who is associated with Harvard Medical
School, distinguishes in his compassionate study *Loneliness: The
Experience of Emotional and Social Isolation* between the kind of
agonized, debilitating loneliness which caused Vernon Matthews to feel the momentary desire for a child and that
growth-inducing state which Vernon also experienced: ". . .
a time in which one is not only alone but able to use one's
aloneness to recognize with awesome clarity both one's
ineradicable separateness from all else and one's fundamental
connectedness . . . a time . . . after which one can recognize
one's true self and begin to be that true self."[2]

It is only natural in the transition from the married to the
single life for the childless person to feel strangely rootless.
Children, after all, though they often bring more heartache
than joy at this stage, still offer a source of continuing love, a
pressing need for getting up in the morning, an intimate re-
membrance that a marriage did once exist. With no child to
care for and worry about, no child to resemble the lost mate,
it can seem almost as if the two adults had never been a

twosome. Eileen Simpson, in her sensitive novel *The Maze,* which deals with the disintegration of a marriage, describes the scene in which the relationship ends. Afterward, the wife says to herself in pain and disbelief: "How easy it is to undo a marriage when there are neither children nor money! The whole thing hadn't taken ten minutes!"[3]

Compounding the loss for many a newly single person is the frightening realization of how close he or she had been to the mate—even if the marriage ended in terrible discord. As we have seen, childless marriages, especially those of some duration, tend to be intimate, with a lot of dependency on both sides. Characteristically, in the absence of children, husband and wife take on the role of parent and child to each other, whether consciously or not. Once the mate is gone, so is that pretend child and/or parent.

Especially in the early stages of aloneness there is a tendency for the divorced or widowed person, if voluntarily childless, to dwell anew on the choice made, perhaps decades ago, not to have children. Was it a wise decision? Had it been discussed sufficiently? In the case of a divorce, might a child have saved the marriage? What if the former mate marries again and has children of his or her own and/or becomes a stepparent? That can appear an act of betrayal.

Those who made their decision about children carefully, rather than superficially, are less likely to indulge in such backward glances. Donna, a thirty-four-year-old Washington, D.C., research librarian who was recently separated after a ten-year marriage, told me that many years ago she had realized the childfree life style was right for her as an individual; her husband came to the same conclusion about himself. Theirs was a joint decision made upon individual needs instead of upon the marriage itself. Hence the separation, though painful, at least did not cause her to requestion that one area. "I wasn't taken in by some of the myths that society pushes on you—you know, 'Now you are alone, and you don't even have a child who is part of you!' "

Marital separation or the death of a spouse causes some childless people to become belatedly obsessed with issues of heritage and family line. Gail Sheehy, in her widely read book *Passages,* has written: "With your own role as child to your parents intact, you still feel secure. With the death of your father or mother, you are exposed. . . . The death of the remaining parent has been documented as one of the most constant crisis points in the individual's evolving sense of self . . . for you . . . are abruptly flung to the front of the generational chain, followed only by your own children."[4] The childless, however, are followed by no one.

A forty-year-old registered nurse to whom I spoke is painfully aware of this. Divorced, childless, and without siblings, she now has only a mother, to whom she is very close, in her immediate family. "Sometimes," she told me, "I think that if I had had a child that would take the edge off the grief in a practical sense when my mother dies. A child would have been something to link me to life instead of always looking back as if the clock had stopped."

Intertwined with this feeling is the cry: "Who will take care of me when I'm old?" Parents tend to expect (not always realistically) that they will care for each other until one of the two dies and that their child or children will eventually assume responsibility for the one left. Having no offspring, and with the mate lost through death or divorce, one seeks a way out of the loneliness as well as an answer to the most unanswerable question of all: "Why am I here?"

Mel is a Philadelphia artist and author in his fifties, divorced for many years after a three-year childless marriage. A bearish-looking man given to gentle wit and philosophical meanderings, Mel doesn't talk much about children but, when asked, admits to thinking about them a lot:

"Like when I'm on trains or planes or doing the laundry. I enjoy watching babies being wheeled around in carriages—it's such a nice way to travel."

"I like children. I am a child myself as the result of not having children. I watch people buying giant boxes of Pampers with great admiration and with a sense of relief that *I* don't have to do it.

"On the other hand, it's hard to think that you haven't made anybody in your own image like God did. And that you *could* have, you had all the technical apparatus to do it, all those sperm . . . my God, 60,000 sperm just dancing around at the top of a needle. Having children it seems to me, at least on the surface, is a reason for living, and if you don't do that somehow you've not fulfilled your purpose."

In learning to live alone again, childless people may turn to pets for company and comfort. Dogs and cats, in particular, are known to take the place of children in some marriages, but the extent of that displacement may not become clear until the couple is separated. (Back in the 1930s Hollywood poked fun at this situation in a film called *The Awful Truth*, which co-starred Cary Grant and Irene Dunne as the estranged, childless mates who go into court over custody of a fox terrier.)

Other people do not foist a child's role upon their Persians and poodles, yet suffer guilt when a new job or life style makes the maintenance of a pet untenable. Thirty-two years old, Suzanne Zumbrunnen of Atlanta, who was sterilized after her divorce, is the kind of person who knows what she wants out of life. One wouldn't expect her to become victim to a ball of fur. "When I was married, we had a cat named Sam," Suzanne told me. "After the divorce I moved into an apartment and went back to school. I didn't want anything tying me down when I simply was having a hell of a time being responsible for all the logistics of living by myself. So I asked John, my ex, to take Sam. He did.

"Well, it turns out John goes out of town a lot, one weekend a month. I started worrying, I started getting really sad, having extraordinary guilt feelings about abandoning this cat. Now the cat can take care of itself. It has a litter box; you can put food down for a weekend now and then. But not every four weeks.

"So I called up John and said, 'Look, I've been thinking about this. Why don't you drop Sam off and I'll keep him the weeks you're out of town? We'll try and work this out.' Now we phone back and forth. It's like visiting rights. And it's crazy. It's just an animal. I mean, the cat looks at me and I wonder what it's thinking. If a kid said, 'Why isn't Daddy living here anymore?' I think I would jump out the window."

People sometimes assume that those who are childless are less committed to their marriages and are more likely to end up among our nation's high divorce statistics (estimated at being between 33 and 40 percent of all first marriages). Elizabeth Whelan, in her book *A Baby? . . . Maybe,* writes that couples without children do statistically show a higher divorce rate than parents. However, she also points out that a significant number of all first marriages which end in divorce do so early in the marriage, when there is a higher probability that no children will have been born.[5]

Professionals with long experience generally agree that commitment to a marriage increases with the number of years spent together, whether or not there are children. "I would say the partners in a childless marriage are as committed to each other as are parents if the marriage has lasted for ten years or more and if the partners are at least in their thirties," says Philadelphia psychiatrist Martin Goldberg. Some go so far as to claim that not having children adds substantially to the chances of marital survival. Harold Feldman, professor at Cornell University's Department of Human Development and Family Studies, has written extensively in this vein. He maintains that children are disruptive to marital communication and to mutual satisfaction, with husband and wife feeling less close to each other and more prone to conflict.[6]

Hence one cannot make a direct cause-effect link between childlessness and divorce, especially today when children are hardly a deterrent to marital breakup. (Every year, according to *Newsweek* magazine, one million American children under age eighteen see the dissolution of their families.)[7] Nonetheless, it is obvious that couples without children normally find it easier to end a poor marriage than do parents. "Knowing how long it took me to get out of a bad situation with just the complication of a husband," an eight-years-married southern divorcée told me, "I am sure that if I had had even one child

I never would have left. I mean I just wouldn't. It would have been so much easier simply to stay."

There are some special situations in which not having children is deeply intertwined with the failure of the marriage itself. Infertility is acknowledged to cause great strains even in the strongest of relationships, and all too frequently it results in divorce. One such case I learned of had an ironic twist: Julie and Pete entered their marriage having been told they were both infertile. This shared problem was something that drew them together. However, it turned out that Julie was *not* infertile; the diagnosis had been incorrect. Eventually, the very basis of the relationship having been shaken, she left Pete to seek marriage and parenthood with another.

In other cases the catch is not infertility but a sharp difference of opinion between husband and wife about children. More characteristically it is the wife who wants children and the husband who does not. But with Sandra, a successful East Coast physician in her thirties, it was the opposite. Her husband, Igor, Russian by birth, very much desired a family, partly because this would help him reaffirm his ethnic identity in a foreign country. Since her marriage meant a great deal to her and she felt that Igor was the only man with whom she could ever have children (he was very sympathetic to the women's movement and willing to take more than his share of the responsibility in child care), Sandra tried to become more amenable to the idea of motherhood. But she could not.

"I don't respond to some of the brightest kids," she admits, "if they aren't mirror images of myself, liking the things I am interested in, be that Renaissance music or book binding. So it would not be fair either to a child or to myself." Largely because of this irreconcilable difference, the marriage ended.

Whatever the circumstances of the divorce, and despite the grief that accompanies its early stages, most childless people realize that to romanticize the notion of children as a major supportive force in such times of crisis is quite unrealistic. In truth, especially when young, children can be more of a handicap—socially, emotionally, and monetarily—than a help to their newly single parents. In a sense, then, those who are childless have some decided advantages in dealing with the "alone again" period of life. How they react depends, of course, on a great number of variables: their basic adaptability and sense of self-esteem, the status of finances and career, health, age, the support of their circle of intimates, and whether the childlessness was voluntary or not.

In the main, the childless separated and divorced people to whom I spoke expressed a great sense of relief that they were not carrying the burdens of parenthood. They did not have to face hassling with the former mate over custody and child support. They could develop their careers to the fullest, enrich their lives through new friendships and different life styles, move to another city. They didn't have to think about bills for orthodontia, the quality of day care and school systems, geographic proximity to in-laws, the availability of babysitters. They could become involved sexually as they wished without worrying about how this might affect a son or daughter. Above all, they didn't feel that terrible guilt over having shaken the foundations of a child's life.

Divorced people without children lead lives that in many ways are like those of individuals who have always been single. However, the experience of having been married can be used to great advantage in their present life. Without the responsibilities of parenthood they can maximize that newly single state, whether it be temporary or permanent. Among those who seemed in my interviews to be most content were several women who, having married young before they had had the opportunity to develop professionally, were now making full use of their freedom by embarking on exciting and demanding careers. One, Nora, married at twenty and divorced at thirty, is now a ticket agent for a major airline, spending as much time on treks in Nepal as behind her New York City desk. Though she would like to marry again, Nora is not about to give up her peripatetic ways for any man, or any child.

Carol Holcomb, whose seven-year marriage ended two years ago, is a charming, quietly assured divorcée of thirty. A social worker, she lives in Chapel Hill, North Carolina, where she shares a home with another professional woman. Employed at Duke University in the obstetrics-gynecology unit of the full-time nursery, Carol sees newborn babies daily. "The first time I walked into the nursery," she recalls; "I began to cry. I was just overwhelmed by the miracle of birth. Yet I never really wanted my own children."

In the early years of her marriage Carol was convinced the relationship would last forever. Children were put off ostensibly because of finances, though Carol did recognize the more basic fact that she did not want the responsibility of motherhood and that in her particular marriage she probably would have had to assume the role of "caretaker" to any offspring. Carol supported her husband through his master's degree and doctorate. When the marriage began to fail, he suggested having a child as a means of revitalizing it, but she refused. "We still would have had the problems and there would have been a great deal of added responsibility."

Once the break occurred, Carol focused on her own personal growth. She feels fortunate to have had that opportunity. "I see many women my age who are in the same situation but with children, and whereas the kids provide some things for their mothers that I don't have, it seems to me the advantages do not outweigh the disadvantages.

"I have a friend who is a professional woman, divorced with two children. She is envious of my life style and feels guilty that she is not a fit mother, that maybe she should let the father have them because she's always running off to meetings and having a career. That gives me a lot of affirmation that my choice has been the right one.

"Yes, I may be missing a big part of life by not having a child, but I am also experiencing a lot, too. I have my independence, the chance to be spontaneous. I'm going to graduate school.

"I am a seeker by nature. I know that in my marriage I totally lost myself and gave up a lot, though I didn't realize it at the time. I've struggled the last couple of years to regain me, my identity, my autonomy, and I'm still doing that every day, discovering things about myself. Life for me is to continually grow, to understand relationships better. Intimacy. And career—not necessarily being a do-gooder and achieving something great for the world but using my potential, whatever that is."

Being widowed, as Vernon Matthews articulated so well, brings a special kind of grief that sometimes causes even the voluntarily childless person to wish momentarily that there had been children as a means of bringing back in concrete form the partner who is gone forever. The pain can be especially great when it is combined with guilt at having denied that partner children he or she deeply desired.

Rita, an administrator at a large midwestern hospital, lost her engineer husband Monte three years ago in an automobile accident when she was forty-three and he forty-five. They had been married for fifteen years with no children.

An only child and a southerner by birth, Rita was raised by genteel parents in an elegant home. Today, in her professional environment, she has opted for a distinctly feminine look, her tiny figure enhanced by designer clothes and furs, her nails delicately polished. But behind the polish and perfume resides a woman of political savvy and irreverent wit.

"I was the one who didn't want children," Rita told me. "I'm not a homemaker and I don't like kids until they are seven or eight and you can talk to them like adults.

"But Monte wanted them very badly. And children adored him. Any age, didn't matter. Little tots up through teenagers.

"Monte should have settled down with some nice sweet thing who would have two, three kids and look at him with big eyes and say how brilliant he was. But he didn't want that. When I met him I realized I was going to marry him or be lonely all the rest of my life. If you're the praying kind . . . I used to pray that I would have the strength not to marry him, but I didn't.

"I kept promising him I would think about children. Well, I thought about it. And I never could change my mind. All the time I felt guilty. In the six or seven times in the fifteen years that he ever mentioned it, I would say, 'Yes, dear, you're right.' And I wasn't doing it to kill the argument. It was that he *was* right. At least as society points to everything, he was right. And he was still at it within weeks of his death. Wouldn't I change my mind? I said, 'Monte, I'm forty-three, this is ridiculous. I'm so old now it could kill me!'

"But he would also be very dear. He would say, 'You know, I won't say that I didn't want children, but I would rather have you under any circumstances than all the children in the world,' and then, of course, I would feel worse. I'm sorry about it. I'll always be sorry. But I would have been a terrible mother. And I think Monte would have smothered a child. The way my father did me.

"I was born when my parents were in their mid-forties and had given up on being able to have a child. They really were very fine. I loved them dearly, but when I came on the scene the sun rose and set on me and they proceeded to change their whole lives. They gave up golf. They gave up their friends. I never knew a babysitter—my parents waited up for me until I got married.

"My mother would tell me, 'When you have children, your life changes.' I could *see* it. I didn't have to be told. There was no way I was going to do that. I'm not a basically nice person. I'm very selfish. I want a life of my own.

"I would have been terribly wrong to have a child, because I didn't want one. Often I wondered, suppose I *did* have a child, how would I keep from that child the fact that I didn't want it? Monte kept saying, 'Well, when it's your own you'll love it.' What a hell of a risk to take! Suppose you *don't?*

"There's another aspect, too. Jealousy. I don't know how I would have reacted to sharing Monte with anybody. In a way, in giving me love he was giving love to a child, because he treated me as if I were a total incompetent, and I loved it. He cooked and he cleaned and he said, 'No, dear, you can't do that,' and I said, 'Yes, you're right, I can't do that.' I don't think I loved Monte nearly as much as he loved me. I mean it was a very uneven relationship. I was the recipient of most of it. And it was delightful. I was the center of my parents' universe, and I became the center of his universe."

A few days after our interview I received a letter from Rita. She had been thinking about our talk and there was something she wanted to add "which I find too painful to contemplate for very long. I always found it difficult if not impossible to make a spontaneous gesture of affection—to say, 'I love you,' or to give a quick hug or kiss. To have had children would have required a major change in my life and attitudes, but to show some outward signs of love would have given joy out of all proportion to the effort. I could have given joy and I gave pain, and that is tough to live with forever."

One of the dilemmas that divorced and widowed people with or without children face is whether, in the reality of slightly higher divorce statistics for second marriages than first, they want to marry again. Most do take the chance: 80 percent of divorced people marry again as do 50 percent of those widowed.

An issue of particular concern for the voluntarily childless still of childbearing age is whether to consider having a child or children with a different mate. Some say no, absolutely not. I met more than one man and woman who were sterilized *after* the divorce to prevent just such a possibility. Others say they would rethink the matter if, and only if, the circumstances were right: money, child-care resources, sharing of home responsibilities, and so on. Still another group maintains that with the right mate they would feel much more positively about parenthood than they did the first time. I found by chance two couples—articulate, personable, successful—who, the second time around, had found that right relationship. But time had just about run out on them both.

Lillian, forty-two, and Art, thirty-eight, were married a few years ago after childless first marriages which ended in divorce. Both teach political science at a prestigious academic institution in the western part of the country.

The success of their relationship is deeply gratifying to Lillian and Art. "What was it Samuel Johnson said about a second marriage?" recalls Art. "That it was a triumph of hope over experience. With Lillian and me it has been very successful and we appreciate what we have all the more because we didn't have it with our previous mates."

Art considers the childlessness in his first marriage "to have resulted perhaps from inertia. We never thought much about children, partly because my ex-wife was so absorbed in her profession and might not have made a good mother." Nor is he the kind of man who missed fatherhood greatly. "As a child, I was rather solitary, and I don't have much of a sense of family life." Art's father was killed in World War II; his only sibling, a sister, is several years his senior. "So I certainly didn't grow up in the kind of Kennedy syndrome where family was an obsessive thing."

As a result, Art feels rather ambivalent about full-time exposure to parenthood, commenting half seriously: "If I had children, I'd sort of want them to be defrosted and then put back in the freezer—though I'd hate for that to be used as evidence against me!" At the same time, it seems clear that, with a more compatible and maternally inclined mate than his first wife, he would not have been averse to fatherhood.

Lillian provides just those qualities. Yet she too did not want children in her first marriage. "We were voluntarily childless," she says, "probably because we simply were not happy enough together." At that time, however, she did not clearly perceive this; career had become all-important, masking the marital problems.

With Art, Lillian feels very different about motherhood. She also has seen him interact with her sister's children and describes that as "an enchanting experience." Hoping that she could still conceive and give birth, Lillian recently consulted her gynecologist. "His advice regarding pregnancy was so very discouraging and negative that that door is closed." Now she is considering other alternatives.

"I like to help stray things, and Art has been awfully good about tolerating me in this regard. We are always rushing out and grabbing dogs and cats and bringing them home when they look like they're lost. We're even considering whether there aren't stray human creatures, not necessarily infants, who need help as much as animals." But it's a big step toward which they haven't made concrete moves. Lillian says perhaps what will happen is that she'll make a career switch from teaching to administration. "And, if we don't adopt, we'll get a golden retriever."

A couple with whom Lillian and Art share a similarity of outlook, though the circumstances differ significantly, are Claudia and Carl. Claudia, a forty-three-old classics professor in Philadelphia, was divorced from her lawyer husband after a fifteen-year marriage without children. She is now living with Carl, a similarly divorced and childless bank executive, forty-nine.

"I was pregnant twice during my marriage," Claudia told me. "The first time it was by accident, and I had a miscarriage early on. I went to the doctor and he said there wasn't anything the matter with me, just that if I wanted to have a child I would have to be careful. In those days I was doing graduate work, holding down a job, and was responsible for most of the housework; probably I was working ninety hours a week. So I'd been anything but careful. The second pregnancy was kind of intentional. Even so I paid no attention to the doctor but ran around as much as ever. That time I had a miscarriage at three months, a very messy affair. I was sorry at the time but not really broken up about it, and after that I took care not to get pregnant.

"Later, many years later, I wondered why I had acted in such a lackadaisical fashion. It wasn't really until the summer before last when Carl and I got together that the light went on and it suddenly dawned on me that the reason I had been so careless was problems in the marriage itself.

"I know now that if it had been Carl I was married to back in the 1960s, and if I had gotten pregnant with *his* child, I would have acted very differently. I would have taken care of myself for sure. And, if something had gone wrong, I would have taken all the necessary precautions the next time.

"There's something else, too, and that is I always felt I would not be a very good mother. This has to do with hangups about my own mother. It certainly is a very deep-seated reason why I was careless with those two pregnancies. But probably —I will never know for sure—probably with Carl I would have been able to get over the 'I will be a bad mother' complex. And I very much regret that we met at this stage in life where for all practical purposes we're too old for that kind of thing."

Carl acquiesces. His own first marriage was childless because his wife was unable to conceive, but in his case, too, he believed having a child merely would have glossed over a seriously flawed relationship. Were Claudia to become pregnant now—something they feel would not be quite fair to a child, given their ages—"I have to admit, it would thrill me no end."

Lillian and Art, Claudia and Carl, Vernon Matthews and his wife Connie—there is a common thread in all these relationships. Childless from their first marriages, each found (and perhaps sought out, consciously or not) a similarly childless person as a new mate: someone who would bring the experience of marriage without the baggage. This is only natural. New relationships are difficult enough to form without having other people's children, especially young ones, in the picture. But they aren't so easy to avoid. After all, most people who divorce or are widowed do have children; the childless person seeking a new mate is likely to run into more than one of them.

Caution is hardly cowardice in this highly flammable area. Various studies, including one in 1976 by L. Messinger, indicate that the biggest source of differences in second marriages, and hence a main reason for the high rate of divorce, is the children.[8] (Some would argue this; psychiatrist Martin Goldberg, for one, feels that children are less the cause of such breakups than are personal battles between the new partners, with the children serving as battleground.) Nevertheless, working out acceptable stepfamily behavior is surely not easy, even in the most successful of marriages.

There is also a difference of opinion as to whether childless people make better or worse stepparents. Writing in *Washingtonian Magazine,* Kim Hetherington stated plainly: "People who have never raised children of their own have the most illusions and suffer the most exhaustion and despair."[9] Accustomed to the peace of an adults-only environment, the childless person may be unable to adjust to the frenetic activity and noise that come with children. He or she may also find it difficult to sometimes take second place in the family hierarchy. In her book *Widow*, Lynne Caine wrote poignantly of the loss of her husband and the importance of their two children in her new life: "Any man with whom I want to have a . . . serious relationship must be able to establish a rapport with my son and daughter. . . . To care enough to put himself second at times."[10] David Knox, author of the book *Exploring Marriage and the Family*, adds that the childless person who marries into a family with children has great difficulty in penetrating the "closed system of interdependency" between parent and children.[11] Still, some specialists maintain that the childless person is potentially a better mate for the divorced or widowed parent than is another parent. Why? Because so many problems derive from the so-called "blended" family (a mix of children from both sides). With one adult childless, this potential source of trouble is avoided.

However you look at it, stepparenthood is "in" today. According to *Newsweek*, in 1980 there were 6.5 million stepchildren under eighteen years of age in our nation and 12 million stepparents.[12]

I asked a lot of people I interviewed how they felt about this sensitive matter, and I received a lot of different answers.

Carol Holcomb, the Chapel Hill resident who works at Duke: "Well, I swore I'd never divorce and I did, and so I can't absolutely say 'no' to stepparenting either. To marry or live with someone who already had children would be a hard decision and I'm not close to being there. But, if I cared enough about the man and he was important enough to me, I don't think children would be a big obstacle. Besides, I don't feel someone else's children would be basically my responsibility. There is a difference between having your own and accepting someone else's."

Suzanne, the lady with the weekend cat: "No thanks. I'm grown up now and I didn't enjoy growing up. I don't want to deal with all that again unless . . . well, maybe if the kid was around twenty."

Betty, thirty-nine, a stately, green-eyed tennis instructor at a country club in North Carolina, divorced after an eight-year marriage: "I'm glad I never had kids of my own, not only because the marriage broke up but because I just do not like babies. But I do like older children. I'm going now with a man who has two daughters, twenty-six and sixteen. We get along extremely well. In fact, they have a far better relationship with me than they do with him. He wants to be close to them but just doesn't know how to go about it. Yes, I think it could work out nicely if we were to marry. It would be just perfect —I would have the pleasure of children and none of the problems."

Of the divorced men I spoke with, Jerry was the one who seemed most sure about what compromises he would be willing to make regarding children—his own or those that came along with a hypothetical new mate. He was also particularly frank about his marriage and its breakup.

Thirty-three years old, Jerry is a Los Angeles attorney, divorced and voluntarily childless. He came to the interview wearing blue jeans and a T-shirt that read "Soup 'n Stuff." A trim, slight man, bearded, with a gentle, open face, he looked at the bar setup that my hosts had made available and then said plaintively: "Don't you have any junk food?" We raided the kitchen and began to talk, while outside in the car Jerry's fifteen-year-old dog, a tiny lovable mutt, sat awaiting the ride home.

The story began with an example of pronatalism so blatant as to be almost unbelievable. Jerry's ex-father-in-law, who was very wealthy, had long been obsessed with becoming a grandfather. To achieve this exalted state, he bribed Jerry: he would give him and his wife Liza $100,000 if they would produce a baby—preferably male. "I have clients now," Jerry told me, "like from the Arab countries, who are fabulously wealthy, and they toss around money so much that I have to keep the expression on my face from looking weird. But ten, twelve years ago $100,000 to me was an incredible amount of money, since Liza was an undergraduate and I was in law school, and we barely had enough for food."

Jerry and Liza turned down the offer. "We both had a little laugh and a little cry about how people could want a grandchild so much that they would resort to bribery." It wasn't that Jerry wouldn't have taken the money if he and his wife had really wanted a child, but the timing, in terms of career and economics, was all wrong. So, it turned out, was the marriage itself.

"I've learned that how well a person can make permanent commitments depends on how happy and healthy a home life one had as a child," he told me. "My ex's family was a very unhappy one, and the dynamics were incredibly sick. I didn't realize *how* sick until after the marriage started not to work and that was about five years later.

"My wife did some really heavy-duty numbers on my head emotionally. Like she went away with a guy for a weekend, and then she said she wanted to keep both of us. She and I went into therapy but it was too late for me.

"Looking back, the early years were good ones and worthwhile despite the pain at the end. It still hurts when I think about it, but I'm willing to be vulnerable and try again. I think a lot of people are trained not to be in touch with their feelings, and some men go even one step further, which is to hide their feelings when they have them. And that's very bad for relationships."

How does he feel about children in his future?

"All I know is that right now I don't want more than one child of my own. I was in a relationship after my divorce that, as soon as it assumed the possibility of permanence, she started telling me how much she loved kids and wanted lots of them. I tried to explain to her that it's not for me. This isn't a matter we can compromise on. It's one of those essential things that, if we don't agree on, we don't belong together.

"I said to her that if I had one child I might want more. I might want five more. I'd gotten past the point in life where I made permanent promises and had permanent promises made to me, and I don't state things categorically anymore.

I'm not writing it in stone. But I honestly believe that I might want to have one child, and I honestly believe I wouldn't want more than one."

What about a child or children that come along with the woman? Here Jerry is willing to be more flexible. He told me that in the five years since his divorce he has met perhaps two or three women that he "might be able to live with. When I was first divorced I had all these rules. No this, no that, and then I realized I would be eliminating a lot of women who might be interesting to me. Now I wouldn't reject anybody just because she had children. It's hard enough to find someone with whom you have a serious enough chance of being compatible. And I don't have that need of fathering my own child; if somebody I loved had a child or children, that would be enough."

Jerry finished up some pretzels, took a last swallow of instant coffee, and walked outside to rescue his dog from boredom.

8

The Later Years

•"Suppose I'm old and Tom is dead and I have to go into a nursing home and nobody will care about me and nobody will know if I'm alive from day to day. That's very irrational when I think about it, but it concerns me." These are the words of a married and voluntarily childless female educator, aged forty, from Philadelphia.

•"No, children won't bring me comfort in old age. Money will." A San Francisco college professor, male, age forty-eight, married and voluntarily childless.

•"It's not whether or not you have children that makes the difference in old age; it's how you view the world." Diane Elvenstar, twenty-eight, Los Angeles psychologist, married and voluntarily childless.

•"It's very sad, the whole picture that comes to mind of old people, most of whom have children out there somewhere, and if the children don't care about them they are not only alone; they're hurt, they're disillusioned." Vernon Matthews, fifty-one-year-old Illinois biology teacher, married and voluntarily childless.

•"No, I don't worry about being lonely later. I have a lot of friends. They are my children. They are my peers." Addie Herder, New York artist, divorced and involuntarily childless, fifty-nine.

•"I sometimes wonder, am I going to be sorry in twenty or thirty years, but I know it's wrong to have a child now in hopes that eventually I'll be glad." A thirty-two-year-old female music teacher from Boston, married and voluntarily childless.

•"For a lot of our readers the decision to have a baby is made backwards; instead of considering what they want now, they worry about whether they'll be lonely when they're old." Kate Rand Lloyd, editor of *Working Woman* magazine.

•"What if your kids are in California and you're in Philadelphia? Or if they hate you? Or *you* may end up having to support *them*." A thirty-eight-year-old male banking executive, residing in Bucks County, Pennsylvania, married and voluntarily childless.

•"Very often my mother gives me a piece of jewelry and says, 'I want you to have this,' and I think, why is she passing this on to me when I don't have anybody to pass it on to?" A forty-three-year-old female writer from Los Angeles, married and voluntarily childless.

•"I feel you come into this life alone and you have to go out alone. You can count only on yourself." A real-estate agent from San Francisco, female, married and voluntarily childless.

•"I don't believe in getting older. I believe in getting better." A fifty-two-year-old Manhattan painter, female, married and involuntarily childless.

•"People keep telling me you can't depend on kids to take care of you but I don't believe it. There's at least a fifty-fifty chance." A forty-four-year-old female public-relations consultant from New Orleans, divorced and voluntarily childless.

•"When I read of other people's children and grandchildren, I regret the fact that I haven't got a child. I am bored to death with most things that happen to people my age. For God's sake, I mean what do they *do* with their lives?" A Los Angeles television actress, aged sixty, married and involuntarily childless.

•"You know I can't worry about old age now. I might not live that long." A thirty-nine-year-old married, involuntarily childless housewife in New Jersey. Adds her husband, an appliance-store owner, forty-two: "I think we'll be loved as much as any parent would be."

Loneliness, nursing homes, isolation, widowhood, illness, medical bills, death: a pervasive cycle of fears that invades one's peace of mind—sometimes from young adulthood, frequently not until the middle years. The childless think and talk a lot about old age before they actually get there, as the preceding quotes illustrate. In large measure their concerns are similar to those of parents. But there is one nagging difference: the childless theorize abstractly about whether children and grandchildren would have given meaning to their advancing years, while parents, with the concrete reality of their offspring before them, ask if that younger generation will really come through for them in terms of affection, understanding, and, when they need it, concrete help. (Among the latter, writer Erma Bombeck approached the issue with her customary wit: "I worry . . . that one of my children will marry an Eskimo who will set me adrift on an iceberg when I can no longer feed myself.")[1]

Though some people are less obsessed than others with old age, professionals working with young couples who are still in the decision-making process regarding parenthood report that, even if no other reasons for considering children are cited, the fear of an isolated, lonely old age is almost always brought up. But what about the reality—thirty or forty or fifty years later?

The people I interviewed for this book who had reached that stage encompassed an age range of from sixty-five to ninety and included widows and widowers as well as couples still together; some were voluntarily childless and others involuntarily so. The former were far less numerous since voluntary childlessness, as a defined life style, did not exist until the 1960s, and birth control was hardly the household word it is today. But there were exceptions: people with surprisingly modern views about career and overpopulation and priorities in life who attempted consciously to avoid parenthood—and did so. One such individual is Henry Beetle Hough, a resident of Martha's Vineyard, Massachusetts.

Hough was eighty-three years old when I spoke with him. He had been widowed in 1965 after a forty-five-year marriage, during which entire time he and his wife Betty were editors and publishers of a weekly newspaper, the *Vineyard Gazette* (the paper was a wedding gift, bought for them by

Hough's father). He also found the time to write some twenty books, ranging in subject from Thoreau to whaling, so his name is known in a quiet sort of way to generations of readers.

We talked at Hough's home on a wet, chilly day of fall when his beloved island, thirty miles by sea from the mainland, was empty of the tourists who packed it in warmer weather. A gentle, balding man with smooth skin and an understated, matter-of-fact New England manner (though he admits to being "sentimental as hell"), Hough looks younger than his years.

Henry and Betty Hough came to the realization after their marriage in 1920 that they did not really want children. The responsibility of a weekly newspaper was simply too great to combine with a family, and money was tight. Additionally, both were aware of the dangers of overpopulation and were strongly in favor of birth control. The decision was made easier because neither was truly child-oriented. "I never saw a beautiful baby," Hough admitted to me.

"I don't remember making any major decision about children or facing up to any great fact of life," he continued. "We just drifted into childlessness as the most practical, most congenial way. And I don't think there were any moments of regret through the years for either of us. I don't think I ever missed having children. I never thought I would make a good father, and as time has gone on the family as I knew it has just disappeared. I pity someone who tries to have children nowadays. Family has no influence at all.

"Also, I like to escape unnecessary responsibility. I think of myself as a responsible person, but I want to limit my obligations."

Nonparenthood proved to be a wise choice for Henry and Betty Hough. The marriage was rich in shared experiences, contacts, causes. In his autobiographical book *Mostly on Martha's Vineyard,* Hough wrote: "We were devoted to the end. We had common interests. I don't think we ever fought about important things."[2] Above all, the bond was the *Gazette,* which under their management became a prime example of a local newspaper committed to the news and causes of the Vineyard.

Hough told me he is close to the young people in his family, especially those from around fifteen up. He does not enjoy the companionship of the middle-aged nearly so much.

Middle age in general was not to Hough's liking. "I think it is the most undesirable time and that it's a good thing you get out of it. I fortunately am out of it."

Why that attitude? "Because it is an age of disappointment. It's the age of being fed up, dissatisfied. You know, some philosopher said, 'The future is pregnant with an infinity of present possibilities.' It's so much richer than the future itself. By the time you're in middle age, you realize that the infinity of present possibilities has dwindled."

Old age is a much more agreeable stage for Hough. "I enjoy life now. This is a very, very happy time. I don't think anyone old is in perfect health, you know. I have troubles, but I get along all right. Somebody asked me last night what I'd say if I was given the choice of being any age. I said, 'The age I am now.' I'm so happy to have reached it. I'm very happy to be here."

Henry Hough told me he is "partly retired" from the *Gazette* and works at home on editorials and obituaries. However, he added: "I'm over there three or four times a day."

"I think, to wind up the story," he said, as I prepared to leave, "I should tell you that I'm going to remarry, probably next week. It just comes about; it's principally to perpetuate a good friendship." There was a hint of a twinkle in his eye as he added: "And at our age there isn't any question of having children."

Hough proceeded up the creaky staircase while I waited for the taxi that would return me to the ferry. Within moments I heard his typewriter clattering furiously.

As I think of Hough, I am reminded of a phrase in his autobiography regarding the decision made a half century ago to be childless: "We could see that . . . there were choices in the paths to fulfillment in life."[3]

Another individual who made the choice of nonparenthood

is veteran actor Sam Jaffe, known for a host of theatrical and cinematic performances (among the latter are *Asphalt Jungle, Gunga Din* and *Lost Horizon*) and also for his sympathetic representation of Dr. Zorba in TV's *Ben Casey.* Jaffe's second wife, actress Bettye Ackerman, was nurse to physician Casey in that series; southern-born, she married Jaffe twenty-three years ago. He had been widowed after a first marriage which was also childless.

Sam Jaffe is a man of quiet dignity, slim and erect with a halo and beard of reddish white hair. "It isn't a denial of children that I believe in," explained the actor. "It's rather that when you have children it is a complete undertaking. You can't let them grow up in the streets. You have to take care of them, guide them. But being a parent is a responsibility the creative man can't give sufficient attention to because his mind is a single-track one. Especially if you are married to someone who also has a career—like my wife who is gifted in both the theater and as a painter—motherhood might prevent her from fully realizing those ambitions.

"For the same reason we don't have animals. To put them in a kennel when we go away would be unfair. It's a great responsibility and I love animals."

Jaffe is very sensitive to the problems children have in coping with famous parents, especially those children raised in the glamour and instability of Hollywood. His feelings are colored by memories of his own childhood. When his father deserted the family, Sam, then an infant, was left in the care of an aunt and uncle. "I only got to know my mother years later. But by then my aunt was my mother."

Jaffe gives much thought to the concept of selfishness and how to avoid it while still fulfilling oneself. "I would say that selfishness is not learning to express yourself in a way that will help others." Reciting in Hebrew from the Talmud, Jaffe adds: " 'If I am not for myself, who will be? And if I am only for myself, what am I?' "

Sam Jaffe does not regret not having children, though Bettye admits to having much wanted a son when they first married. ("I felt someone as precious as Sam should go on forever," she told me.) Today the Jaffes have many friends who are parents. "We cash in just being on the fringes of the young people's lives," according to Sam. He and Bettye are very close as a couple, being free to travel together when one or the other is on assignment.

"Anyway," says Jaffe, smiling, "you have to remember that our marriage was a kind of December-June one, and I didn't want any child of mine calling me grandfather!"

Both Sam Jaffe and Henry Beetle Hough chose to be childless and do not regret that long-ago decision. But what about those who very much desired children and could not have them? How long does the pain last and does old age have any compensations?

Louise and Ellie are sisters in their seventies, widowed and involuntarily childless, who live together in Louise's home in an attractive suburb of Baltimore. Each is quick to admit that not having children constituted a serious deprivation. When I first spoke with Louise by telephone, she volunteered this statement: "I always wanted kids, I always regretted not having them, and I still do." Married while in her forties to a physician ten years her senior, she did not conceive and sought help at a fertility clinic. The problem, she learned with surprise, was less her own age than her husband's low sperm motility. Artificial insemination was unsuccessful. "After a point," says Louise, "I just reconciled myself to the situation and decided that probably it was a good thing that we were childless. My husband, though very bright, was an erratic and unstable man who demanded a great deal of my attention. Also, given our ages, by the time a child would be grown up we'd have been so old there would have been little companionship with him or her."

Louise poured all her love of children into those she worked with as a schoolteacher. "I took the attitude that I was a surrogate mother and I gave the children as much love as I could." After the death of her husband and thirty-five years as a teacher she retired, feeling that it was time for something new. "I wanted to study music. I bought a clarinet and began

to take lessons. It was really a very difficult undertaking."
Eventually Louise joined an amateur orchestra. She also became active in charitable organizations. "Since I can afford it,
I am swamped with requests for money. I do give a lot. Financially I am a great deal better off than I would have been if
I had had to worry about supporting children through college
and all that. So there are things to balance. That's always true
in life.

"And I have my sister. We are very fortunate to have each
other. We get along very well together."

Ellie was married to a divorced man whose two children
lived with their mother. Like Louise, Ellie was unable to conceive, though in her case no particular cause was determined.
She too still regrets her childlessness, yet developed similarly
to Louise: she directed her working life to children as a designer of infant wear. Both say they considered adoption but
decided against it.

The two sisters began to live together after the death of
Ellie's husband. Their companionship takes many forms,
music being very meaningful to both. Ellie is a pianist and
serves as Louise's accompanist. They also look after each
other; Ellie is more frail and in need of physical help.

I asked when in their lives they had most felt the lack of
their own children. Both responded: "In the early years."
Ellie said, "I've forgotten about it. What can you do? You
have to accept it."

Within a few months of our meeting, Louise and Ellie were
planning to sell the house and move into a retirement community which would offer them lifetime care. They had taken a
two-bedroom apartment with kitchen where they will prepare
breakfast and lunch; dinner will be eaten in the main dining
room with the other members of the community.

Louise: "This is the way we are solving what to do when we
become seriously ill. When I read about this place I thought,
this is it. This is the solution for us. Because if I should die first
I don't know how Ellie could manage. Or, if she gets sick, I
would find it very difficult, too. You pay a fairly large amount
down and a certain sum every month, but it's lifetime care.

"People I know pretty well are going to this same place. These are people I like and admire. They look like me, they're not all bent and decrepit, though some use canes and walkers. They're intelligent and alert. They're well dressed."

What about contact with young people? Louise: "We have younger cousins and a nephew—it's a nice relationship. We'll invite them to see us. Yes, we'll probably miss having children in the neighborhood but, on the other hand, children are hard on you when they make a lot of noise."

I asked the sisters how they respond to today's voluntary childlessness. Ellie said: "I think it's a horrible thing." Louise feels that the people who are electing to be nonparents are the educated, financially advantaged segment of the population, who should be producing children.

In their own lives the two have dealt as positively as they could with a situation they did not choose. They also have made the most of something many others do not have: each other.

Old age is a stage of life which human beings have regarded throughout history with contradictory attitudes: reverence and revulsion, respect and ridicule—the "golden years" vs. a time of decay. Especially in the United States, advancing age until recently was considered so distasteful a repudiation of our self-image as a young, brawny nation that it became almost a nonsubject.

Among the few classic works to have appeared on this period of life is the book *The Coming of Age* by Simone de Beauvoir, first published in France in 1970. Within a vast historical framework, de Beauvoir deals with feelings of and toward the elderly. Old age, she contends, fills people with more aversion than death itself. It is a time constrained by "a limited future and a frozen past." Specifically, she refers to the American tendency to strike the word "death" from the vocabulary and to treat great age as a "shameful secret."[4]

Finally, both these neglected, and intertwined, aspects of human existence are receiving belated attention in our country—and hardly too soon. At present, adults aged sixty-five and over make up an estimated twenty-five million people or 11 percent of our total population, and it is projected by most demographers that that number will probably reach 16 percent—and perhaps several percentage points higher—by the year 2030. (The idea of old age beginning at sixty-five is, incidentally, arbitrary, especially as the life span increases; its use became official with the establishment of the Social Security program back in 1935.)

Currently, life expectancy is approaching eighty for women and seventy for men. Women sixty-five and older are the fastest-growing segment of the U.S. population. There are 150 for every 100 men of that age, and of the elderly in nursing homes, over 70 percent are female. Because of this disparity in longevity, older divorced or widowed men find it much easier to remarry than do women.

In recognition of the rapidly multiplying numbers of older people whose usefulness to society and opportunities for personal fulfillment were not being maximized, Congress in 1974 passed the National Research on Aging Act which, in turn, created the National Institute on Aging (NIA). With this formal recognition of a long-ignored field, the study of gerontology swiftly emerged as a leading addition to the social sciences. The issues it must address are enormous in scope: from a better understanding of the physiological changes within the aging body to the ways—positive and negative—that retirement can affect people, from a better community support system for the elderly to a recognition of senior citizens as an influential political force. Among other questions of importance are: How much do children ease the burden and enhance the lives of their parents in old age, and, in lieu of children, what can the childless expect of their later years?

There is little question that support networks of some kind are essential to the aged, and research to date tends to support the belief that there is a direct relationship between the vitality of family and friendship networks and the physical and mental health of senior citizens. It also seems clear that "at this time, the major social resource of the elderly in the U.S. and other countries is their adult children" (Ethel Shanas, professor of sociology at the University of Illinois). Particularly during the stressful experience which most older married women face of widowhood, adult children can be of great help. According to an NIA report published in 1979, research has shown that, although older women socialize with friends, "children are the most important [resource] for personal exchange and for access to other services." "Contrary to the myth of older women being abandoned by their children," claims the report, "many older women's emotional relationships to their children have been found to be highly significant and lasting."[5]

There is a feeling among scientists and the general public that the childless tend to be more socially isolated, though actual studies in this area are still sparse. Results of a poll by Louis Harris and Associates in 1974 indicate that more elderly nonparents live alone than do parents. Of those polled more than 83 percent of the childless widowed, separated, and divorced lived alone as compared with 65 percent of elderly parents who were no longer married. This difference reflected the fact that roughly 22 percent of the previously married parents lived with a child. The childless do not seem to make up for the lack of children by living with other persons; shared living with relatives apart from children was, in fact, only slightly higher among the childless than among parents, and residing with nonrelatives was rare in both groups.[6]

One must take into consideration, when analyzing data of this kind, that living alone can be by choice. In fact, the ability to remain independent is frequently cited as being highly valued by older adults. Nonetheless, according to an article in *Intercom* by Christine A. Bachrach,[7] who is currently a statistician at the National Center for Health Statistics, the elderly childless in the Harris poll "did tend to express greater feelings of loneliness and lower levels of satisfaction with their lives than persons who had children." These differences, though small, she writes, appear to be largely attributable to lower levels of social contact. The data suggest, writes Bachrach, "that childlessness may be accompanied by a higher than average risk of social isolation in old age, when isolation is defined in terms of the chances of living alone and in terms of the presence of others in one's day-to-day life." Particularly when the older person suffers a decline in health, mobility, or economic resources, she continues, the need to depend on others tends to increase. Children are a central source of support for parents at such times. Do the childless elderly have "alternate means of support . . . or do they simply make do without the help they need? To date, these questions have not been adequately explored."

Bachrach does caution that "the importance of having grown children as a safeguard against isolation in old age may well decline in the future" as geographic mobility and the participation of younger women in the work force make contact between the two generations more difficult. "Community supports designed to supplement or replace the family in providing care to needy elderly may thus become increasingly important in the future."

Other investigators point out that people have a tendency to confuse the mere fact of an elderly parent/adult child relationship with its quality. It was reported in a publication of the Population Reference Bureau, "The Elderly in America," that researcher Robert B. Brown had reached such a conclusion. Of his sample of elderly people, although 68 percent saw a child at least once a week, only 17 percent reported close affectional ties; many said they felt more like guests in their children's homes than like integrated family members.[8] This finding, however, is questioned by a number of other investigators, whose studies of a more representative population conclude that the elderly parent/adult child relationship is characteristically a much more positive one.

Working in a related area, Beth B. Hess, a sociologist at New Jersey's County College of Morris, and Joan M. Waring of the Russell Sage Foundation pointed out in 1977 that reliance on children hinders some parents from developing or maintaining friendships and interests outside the family.[9] Bachrach told me that her data showed similar findings: 55 percent of the parents living with a child had seen friends and neighbors during the past day or two, as compared with 69 percent of the parents not living with a child. However, she does not agree with the suggestion of Hess and Waring that nonfamily networks may actually be more reliable emotional resources than adult children. "They may be more rewarding but I would not say that they are more reliable," says Bachrach, "simply because you have to stay healthy to enjoy them. Many studies, including mine, show that non-kin contact declines as health deteriorates."

Less subject to disagreement is the thought also expressed by Hess and Waring that the childless aged who are profoundly affected by the absence of children are those "whose social resources were never very ample." When nonparents do not develop networks of support, write the two researchers, their old age is likely to be as socially isolated and bitter as that of the all too typical parents whose children fail to meet expectations.[10]

There are various kinds of support networks that older people without children can take advantage of. Henry Beetle Hough, the editor on Martha's Vineyard, maintains a close tie to the town where he has lived for over half a century and where the year-round residents look out for each other. He remains active as a writer. He has one dog of his own and another that is convinced it belongs to him. He has many friends and, after being widowed for some years, remarried. Actor Sam Jaffe has a devoted wife and a large circle of friends of all ages, largely deriving from his active professional life. The two sisters I visited, Louise and Ellie, depend on each other and a few relatives; they expect that the retirement community to which they are moving will provide new ties with old friends and, hopefully, new friends as well.

Some childless couples are fortunate to reach and spend their old age together. One such couple is Emma, a retired schoolteacher, and George, formerly the owner of an auto body shop, now also retired. Since George was recovering from a leg injury, I spoke with Emma alone. Seventy-three years old and a native of North Carolina, she was as comfortable to be with as her furniture was to sit on—the kind of person one would expect to be a grandmother many times over.

Emma did not marry until she was forty-four years old. Her life was dedicated to teaching first-grade students, which she did for a total of thirty-five years. "My teaching was a hobby as well as a job," she told me in a deep southern drawl, "because I liked it so much. I never had a first grade that I didn't enjoy." Not meeting anyone in her youth that she wanted to marry, she fulfilled her personal life in other ways, like caring for her brother until he married (both their parents had died young) and then building her own home. "I was building that house to be an old maid schoolteacher in!" she recalls, laughing gleefully. Summers she would go off on vacation with another teacher, mostly to paint in New Hampshire. "One summer we painted boats on the water and everything was blue. Went up to the mountains another summer and everything was green. I've gone up there since on my own to paint and I found the happy medium between blue and green."

When George came into Emma's life, he was a childless widower. "I was getting older," she says, "and he just sort of struck my fancy." Already she had been teaching long enough to have her first "grandchild" (a student whose mother she had also taught) presented to her by the principal. "That's when I decided I better get married and move on to another school!"

Emma's new husband came from a family of thirteen. Quickly she became part of their lives, sharing in the joy of his parents' fiftieth wedding anniversary. "When I married George, I got a whole new family. I'm proud of it. It's made my life complete. I would have liked to have children because George didn't have any by his first wife, and I knew he would have loved to be a father. But I had to have a hysterectomy a year after we were married. I was disappointed not to have children. I always wanted them. Still, I sure enjoyed teaching everybody else's."

In their retirement Emma and George allow each other a

lot of freedom. "I felt," says Emma, "that both of us should be allowed to have and do what we want so long as it didn't hurt the other. That's wound up by us going together on most things."

Keeping busy and holding on to her strong sense of humor are Emma's keys, she says, for her buoyancy and upbeat attitude. "Above all, keep your sense of humor. We're here such a short time." She even laughs when all her nieces and nephews go around her house pointing out which things they want when she dies. She mimics: " 'Aunt Emma, I want this! Aunt Emma, I want that!' But I enjoy 'em, every one."

Emma describes the beginning of her retired life. "One day George says to me, 'Emma, I'm going to retire this year.' I say, 'What are you going to do with yourself?' He says, 'Pack my bags and go somewhere.' I said, 'All right, I'll retire and pack my suitcase, too.' We bought us a trailer and put it behind our car and we went to Florida. Then we bought a motor home and we still go places in it. We go to the lake for a weekend and we cook in it. We live in it. We've a bed apiece in it."

Retirement homes probably will be built in their area. "But I say, 'George, we're staying right here in this house and looking after each other. This is something we've worked for all our lives. Of course, in some cases you get too sick, but we're going to try as long as we can."

I had met Emma through her neighbor who was a friend of mine. On our departure, Emma handed my friend two jars of home-grown beans, then, after we were on our way, came running after us, shouting: "You better take some grape jelly, too. How come it took you so long to eat up the last batch? Don't be so stingy next time!"

Mollie Desiderio, the oldest person I interviewed for this book, was widowed almost thirty years ago. She lives with a middle-aged niece and spends her weekdays at a retirement center.

Mollie is a tiny spry lady who, when I saw her the day after her ninetieth birthday, was dressed in a tailored skirt and blouse, her white hair tied in a neat bun and her large blue-green eyes reflecting the colors of her cardigan sweater. Her manner was gracious, of an old-world formality.

Russian-Jewish by birth, Mollie came to the United States in 1923. Here she met and married an Italian Catholic widower who worked in the same tailoring shop where she was employed. Mollie never conceived, "not because I did not like children but because I liked them too much." She had been responsible since her teen years in Russia for the care of other people's children—her sister's, her brother's, and, later, her husband's from his first marriage. "The economic conditions were bad when I came here and in 1929, 1930 the Great Depression started. Was that a time for me to have a child?" Mollie both feared that she would become pregnant and grieved that she did not. Hers was a voluntary but imposed childlessness. Fortunately, she has never considered herself "childless" since the young relatives for whom she cared from their earliest years were devoted to her as she was to them. Of the niece with whom she lives, Mollie says: "She is my child, and so is her sister."

Mollie Desiderio retired twenty-five years ago. She still arises at six o'clock each morning as she did while employed. Every weekday she takes two buses from her suburban home to downtown Philadelphia's Charles Weinstein Geriatric Center. Neither sleet nor heat nor crowds deter her from this schedule. Life at the center, which Mollie first joined with her husband, provides a focus to her life. Open to retired people aged sixty-two and over, it has recreational and educational facilities of every variety—classes in writing, arts and crafts and health, theatrical performances, a chorus, movies, political discussions, day trips. Mollie is active not only as a participant but as a member of various committees. She leaves there at four o'clock daily in order to prepare dinner for her niece and herself.

It is tempting to romanticize the youthfulness of this seemingly indomitable little lady. But Mollie does not allow that: "I am my age in every way." Still, she says that she keeps on growing and learning. She is trying to accept others and herself. "You have to give people the chance to grow up. I miss a lot of what goes on around me, even now. I need the chance, too. I learn from yesterday."

I asked Mollie whether she feels her old age would have been happier had she had her own children.

"No, that doesn't make sense to me. First of all, that never did work perfectly. It is not a pleasant thing to need your children. Youth always wants not to be bound. And now conditions are changed. Suppose I would have children, they go to school, and after that they start to work. Maybe they want to change jobs or the job takes them somewhere else and they move away. Would I be guaranteed that they stay with me? Would I like it that they stay with me? I wouldn't like it.

"The children of my relatives are just as dear to me as my own. Children are children. And, even if I had been alone, I don't think I would have chosen to have a child to better my condition.

"It's true, I cared about my parents a lot. I was devoted until the last days of their lives. But that does not mean it would have worked out the same if I had had my own. People are different. We are all different."

Being childless in old age carries with it what many consider to be a great deprivation: missing out on grandparenthood. Simone de Beauvoir writes: "The warmest and happiest feelings that old people experience are those that have to do with their grandchildren."[11] Free of the responsibilities but rich in the knowledge that they have gained as parents, older people can love their grandchildren in a generous, accepting manner, in turn receiving a great deal of affection.

A close relationship between young and old need not, however, be limited to grandparents and grandchildren. Again de Beauvoir: "The friendship of the young is very valuable to old people, quite apart from any family tie: it gives them the feeling that these times in which they are living are still their times; it revives their own youth; it carries them along the infinity of the future and it is the best defense against the gloom that threatens old age. Unfortunately," she continues, "relations of this sort are rare, for the young and the old belong to two worlds between which there is little communication."[12]

There are, however, people working today in both their professional and personal lives to bring together these two worlds. I met one of them in Laura Huxley, the widow of the British-born literary giant Aldous Huxley.

In 1978, with the support of such renowned individuals as anthropologist Ashley Montagu and family therapist Virginia Satir, she founded in Los Angeles Our Ultimate Investment, a nonprofit organization devoted to creating an environment where the human potential can be nurtured, especially during the crucial first years of life.[13]

"It is," says Mrs. Huxley, "at the two extremes of life that loneliness is most acutely felt—for in the years in between, action and involvement absorb our time and energy."

Her philosophy is expressed concretely in several Project Caressing centers where, in serene pastel-colored rooms furnished only with rocking chairs and pillows, working mothers and fathers leave their babies in the care of volunteers over age sixty who spend an hour or more each day caressing and rocking the babies. "In this room the new and the old loneliness meet and dissolve," says Huxley.

What makes her project particularly interesting is that Laura Huxley, sixty-six years of age and childless, has filled her own life in a similar fashion. Married to Huxley from 1956 (he had been widowed and was a father) until his death in 1963, she was a professional musician and writer as well as helpmate to her husband in his literary and scientific efforts. "We didn't have children," she told me, "because first of all it probably would have been too late for me and secondly our lives were so full."

But some years after Aldous Huxley's death all that changed. Laura Huxley came to know an eight-month-old baby, the daughter of a single mother. The visits became more and more frequent, and eventually she became the child's legal guardian.

"That child has become the center of my life, and I am going through all the events a single mother or, rather, a single grandmother, goes through," Huxley told me. "I realize now that I am barely old enough to do this because parenthood is the most difficult of the things I've done in my life. Physiologically, of course, one has to be young to produce a child, but psychologically and emotionally, one is more prepared later on to be with a child and to give up many things without regret.

"I am planning for my child's life; I am building around her an extended family which all single mothers should do, for a child has to have a relationship with many loving people."

Mrs. Huxley believes that "only an extraordinarily intelligent and energetic career woman who has a dependable support system to back her up can have a demanding professional life and be a good mother as well. In general it is asking too much because career and motherhood are both full-time undertakings."

Laura Huxley laughingly refers to herself as "the oldest single grandmother in America. I don't write now. I barely take care of emergencies and the mail. My life has been restricted, but in my case it is a golden age."

Also in a "golden age," surrounded by "grandchildren" are Floyd and Norma Souders of Cheney, Kansas, aged seventy-six and seventy-two, respectively. I did not meet the Souderses personally but corresponded with Norma.

They have been married for half a century. For the first ten years Norma was a housewife. "I presumed I would have children," she wrote me, "but none came." Had she and Floyd become parents, she feels sure she would not have become an active career woman, at least until the children were grown. But, without a family, she and Floyd formed a family outside, one whose numbers they can't even begin to count.

Probably the most dramatic of their efforts was the creation some twenty years ago of the Souders Historical Farm Museum, located on a piece of family land in Cheney. Complete with every kind of farm implement and machinery used in the area, the museum also has replicas of an old-time schoolroom, chapel, washhouse, law office, and post office. The Souderses have guided thousands of visitors—many of them schoolchildren—through the exhibits, and recently they presented the museum plus ten acres of the land on which it is situated to the Kansas State Historical Society.

The two were well equipped to bring this project to fruition. Floyd had been a working farmer since 1924, earning many awards for his conservation projects. Both knew children well. Norma, having been a public and Sunday school teacher, wrote me, "I taught nearly three hundred little ones, and I loved them as my own." Floyd also has been superintendent of schools and served on the state board of education and the governor's conference on education.

As if life weren't busy enough, for thirty years the Souderses were publishers and editors of a newspaper, the *Cheney Sentinel,* and wrote a book about Friends University, from which Floyd graduated and which awarded him an honorary doctorate. Norma devoted her spare time to starting a library for the town of Cheney, an effort with which she was connected for thirty years.

Almost every facet of their lives either directly or indirectly reaches out to young people. "Our work with children . . . has replaced children of our own," wrote Norma Souders in her letter.

Reading her comments reminded me of one of the most charming fictional examples of surrogate parenthood: the eccentric but beloved English schoolmaster in *Goodbye, Mr. Chips* by James Hilton. Chips, alone after the death of his lovely young wife and newly born first child, devotes his long life to instilling in his pupils the principles of Latin, Greek, and life. On his deathbed, Chips, an octogenarian, overhears some of his younger colleagues whispering. "Pity," says one. "Pity he never had any children." Chips pulls himself back to consciousness:

"I thought I heard you—one of you—saying it was a pity—umph —a pity I never had—any children . . . eh? . . . But I have, you know . . . I have. . . ."

The others smiled without answering, and after a pause Chips began a faint and palpitating chuckle.

"Yes—umph—I have," he added, with quavering merriment. "Thousands of 'em . . . thousands of 'em . . . and all boys."[14]

Old age. Childlessness. Both words conjure up a sense of isolation. There is no question that old age can be—perhaps, more often than not, is—the most difficult of life's stages, particularly if health, monetary resources, and human contacts are lacking. And childlessness, whether or not it is by choice, does mean knowing that one will die without having passed on one's essence in that direct, generational fashion that gives a special meaning to life. To argue this seems foolish. To deny that if one had had children they and their children might— which is not to say "would"—have brightened and lightened old age is equally unrealistic.

However, the mere fact that one is old and, at the same time, childless, does not automatically add up to a solitary, miserable existence any more than being old *with* children means a happy life in the glow of intergenerational love. The childless people I met revealed that clearly. They were, without exception and in differing circumstances, demonstrating a strong ability to cull richness and meaning out of the later years. How were they doing it?

One answer is work, hobbies, interests—time spent learning and growing. Once again Simone de Beauvoir says it well: "The greatest good fortune, even greater than health, for the old person is to have his world still inhabited by projects; then, busy and useful, he escapes from boredom and decay."[15] Commitment to useful activity means escape of another kind: from the loneliness that is a part of every life whether we are parents or not, married or not, living alone or with others, young or old. "Even when I'm alone I'm not lonely," Sari Dienes, the eighty-two-year-old childless artist said to me. People like her and like editor-writer Hough are fortunate in that they need not retire at a given age but can continue with their life's work. Others, like the widow Louise who retired from teaching, take up a demanding new interest—in her case, the clarinet. Planning ahead is something that gives vitality to life, whether fifty years lie ahead or two.

There is a more painful kind of planning ahead that the elderly must think about: giving away their worldly possessions. Not having children and grandchildren to leave these to, nonparents—if they value themselves and their possessions of a lifetime—look to others in the family, to friends, causes. One of the most treasured items I have is a small vase given me by a childless widower of eighty whose wife had recently died. They had been a devoted couple. He chose with care a number of remembrances from among her personal possessions and gave one to each of her friends, wanting to see their pleasure during his own lifetime.

Childless people whose old age is rich in social contact do not just reach age sixty-five and call into instant being a human support system. They develop it gradually, particularly during their middle years, through careful nurturing of their circle of friends and family; by the time they reach old age this network is an established part of their lives. (Here they often have the advantage over parents, who, tending to depend heavily on their children, may not develop such resources.) Emma, the self-styled "old maid schoolteacher" from North Carolina, has doubtless been dispensing grape jelly, green beans, and homespun advice for many years, and the recipients of it all keep coming back for more. Obviously such networks are most naturally created when one remains in the same geographic area—as each of the people I interviewed has been able to do.

Another trait of the individuals I met was adaptability. They had suffered tragedies and setbacks and disappointments like everybody else; they had made mistakes. But, instead of focusing on what might or should have been, they made the most of what was. The widower remarried (and, having no children, did not have to account for his choice). The sisters, realizing that they could no longer go on living independently in a large home, took advantage of the savings they had been able to accrue and moved to a senior community setting. The widow took on a "grandchild" and opened a center where old and young loneliness "meet and dissolve."

Youth and age together. Perhaps that was the most interesting revelation: that being childless need not mean being removed from children. This was, in fact, a key to the vitality of the people I met. Though peer support was vital to their well-being, they were reaching out as well to the generations that came after them—and this had little to do with whether they were voluntarily or involuntarily childless. For some, like Mollie Desiderio, who lives with a niece, this took a very direct one-to-one form; for others, like Floyd and Norma Souders, who began a museum, the relationship was with dozens, hundreds of young people. This is not to say all old people should be around two-year-old babies. Henry Hough, for one, did not find babies the slightest bit appealing. But it does mean that to isolate old from young intentionally is detrimental to both. Youth learns from age, age from youth. Our society is not structured with that in mind, and especially for the childless this constitutes a danger, requiring imagination and courage to overcome.

There is a tendency, when speaking of aging in America, to consider this as a fixed state. In truth, the life of the elderly has been changing greatly in our country and will continue to change as our society undergoes vast permutations. Hence, the middle-aged of today will, when they become old, lead a far different life from the current over-sixty-five population, and today's youth will become aged in a world of which we can barely see the outlines.

In some ways the lot of the elderly, both parents and nonparents, is improving significantly.[16] Many new living arrangements are possible, such as retirement communities, mobile-home parks, and congregate housing, where older people who are not fully self-sufficient help each other. Research has been done (by Irving Rosow)[17] which shows some evidence of "compensatory neighboring" among older people with few child contacts who live in apartment complexes with a high density of older people. Daytime senior recreational and service centers are abundant. Employment agencies geared entirely to the elderly now exist, and careful attention is being given to the ideas of eliminating mandatory retirement and making possible early, voluntary retirement. More and more senior adults are taking tuition-free college courses. There is a growing recognition that the mature adult needs and thrives in a life full of activity, that sexual pleasure does not cease in mid-life, that senility results as much from disuse of the mind and body as from the physiological aging process.

In other ways the elderly have many and serious problems to face, among these being the decreasing strength of the family unit. Given such factors as geographic mobility, the growing numbers of women in the work force, severe demands on family income, and high divorce statistics, the elderly are often left on the fringes of the family. Of them, 5 percent live in nursing homes, a proportion which at first glance seems small but which in actual numbers is not and which some authorities feel will mushroom. (Bruce Vladeck in his book *Unloving Care,* published in 1980, estimates that at present rates one of every five who live past sixty-five will spend time in a nursing home—perhaps unnecessarily.)[18]

These developments have an important implication: that elderly parents and nonparents may increasingly find themselves in similar situations and adopting similar life styles, with their support system moving away from the family into the larger community. Furthermore, if low fertility rates continue as they are expected to do, it may well be that a half century from now there will be as great a percentage of childless elderly people as there are today—or greater. (Some 22 percent of women now in their seventies never gave birth to a child as a result of the Great Depression and World War II. This constitutes the lowest fertility of any cohort of women in U.S. history.[19] Gerontologists realize that careful studies of this group might tell us much about childlessness in old age, but as yet these have not been carried out in depth.)

There is an urgent need for more research, followed by action, on the elderly in America, among whom the childless constitute a minority of growing importance.

NOTES

1: Marriage Without Children: Then, Now, and Tomorrow

1. Elizabeth M. Whelan. *A Baby? . . . Maybe* (New York: Bobbs Merrill, 1975).
2. Liz Smith, *The Mother Book* (Garden City, N.Y.: Doubleday, 1978).
3. Zero Population Growth, "ZPG Leaflets by Mormons, for Mormons," *ZPG Reporter,* August 1979.
4. Helene Deutsch, *The Psychology of Women* (New York, Grune, 1944–45).
5. Paul C. Glick, "Some Recent Changes in American Families," *Current Population Reports,* U.S. Department of Commerce, Special Studies Series P-23, No. 52, 1975.
6. Ibid.
7. Ibid.
8. Lynda Lytle Holmstrom, *The Two-Career Family* (Cambridge, Mass.: Schenkman, 1973).
9. *World Book Encyclopedia,* Volume 8 (Chicago: Childcraft International, 1979).
10. Leta S. Hollingworth, "Social Devices for Impelling Women to Bear and Rear Children," *American Journal of Sociology,* July 1916.
11. Jean Ayling, *The Retreat from Parenthood* (London: K. Paul, Trench, Trubner, 1916).
12. Simone de Beauvoir, *The Second Sex* (New York: Knopf, 1953).
13. Betty Friedan, *The Feminine Mystique* (New York: Norton, 1963).
14. Gael Greene, "Speaking Out: A Vote Against Motherhood," *Saturday Evening Post,* January 26, 1963.
15. Betty Rollin, "Motherhood: Need or Myth?" *Look,* September 22, 1970.

16. Helen Gurley Brown, *Sex and the Single Girl* (New York: Bernard Geis, 1962).
17. Anna and Arnold Silverman, *The Case Against Having Children* (New York: McKay, 1971).
18. Ellen Peck, *The Baby Trap* (New York: Bernard Geis, 1971).
19. Ellen Peck and Judith Senderowitz, editors, *The Myth of Mom and Apple Pie* (New York: Thomas Y. Crowell, 1974).
20. Shirley Radl, *Mother's Day Is Over* (New York: Charterhouse, 1973).
21. Whelan, *A Baby? . . . Maybe.*
22. Ibid.
23. An interview with Nathaniel Branden, Ph.D., National Organization for Non-Parents, 1976.
24. Diane White, "To Have or Not to Have," *Boston Globe,* January 29, 1976.
25. "What's Happening to the American Family?" a survey conducted by *Better Homes and Gardens,* NON Newsletter, July 1978.
26. Paul R. Ehrlich, *The Population Bomb* (New York: Ballantine, 1968).
27. David Knox, *Exploring Marriage and the Family* (Glenview, Ill.: Scott Foresman, 1979).
28. Susan O. Gustavus and James R. Henley, Jr., "Correlates of Voluntary Childlessness in a Select Population," *Social Biology,* September 1971.
29. Jean E. Veevers, *Childless by Choice* (Toronto: Butterworth, 1980).
30. Ibid.
31. Larry D. Barnett and Richard H. MacDonald, "A Study of the Membership of the National Organization for Non-Parents," *Social Biology,* Winter 1976.
32. John Bartlett, *Familiar Quotations,* 14th edition (Boston: Little, Brown, 1968).
33. Whelan, *A Baby? . . . Maybe.*
34. "Down with Motherhood!" *Time,* July 28, 1980.
35. Eleanor Blau, "Forum and Rite Celebrate 'Nonparenthood,' " *New York Times,* August 2, 1974.
36. Smith, *The Mother Book.*
37. "Research Shows Childfree Marriages Happiest," *NAOP Newsletter,* January-February 1975.

38. Anthony Pietropinto and Jacqueline Simenauer, *Husbands and Wives: A Nationwide Study of Marriage* (New York: Times Books, 1979).

39. Roper Organization, *1980 Virginia Slims American Women Opinion Poll.*

40. Lance Morrow, "Wondering If Children Are Necessary," *Time,* March 5, 1979.

41. John Leo, "Down with Motherhood!" *Time,* July 28, 1980.

42. Nadine Brozan, "New Marriage Roles Make Men Ambivalent About Fatherhood," *New York Times,* May 30, 1980.

43. Whelan, *A Baby? . . . Maybe.*

44. Ann Toland Serb, *Mother-in-Law* (New York: Carillon, 1978).

45. "Tea for 2, Not 3, Thanks," *New York Times,* March 19, 1980.

46. Helen Edey, "Psychological Aspects of Vasectomy," *Medical Counterpoint,* January 1972.

47. Shirley Frank, "The Population Panic," *Lilith,* Fall-Winter 1978.

48. Susan Bram, "To Have or Have Not, A Social Psychological Study of Voluntarily Childless Couples, Parents-to-Be and Parents," doctoral dissertation, University of Michigan, 1974.

49. "Is N.O.N.'s Message Pertinent to Minorities?" *NON Newsletter,* November-December 1977.

50. U.S. Department of Commerce, Bureau of the Census, *Population Characteristics: Population Profile of the U.S.: 1979,* Series P-20, No. 35, May 1980.

51. Charles F. Westoff, "Some Speculations on the Future of Marriage and Fertility," *Family Planning Perspectives,* March-April 1978.

52. Thomas J. Espenshade, "Raising a Child Can Now Cost $85,000," *Intercom,* September 1980.

53. "The Baby Boomers Come of Age," *Newsweek,* March 30, 1981.

54. Alvin Toffler, "A New Kind of Man in the Making," *New York Times Magazine,* March 9, 1980.

55. "Sinfully Together," *Time,* July 9, 1979.

56. Nathan Glazer, "The Rediscovery of the Family," *Commentary,* March 1978.

57. Veevers, *Childless by Choice.*

58. Richard A. Easterlin, "What Will 1984 Be Like? Socioeco-

nomic Implications of Recent Twists in Age Structure,"
Demography, November 1978.

59. "Poll Finds People Feel Family Life on Decline," *New York Times,* June 3, 1980.

60. Lawrence Van Gelder, "The State of Marriage: Is It Dying, Evolving or Just Fine?" *New York Times,* November 5, 1979.

2. Childless by Choice: Making the Decision and Living With It

1. Jean E. Veevers, *Childless by Choice* (Toronto: Butterworth, 1980).

2. Erika Jong, *Fear of Flying* (New York: Rinehart and Winston, 1973).

3. Kate Harper, *The Childfree Alternative* (Brattleboro, Vt.: Stephen Greene Press, 1980).

4. Beverly Toomey, "College Women and Voluntary Childlessness: A Comparative Study of Women Indicating They Want to Have Children and Those Indicating They Do Not Want to Have Children," doctoral dissertation, Ohio State University, 1977.

5. Susan Bram, "To Have or Have Not, A Social Psychological Study of Voluntarily Childless Couples, Parents-to-Be and Parents," doctoral dissertation, University of Michigan, 1974.

6. "Childless by Choice," *Newsweek,* January 14, 1980.

7. Veevers, *Childless by Choice.*

8. Kahlil Gibran, *The Prophet* (New York: Knopf, 1923).

9. Isaac Bashevis Singer, *Enemies, A Love Story* (New York: Farrar, Straus and Giroux, 1972).

10. Veevers, *Childless by Choice.*

11. Barbara Varro, "Couples Choose to Be Child-free," *Boston Globe,* May 12, 1980.

12. Nancy Friday, *My Mother/Myself* (New York: Delacorte, 1977).

13. Rogers Worthington, "He's Still as Young of Mind as Ever," Philadelphia *Inquirer,* March 28, 1980.

14. Barry Schapiro, "Predicting the Course of Voluntary Childlessness in the 21st Century," *Journal of Clinical Child Psychology,* Summer 1980.

15. David Knox, *Exploring Marriage and the Family* (Glenview, Ill.: Scott Foresman, 1979).
16. Cynthia Ringholz Cunningham, "Letters," *Newsweek,* February 4, 1980.
17. Veevers, *Childless by Choice.*
18. Liz Smith, *The Mother Book* (Garden City, N.Y., Doubleday: 1978).
19. "At Long Last, Motherhood," *Newsweek,* March 16, 1981.
20. Oriana Fallaci, *Letter to a Child Never Born* (New York: Simon and Schuster, 1977).
21. Harper, *The Childfree Alternative.*
22. Johanna Garfield, "The Overrated Joys of Motherhood After 30," *McCall's,* March 1980.
23. Veevers, *Childless by Choice.*
24. Stephen Steiner, "The Ambivalence of Motherhood," *Cosmopolitan,* January 1979.
25. Veevers, *Childless by Choice.*
26. Ibid.
27. Ibid.
28. Ibid.
29. Ibid.
30. Larry D. Barnett and Richard H. MacDonald, "A Study of the Membership of the National Organization for Non-Parents," *Social Biology,* Winter 1976.
31. National Organization for Non-Parents, "An Interview with Nathaniel Branden, Ph.D.," 1976.
32. Veevers, *Childless by Choice.*
33. Ibid.
34. John Updike, *Couples* (New York: Knopf, 1968).
35. Linda Silka and Sara Kiesler, "Couples Who Choose to Remain Childless," *Family Planning Perspectives,* January-February 1977.
36. Veevers, *Childless by Choice.*
37. "Parenthood as a Development Stage and Its Relationship to Achieving Full Adulthood: A Study by Kathryn Welds," *National Alliance for Optional Parenthood Newsletter,* May 1978.
38. Judith Guss Teicholz, "Psychological Correlates of Voluntary Childlessness in Married Women," speech presented at the Conference of the Massachusetts Psychological Association, Boston, May 1979.
39. David Knox, *Exploring Marriage and the Family.*

40. Graham Greene, *The Human Factor* (New York: Simon and Schuster, 1978).

3. Sterilization: The Active Decision

1. Nell Gifford, "She Didn't Want Children. Not Even a Few," *Chicago Tribune Magazine,* November 3, 1974.
2. Liz Smith, *The Mother Book* (Garden City, N.Y.: Doubleday, 1978).
3. Betty Gonzales, "Psychosexual Aftermath of Voluntary Sterilization," presented at the Society for the Scientific Study of Sex, Eastern Regional Chapter, Leonia, N.J., April 30, 1978.
4. Arthur B. Shostak, "Abortion as Fatherhood Lost: Problems and Reforms," *The Family Coordinator,* October 1979.
5. Betty Gonzales, "Psychosexual Aftermath of Voluntary Sterilization."
6. Ronald H. Magarick and Robert A. Brown, "Social and Emotional Aspects of Voluntary Childlessness in Vasectomized Childless Men," presented at the 104th meeting, American Public Health Association, Miami Beach, October 21, 1976.
7. Betty Gonzales, "Psychosexual Aftermath of Voluntary Sterilization."
8. Steven A. Leibo and Jennifer L. Santee, "Sterilization for the Non-Parent: Preliminary Findings from a Study of the Psychological Aspects of Fertility Termination," *NAOP Newsletter,* January-February 1978.
9. Nancy D. Kaltreider and Alan G. Margolis, "Childless by Choice: A Clinical Study," *American Journal of Psychiatry,* February 1977.

4. Infertility: Those Who Can't Have Children

1. Edith Sitwell, *The Queens and the Hive* (Boston: Little, Brown, 1962).
2. *Encyclopaedia Britannica,* eleventh edition, vol. 28 (New York: Encyclopaedia Britannica, Inc., 1911).
3. Miriam D. Mazor, "Barren Couples," *Psychology Today,* May 1979.
4. Will and Ariel Durant, *The Story of Civilization: Rousseau and Revolution* (New York: Simon and Schuster, 1967).
5. Dena Kleiman, "Anguished Search to Cure Infertility," *New*

York Times Magazine, December 16, 1979.

6. Mazor, "Barren Couples."
7. Ibid.
8. Ibid.
9. Kleiman, "Anguished Search to Cure Infertility."
10. Mazor, "Barren Couples."
11. Barbara Eck Menning, *Infertility: A Guide for the Childless Couple* (Englewood Cliffs, N.J.: Prentice-Hall, 1977).
12. Mazor, "Barren Couples."
13. Jacqueline Horner Plumez, "Adoption: Where Have All the Babies Gone?" *New York Times Magazine,* April 13, 1980.
14. Hesketh Pearson, *Bernard Shaw: His Life and Personality* (London: Methuen, 1942).

5. Careers and Childlessness

1. Terry Rubenstein, "Ellen Goodman on Women and Their Roles," Baltimore *Sun,* October 27, 1979.
2. Roper Organization, *1980 Virginia Slims American Women Opinion Poll.*
3. Jean E. Veevers, *Childless by Choice* (Toronto: Butterworth, 1980).
4. Ibid.
5. Denzel E. Benson, "The Intentionally Childless Couple," *USA Today,* January 1979.
6. Veevers, *Childless by Choice.*
7. Ibid.
8. Ibid.
9. Rebecca and Jeff B. Bryson and Marilyn F. Johnson, "Family Size, Satisfaction and Productivity in Dual Career Couples," *Psychology of Women Quarterly,* Fall 1978.
10. Caroline Bird, *The Two-Paycheck Marriage* (New York: Rawson, Wade, 1979).
11. National Organization for Non-Parents, "Happy Non-Parents' Day—August 1, 1978," *NON Newsletter,* July 1978.
12. Roper Organization, *1980 Virginia Slims American Women Opinion Poll.*
13. Leslie Bennetts, "Charlotte Curtis' Pursuit of Excellence," *Diversion,* September 1979.
14. Bird, *Two-Paycheck Marriage.*
15. Tillie Olsen, *Silences* (New York: Delacorte, 1978).

16. Ibid.
17. Quentin Bell, *Virginia Woolf: A Biography,* vol. 2 (London: Hogarth Press, 1972).
18. Olsen, *Silences.*
19. William Drake, *Sara Teasdale: Woman and Poet* (San Francisco: Harper & Row, 1979).
20. Anaïs Nin, *The Diary of Anaïs Nin,* vol. 1 (1931–1934) (New York: Harcourt Brace Jovanovich, 1966).
21. Oriana Fallaci, *Letter to a Child Never Born* (New York: Simon and Schuster, 1977).
22. Robert Gould, "The Wrong Reasons to Have Children," *New York Times Magazine,* May 3, 1970.
23. Gail Sheehy, "How Women Can Build Happy Lives," *Redbook,* September 1979.
24. *Newsweek,* "The Superwoman Squeeze," May 19, 1980.
25. Betty Friedan, "Feminism Takes a New Turn," *New York Times Magazine,* November 18, 1979.
26. *Newsweek,* "The Superwoman Squeeze."
27. Marilyn Fabe and Nora Wikler, *Up Against the Clock* (New York: Random House, 1979).

6. The Middle Years

1. Jane Cooper, *Maps and Windows* (New York: Macmillan, 1974).
2. Miriam D. Mazor, "Barren Couples," *Psychology Today,* May 1979.
3. Margaret Mead, *Blackberry Winter: My Earlier Years* (New York: Morrow, 1972).
4. Daniel J. Levinson, *The Seasons of a Man's Life* (New York: Ballantine, 1978).
5. Marilyn Fabe and Norma Wikler, *Up Against the Clock* (New York: Random House, 1979).

7. Alone Again: Divorced, Widowed . . . Remarried

1. T. H. Holmes and R. H. Rahe, "The Social Readjustment Rating Scale," *Journal of Psychosomatic Research,* 11:213–218, 1967.
2. Robert S. Weiss, *Loneliness: The Experience of Emotional and Social Isolation* (Cambridge, Mass.: MIT Press, 1973).

3. Eileen Simpson, *The Maze* (New York: Morrow, 1974).
4. Gail Sheehy, *Passages: Predictable Crises of Adult Life* (New York: Dutton, 1976).
5. Elizabeth M. Whelan, *A Baby?* . . . *Maybe* (New York: Bobbs Merrill, 1975).
6. Harold Feldman, "Development of the Husband-Wife Relationship," report of research to National Institute of Mental Health, 1965.
7. *Newsweek*, "The Children of Divorce," February 11, 1980.
8. David Knox, *Exploring Marriage and the Family* (Glenview, Ill.: Scott Foresman, 1979).
9. Kim Hetherington, "You're Not My Real Mother," *Washingtonian Magazine*, October 1979.
10. Lynne Caine, *Widow* (New York: Morrow, 1974).
11. Knox, *Exploring Marriage and the Family*.
12. *Newsweek*, "After Remarriage," February 11, 1980.

8. The Later Years

1. Erma Bombeck, *If Life Is a Bowl of Cherries, What Am I Doing in the Pits?* (New York: McGraw-Hill, 1978).
2. Henry Beetle Hough, *Mostly on Martha's Vineyard* (New York: Harcourt Brace Jovanovich, 1975).
3. Ibid.
4. Simone de Beauvoir, *The Coming of Age* (New York: Putnam, 1972).
5. U.S. Department of Health, Education and Welfare. *The Older Woman: Continuities and Discontinuities.* Report of the National Institute on Aging and the National Institute of Mental Health Workshop, September 14–16, 1978, Publication No. 79–1897, October 1979.
6. Christine A. Bachrach, "Old Age Isolation and Low Fertility: Is There a Connection?" *Intercom*, January 1979.
7. Ibid.
8. Population Reference Bureau, "The Elderly in America," *Population Bulletin*, vol. 30, no. 3, June 1975.
9. Beth B. Hess and Joan M. Waring, "Parent and Child in Later Life: Rethinking the Relationship," a working paper, presented at Penn State University, April 1977.
10. Ibid.
11. de Beauvoir, *Coming of Age*.

12. Ibid.
13. Kathleen Hendrix, "Our Ultimate Investment: Feting the Birth of a Movement," Los Angeles *Times,* April 11, 1978.
14. James Hilton, *Goodbye, Mr. Chips* (Boston: Little, Brown, 1934).
15. de Beauvoir, *Coming of Age.*
16. Harris Dienstfrey and Joseph Lederer, *What Do You Want to Be When You Grow Old?* (New York: Bantam, 1979).
17. Irving Rosow, *Social Integration of the Aged* (New York: Free Press, 1967).
18. Bruce Vladeck, *Unloving Care* (New York: Basic Books, 1980).
19. HEW, "Older Woman."

Index